TODAY'S HEALTHY EATING

BY

LOUISE TENNEY

Author of

TODAY'S HERBAL HEALTH

TODAY'S HEALTHY EATING

BY

LOUISE TENNEY

Copyright ©1986 by
Louise Tenney

Published by
Woodland Books
P.O. Box 1422
Provo, Utah 84063

ISBN O-913923-09-5

Printed in the United States of America

CONTENTS

DEDICATED

To Adam, Jana, Jenna, Jordan Ann, Jacqueline, Micah and all my future grandchildren in the hope that they will find health and a zest for life through good basic nutrition.

NOTICE TO THE READER

INTRODUCTION

We Americans should become more aware of the publication The Dietary Goals which was prepared by the staff on the Select Committee on Nutrition and Human Needs, the United States Senate, 1977. It is one of the first government publications to cite the relationship of diet and disease. Americans lack proper understanding of the consequences of nutrition-related diseases, for millions of them are sick with diet-related illnesses and do not realize it. The American public is eating without regard to the nutritional values of food, many not getting the nutrients they need--especially the B vitamins, iron and the vital minerals such as zinc. The Dietary report even states that the leading causes of death in the United States could be modified by changing the typical American diet. In the report, Senator George McGovern says, "With medical care expenditures in the United States expected to reach 230 billion dollars by 1980, the estimated savings through an effective preventive nutritional program could be a significant factor in reducing health costs." George McGovern points out that the purpose of this report is to show that the eating patterns of this century represent as critical a public health concern as any now before us. He goes on to say that we must acknowledge and recognize that the public is confused about what to eat to maximize health. If we, as a Government, want to reduce health costs and maximize the quality of life for all Americans, we have an obligation to provide practical guides to the individual consumer as well as set national dietary goals for the country as a whole.

The report states that our diets have changed radically within the last 50 years, with great and often very harmful effects on our health. These changes in diet represent as great a threat to public health as smoking. Too much fat, too much sugar or salt, can be and are linked directly to heart disease, cancer, obesity and stroke, among other killer diseases. Moreover, six of the ten leading causes of death in the United States have been linked to diet.

In the early 1900's almost 40% of our caloric intake came from fruits, vegetables and grain products. Today only a little more than 2% of calories comes from these sources. The consumption of soft drinks has more than doubled since 1960, displacing milk as the second most-consumed beverage. It is also estimated that every man, woman and child in the United States consumes more than 125 pounds of fat (animal fats, saturated fats and cholesterol) and 120 pounds of sugar each year.

What are the risks associated with eating less meat, less fat, less sugar, less salt and eating more fruit, vegetables and whole grains? We have epidemic disease in our population such as heart disease, cancer, diabetes and hypertension. We expect medical science to cure such diseases once they occur and we need public education to emphasize the unfortunate but clear limitation of medical practice in curing the common killing disease. But once hypertension, diabetes, arteriosclerosis or heart disease are manifest, there is very little that medical science can do to return the patient to normal physiological function, the report goes on to say. As a nation we have come to believe that medicine and medical technology can solve our major health problems. Treatment, not prevention, has been the order of the day. The problem will not be solved by more and more medical care.

Millions of children and youth are moving toward hypertension and diabetes. Findings report possible connection between high salt intake and changes in levels of gastric acid secretion, stomach cancer and cerebrovascular disease. Youth need to avoid all salted snack foods such as chips, nuts that have been salted, pretzels, etc. Changing our diets could result in better health, longer active lifespans and greater satisfaction from work, family and leisure time.

The Dietary Goals of the United States suggest the following changes in food selection and preparation:

1. Increase consumption of fruits and vegetables and whole grains.
2. Decrease consumption of meat and increase consumption of poultry and fish.
3. Decrease consumption of foods high in fat and partially substitute poly-unsaturated fat for saturated fat.
4. Substitute non-fat for whole milk.
5. Decrease consumption of butterfat, eggs and other high cholesterol sources.
6. Decrease consumption of sugar and foods high in sugar content.
7. Decrease consumption of salt and foods high in salt content.

The New Anti-Cancer Diet

The American Cancer Society has now admitted that a diet high in whole foods and low in fats can prevent cancer. For years health nutritionists and health conscious doctors have been telling us of the importance of diet in relation to disease, and now the American Cancer Society has outlined a new diet for Americans which they say may cut the chances of contracting breast, colon, prostate, stomach, lung, esophagus, bladder and throat cancers. They intend to educate the people to this new knowledge they have just discovered.

They are also recommending that the American public avoid obesity, moderate alcohol intake and cut back on consumption of salt-cured, smoked or nitrite-cured foods.

GUIDELINES

1. Avoid obesity. Cancer of the uterus, gall bladder, kidney, stomach, colon and breast are more prevalent in obese people.
2. Cut fat consumption. Although still high, the guideline the report gives is that not more than 30% of your total calories should be from fat. Breast and colon cancers are associated with high fat consumption.
3. Eat more high fiber foods such as fruits, vegetables and whole grain cereal. The Cancer Society is not saying these foods well help prevent cancer, but that they provide a good substitute for fatty foods.
4. Eat foods each day which are rich in vitamins A and C.
5. Eat cabbage, broccoli, Brussels sprouts, kohlrabi and cauliflower. These seem to contain something that inhibits cancer growth.

Finally, good nutrition rebuilds and cleans the cells and tissues and prevents fermentation and putrefaction which can eventually lead to degenerative diseases.

BENEFITS WE CAN RECEIVE BY CHANGING OUR EATING HABITS

ALLERGIES TO FOOD--Could be eliminated by 90%.

ARTHRITIS--Could have 50% fewer problems

ALCOHOLISM--Could be reduced by 33%. One of the main reasons drinkers cannot quit drinking is severe nutritional deficiencies.

CANCER--Could be reduced by at least 20%. One in every four persons will die of cancer. Only five years ago it was one out of every eight persons; and about 25 years ago it was one in 25 persons that had cancer. In addition, cancer is the number one child killer.

DENTAL PROBLEMS--Could be reduced by 50% in incidence, severity and expenditures.

DIABETES--50% of the cases could be avoided or improved. Many people are finding help by changing their diets.

DIGESTIVE PROBLEMS--Could be reduced by at least 25%.

EYESIGHT--Could be 20% fewer blindness, cataracts or use of corrective lenses.

HEART DISEASE--Cardiovascular diseases due to nutritional deficiencies could be reduced 20% to 25%.

HYPOGLYCEMIA--80% of the population suffer to some degree. Changing the diet would decrease the incidence of hypoglycemia.

INFANT MORTALITY--Could be reduced by 50%. Fewer infant deformities. Drugs, smoking, alcohol and even aspirin and over-the-counter drugs destroy vital nutrients essential to an infant's body.

KIDNEY AND URINARY PROBLEMS--Deaths and acute conditions could be reduced by 20%.

HIGH BLOOD PRESSURE--25 million Americans suffer and this could be reduced if over-consumption of certain foods were eliminated.

OBESITY--Could be reduced 80%. All of the thousands of diets printed each year have not done the job of eliminating obesity. Obesity leads to many serious health problems, including diabetes and heart disease.

OSTEOPOROSIS (Bone Disease)--Could be reduced by up to 75% if exercise and an increase of calcium, fresh fruits and vegetables are included.

RESPIRATORY and Infectious Ailments--Could be reduced by 20% with diet change.

ULCERS--Could be reduced with a change in eating habits.

AILMENTS AND DIETARY HELPS

ALLERGIES

Allergies are very common and can manifest themselves because of a weakened immune system. A weakened immune system can cause colds and flu to develop, and this in turn can cause a chain reaction of allergies. This happens when foreign invaders (allergens) enter the system through the sinus cavities when we breathe in pollen or any other air pollutant. When the sinuses are healthy they are protected with moist mucous membranes similiar to the skin inside the mouth. When healthy, these membranes are able to wash the pollen out of the sinuses and down the throat and into the digestive tract where it is neutralized and eliminated from the body. The tonsils or adenoids can also trap harmful agents and store them in lymph nodes until a healthy lymphatic system eliminates them from the system.

Imbalanced mucous membranes do not move the agents away from the sensitive lining of the nose, throat and lymph glands as efficiently as they should. When the weather changes with temperature and humidity, and you become chilled from drafts, the body is unable to handle the sudden shock to a weakened immune system, and mucous membranes, having to handle ingested allergen, bacteria, virus and pollutants provide further complications.

Mucous membranes become imbalanced because of the types of foods we eat, and this causes the mucous membranes to become too thin (runny, drippy nose) or too thick (stuffy nose, congestion in the throat). This can cause a scratchy, irritated, less resistant mucous lining in the nose, throat and the stomach. Then we see the beginning of problems. If the lymphatic, stomach and liver are not functioning properly then we rapidly find the cause in a full-blown viral or bacterial infection, common cold or flu.

I personally believe that all of us come in contact with germs, bacterial viruses, allergens and metal toxins, air pollutants, and water pollutants. Yet only those who catch colds, flu or even allergies are vulnerable, due to an internal state of imbalance and a weakened immune system.

Allergies came into prominence at the turn of the century. That is when we became to be a more technologically advanced nation, with hidden additives in food, and antibiotics and hormones added to meat and beef as well as poultry. Fruits and vegetables were sprayed so that they could be shipped all over the nation and still appeal to the eye. We have an ever increasing rate of toxic wastes in the air. Purifying our wheat became very popular, and we traded whole wheat bread for white bread and brown rice for white rice. Over 3,000 additives and preservatives are added to our foods. Take a look at the list of complicated ingredients listed on the wrappers of a modern slice of bread and compare it to a slice of homemade bread of 50 years ago which simply contained whole wheat flour, yeast, non-allergic salt, honey or molasses and water.

SYMPTOMS OF ALLERGIES

Dark circles under the eyes can often be symptoms of allergies to food and chemicals or both. It is estimated that at least 60% of the United States population suffers from unknown food and chemical allergies. It can be a very subtle reaction and may not even be realized, and it is seldom recognized as an allergy. Allergy symptoms are often misdiagnosed and treated for some other disease.

The most common symptoms are sinusitis, headaches, hives, cramps, dizziness, skin problems, high blood pressure and arthritis.

SOME OF THE MOST FREQUENT PROBLEMS ASSOCIATED WITH ALLERGIES CAN BE:

SKIN--Acne, blisters, blotches, circles under the eyes, eczema, flushing, hives, itching, psoriasis.

HEADACHES--probable all types.

EAR--frequent ear infections, loss of hearing, popping of ears, dizziness, imbalance, itching inside the ears, earache, hypersensitivity to noise.

CARDIOVASCULAR--hypertension, heartbeat irregularity, low blood pressure, rapid pulse (very common when allergic to ingested food).

DIGESTIVE--food intolerance, metallic taste, dry mouth, canker sores, tongue stinging, heartburn, indigestion, nausea, vomiting, diarrhea, constipation, intestinal gas, pains, gall bladder symptoms, and food craving.

RESPIRATORY--asthma, cough, frequent colds, hay fever, mouth breathing, nose bleeds, post nasal drip, wheezing, shortness of breath, tightness in chest, rattling sounds in chest.

THROAT--cough, hoarseness, dry, sore or tickly.

UROLOGICAL--bedwetting, frequent urination, difficulty controlling bladder, genital itching, pain or swelling.

MUSCULAR and SKELETAL--arthritis, muscle cramps, spasm and
joint pain, extreme fatigue, sluggishness, neck back or
shoulder aches, lack of coordination.

MENTAL--anxiety, depression, dizzy spells, fatigue, hyperactivity,
insomnia, learning disorders, nervousness and restlessness.

NERVOUS SYSTEM--headaches (variety), drowsiness, confusion,
mental dullness, depression, crying, anger, anxiety, irritability,
hyperactivity, learning and memory difficulties, lack of
concentration, restlessness or convulsions.

Obesity, hypoglycemia and diabetes have also been attributed
to allergies.

It is very important to treat the cause instead of the symptoms
and be aware that frequent colds and flu are often a sign of imbalance
not only in the mucous, but very often in the liver, lymph and
stomach. Allergies indicate a breakdown also in the adrenals.

These areas involved could be one or all four of a breakdown of
function within the system. Making sure these areas are healthy and
protected in advance will be a protection against allergies, colds and the
flu.

1. ADRENALS--those two tiny glands above the kidneys have the job
to produce hormones which render foreign proteins harmless.

2. LIVER--a healthy liver detoxifies the body, preventing harmful
reactions.

3. DIGESTIVE SYSTEM--an efficient digestion is essential to avoid
build-ups of protein substances in the bloodstream, toxic waste, which
cause symptoms.

4. THE MUCOUS MEMBRANES--healthy mucous membranes do
not allow foreign proteins to enter the bloodstream.

SPECIAL DIETARY HELPS

VITAMIN A--Necessary to digest and utilize protein. Builds healthy
mucous membranes to help wash away the pollen and other
inhalants that cause allergens. Use with vitamin E, which
protects the fat in the cell membranes from rancidity. (Rancid
fat causes holes in the cell membranes through which allergens
enter and cause reactions.)

ACIDOPHILUS--Provides natural hydrochloric acid to aid digestion. It
is helpful to a healthy colon, and reduces the toxic wastes in
the large intestine to prevent allergies. With proper digestion
of food allergies could be eliminated.

ALFALFA--Aids digestion and assimilation of calcium and protein.
Contains chlorophyll to clean the blood. It breaks down

poisonous carbon dioxide. Contains a balanced mineral content for complete absorption.

BEE POLLEN--Can help build immunity by acting as a barrier against the inhaled pollen. Start with small amounts. Bee pollen contains 35% protein and high amounts of B complex vitamins, as well as A, C, D, and E.

B COMPLEX--All the B vitamins are needed. They are essential for the general health of the adrenal and can be effective in guarding against allergic reactions.

BIOFLAVONOIDS--Enhance the availability of vitamin C and its utilization by the system faster. Builds the capillaries.

BREWERS YEAST--with grape juice and wheat germ, blended together. All contains nutrients to help the body strengthen its cells and walls to stop the allergens. It works as a natural immunity.

VITAMIN C--A natural antihistamine to detoxify foreign substances entering the body. 5,000 milligrams or more daily. Along with bioflavonoids and B vitamins helps in blocking allergic reactions as well as rebuilding healthy membranes.

CALCIUM and MAGNESIUM BALANCE--Half as much magnesium as calcium. Has an antiallergy effect and may be helpful to repair damage done to the cell membranes which occur as a result of allergic reactions. Cleanses blood, regulates heart beat, helps insomnia and protects the nervous system.

COMFREY and PEPSIN--Very beneficial for cleansing the colon and eliminating toxins out of the body. Provides nutrition and healing elements. Helps to establish normal balance in the whole system.

DIET--Rotation diet, allergies and addictions seem to go together. The most commonly eaten foods seem to fulfill addictive needs.

DANDELION--High in natural sodium and calcium, which helps keep calcium in solution and takes it where it is needed. Cleanses the blood while building. Cleanses the liver. Full of vitamins and minerals. Dandelion and yellow dock together will nourish the spleen and liver.

DIGESTION--Incomplete digestion of protein is believed to be a cause of allergies in some people.

VITAMIN E--Protects the cells and builds immunity against allergies.

ECHINACEA--Has the ability to strengthen and stimulate the body's ability to resist infections while increasing the production of white blood cells. It has a cleansing effect on the lymph glands.

EVENING PRIMROSE OIL--Contains fatty acids that are needed to produce adrenal hormones, helps in utilization of pantothenic acid in intestines.

FOOD ENZYMES--to help digestion of food left in the colon.

GARLIC--contains natural antibiotic properties containing sulfides and disulfides which unite with the irritating allergens and help to inactivate them.

KELP--Feeds the thyroid. An undersupply of thyroid hormone results in exhaustion and susceptibility to colds, flu, and allergies. Kelp is very high in essential minerals.

LICORICE--This herb helps to build up resistance to allergens. It stimulates the adrenal and lymph glands and aids in the production of white blood cells which raises the body's immunity levels. Licorice provides strength and energy to the system.

LIVER CLEANSE--The liver's responsibility is to detoxify poisonous material. A healthy liver produces an enzyme called histamine. If the liver is congested with fats or built-up toxins, it cannot produce this enzyme. Herbs to cleanse liver: alfalfa, dandelion, cascara sagrada, and yellow dock. Food for the liver: sprouts, fresh fruit and vegetables, tofu, yogurt, kefir, millet, buckwheat and brown rice to name a few.

MAGNESIUM--along with calcium strengthens the adrenals.

MARSHMALLOW and MULLEIN--Help relieve and reduce severe inflammations and swelling in those areas of the body most affected by allergies--lungs, throat, neck, sinuses and lymph glands.

MULLEIN--Calming to the nerves, and helps in controlling coughs, sneezes, and spasms. It loosens mucus and moves it out of the body. Contains ingredients that act as disinfectants in the system.

NERVES--It is estimated that 70% of allergies are from nervous disorders. The nervous system needs to be strengthened with nervine herbs, hops, scullcap, valerian and passion flower.

PANTOTHENIC ACID--One of the B complex vitamins which is directly related to the production of natural cortisone. It is increased when under stress, illness, onset of allergies, exposure to toxins (pollens included) as well as rapid growth in children. Use with vitamins E and C, calcium and magnesium for emergency reactions of allergens. Taken for a short time, it can support the adrenals to help produce cortisone.

PARSLEY--Cleansing for the blood stream, rich in iron, vitamin C and chlorophyll. Also rich in vitamin A. Feeds the glands to help regulate the hormones for protection against allergens.

PROTEIN DIGESTIVE AID (HCL)--Hydrochloric acid is necessary for the breakdown of protein and the lack of it can cause the formation of toxic materials and possible allergic reactions.

Hydrochloric acid, along with vitamin C, will harmlessly detoxify nitrites. Lack of it can also lower resistance to infections. Allergies can lead to colds, bronchitis, flu and colds can lead to allergies.

POTASSIUM--Herbs rich in potassium are kelp, dulse, watercress, horsetail and alfalfa. Apples, potatoes, bananas. Potassium protects the cells from leaking. Feeds the nerves and the whole body. Potassium is lost from the body when allergies occur, and this needs to be replenished. Potassium broth is a very tasty way to add to the diet. Potassium strengthens the adrenals.

RED CLOVER--Builds resistance to allergies. Cleanses the blood, which is essential in clearing up allergies. It contains A, C, iron, selenium as well as other vital vitamins and minerals. Relaxes the nerves and builds the blood.

RED MEAT--Full of synthetic female hormones, antibiotics, amphetamines and meat tenderizers. Puts stress on the digestive system.

ROSE HIPS--Supplies the body with the most easily assimilated source of vitamin C. Also contains bioflavinoids, A, E, and calcium.

SPIRULINA--High in protein with all the essential amino acids. Contains vitamin B12. Helps in allergies to supply protein to rebuild cells. It contains potassium for adrenal energy and muscle strength. It helps to remove toxic metals and additives from the system that cause allergies. It contains thyroxine, an amino acid normally produced by the thyroid gland, and is beneficial as a stimulant on the metabolism.

WATERCRESS--One of the best sources of vitamin E. High in A and D also. Acts as a tonic to the system to help regulate the metabolism and the flow of bile. Helps to protect the body against allergies.

WHEY--The powder is an excellent source of natural sodium.

ZINC--Has been proven to help shorten colds if taken at the first sign. Healing to the mucous membranes.

ARTERIOSCLEROSIS
(Hardening of the Arteries)

Arteriosclerosis develops over a lifetime, so prevention should begin early in life. It is the leading cause of death in the United States, not to mention strokes which have afflicted many patients who are in hospitals and rest homes. It has been found that fatty streaks are found in the aortas (main arteries of the body) of children in almost every country, and it is believed that the fatty streaks are the precursors of plaques.

One type of hardening of the arteries is caused by a gradual deposit of un-assimilated calcium in the artery walls, restricting the flow of blood to the cells. Another is a more advanced type of hardening, called atherosclerosis, which is due to the buildup of cholesterol or fatty deposite in the artery walls which cause the degeneration of the arteries.

Obesity, lack of exercise, hypertension, smoking, heredity, stress and poor diet are factors that contribute to hardening of the arteries.

SPECIAL DIETARY HELPS

ALOE VERA JUICE--Rich in vitamin C. Helps in maintaining good blood vessel tone and in promoting healthy circulation. Rich in amino acids and enzymes that provide protein to the cells, and which are essential for strong health. Use with raw apple juice, or any other juice.

ALFALFA--Capsules and alfalfa sprouts. Using 12 or more capsules a day has helped to lower cholesterol. It binds up cholesterol in the intestinal tract, carrying it right through the system to stop reabsorption. Alfalfa is very rich in essential vitamins and minerals.

APPLESAUCE--Raw, grated, contains pectin to help lower cholesterol.

B COMPLEX--Helps in the prevention of atherosclerosis by reducing blood cholesterol levels and by utilizing fat. B6 prevents as well as treats arteriosclerosis and helps prevent the unnatural clotting process that produces strokes. B6 stops the formation of fibrin (a protein substance in blood that encourages clotting) and stops the clustering of those blood cells called platelets which form the clot.

BARLEY--Rich in B complex vitamins. Lowers cholesterol.

BIOFLAVONOIDS (Vitamin P)--Works synergistically with vitamin C. Strengthens capillaries, helps in blood clotting, builds resistance to disease, natural diuretic. Protects against arterial degeneration.

BROWN RICE--Rich in B complex vitamins, helps to lower cholesterol.

BUCKWHEAT--Reduces high blood pressure, especially when using the sprouted buckwheat.

VITAMIN C--Helps in preventing arteriosclerosis and atherosclerosis, fighting bacterial and viral infection, preventing high blood cholesterol, and lowering blood clots in the veins.

CAYENNE or CAPSICUM--Helpful in preventing strokes and heart attacks. It increases the heart action but not the blood pressure. High in vitamins A, C, iron and calcium. It creates circulation in equalizing blood pressure. Cayenne works very well with grlic and hawthorne.

CHELATION THERAPY (Oral)--Use vitamins, minerals, amino acids, glandulars and herbs. Strips deposits from the blood vessels in a natural way.

CHLOROPHYLL--Contains synthesized sunshine and electrial current to revitalize the system. It inhibits the putrefaction of protein in the digestive tract.

CHROMIUM--Helps to utilize fat in the diet; only a small amount is needed.

CURRANTS--Strengthens the heart muscles.

VITAMIN D--Helps the body to absorb calcium and other minerals. It has been found to have hormone effects in the body.

VITAMIN E--A natural antioxidant. Helps prevent blood clot formation. Dilates the capillary blood vessels, enabling blood to flow more freely into the muscle tissues. Strengthens heart muscles, reduces uric acid build-up and improves blood circulation.

GREENS--Fresh. Using leaf lettuce. alfalfa, watercress, parsley, aids in the metabolism of fats in the diet.

GARLIC--Helps cleanse the blood, helps prevent hardening of the arteries, and lowers tension and blood pressure.

GLUCOMANNAN--With lecithin together reduces high cholesterol levels. Glucomannan controls hunger pangs, provides dietary fiber to promote bowel health and reduces blood cholesterol levels. Brain needs oxygen, and lecithin feeds the brain.

HAWTHORNE--Feeds the heart, strengthens the heart and helps prevent blood clotting. High in minerals. Works with garlic and capsicum to feed the heart.

HORSETAIL--Rich in silica; aids circulation. Provides minerals.

KELP--Cleanses the veins while it nourishes the blood. It feeds and regulates the thyroid and the metabolism, which helps digest food. It contains all the minerals considered vital to health. It even contains a small amount of lecithin. It feeds the brain and nourishes the nervous system.

LEMON or LIME JUICE--Fresh used in pure water is considered one of the best blood purifiers.

MAGNESIUM--Aids blood circulation, works with calcium, builds central nervous system and helps keep the veins clean.

PANTOTHENIC ACID--Helps prevent fatigue, essential for fat metabolism. Helps the body eliminate cholesterol and other fatty substances.

POTASSIUM--Essential in helping to prevent heart attacks. Works with sodium to balance the fluids in the body and regulate the heart beat. Helps to prevent high blood pressure, calms nerves, helps oxygen transport to brain. *Potassium Soup*: Potato peelings, celery, onions, carrots, parsley and garlic. Cook and strain.

RYE BREAD--Use more often than wheat bread. Using homemade rye bread can help flexibility of arteries.

SAFFLOWER and SUNFLOWER OILS--Combines with cholesterol and forms a blood soluble lipid which can be excreted from the body.

SALADS--Use fresh vegetables. Aids in the metabolism of fats. Nourishing when used with lemon, whey powder and cold pressed oils for seasonings instead of salt or MSG.

SELENIUM--Necessary for proper functioning of the heart. Works with vitamin E.

SESAME SEEDS--High in calcium with an alkaline reaction, making it an ideal lecithin food. High in protein and other vital nutrients.

SPROUTS--Fresh, home grown. These provide the freshest live enzymes you can have, especially during the winter months. Provide the body with chlorophyll to keep the veins clean. Provide oxygen to the cells. Full of vitamins and minerals. Alfalfa, mung beans, buckwheat, wheat, radish, red clover, fenugreek are a few you can sprout.

TOFU--Use instead of meat; high in protein, low in fat.

WHEY--High in natural sodium with a strong dissolving ability. Holds calcium in solution instead of settling in the joints and kidneys to cause arthritis and kidney stones.

ZINC--Restores sense of taste to help malnourishment which is very common in the elderly. Use zinc with B6.

ARTHRITIS

There are over fifty million people in the United States who suffer from arthritis, and many children are among the group. It is the number one crippler in the nation.

Osteoarthritis is generally found in older people. It usually occurs as a result of aging or inactivity. Exercise strengthens cartilage, muscles, and ligaments, stabilizing the joints.

Rheumatoid arthritis attacks cartilage throughout the body. It tends to be hereditary. Some people have been very successful on vegetable diets to help in arthritis. What you are eating can cause arthritis: White flour, white sugar, red meat, coffee, cola drinks, alcohol, fried foods, pork, fats, and heated oils. Salt-loaded food is bad for arthritis.

Stress causes destruction of protein which is necessary before ACTH (natural cortisone) can be produced.

SPECIAL DIETARY HELPS

VITAMIN A--Helps reduce inflammation and builds resistance to disease.

ALFALFA--Helps remove acidity in arthritis, neutralizes acids, and contains alkaloid for pain. The minerals are increased when sprouted. Beneficial when used with celery juice to draw calcium from the joints. Drink alfalfa tea. Alfalfa seeds ground up in yogurt.

VITAMIN B COMPLEX--Helps in carbohydrate assimilation. Helps prevent hardening of the arteries. B2 helps the body to produce its own cortisone and the pituitary gland to stimulate the adrenal glands. B6 helps in stiffness of the hands. Lack can produce painful joints in hands and feet. The pain causes blood vessels to constrict, leading to arthritis.

BROMELAIN--From pineapple. Reduces inflammation and swelling, helps in tension and pain.

BLACKSTRAP MOLASSES--Unsulphured, helps dissolve calcium in joints and muscles.

BLACK COHOSH--Relieves pain, irritation and acid conditions of the blood.

BRAN--Provides bulk to help keep colon healthy.

BREWERS YEAST--Contains B complex to help prevent hardening of the arteries.

BURDOCK--Reduces swelling and deposits within joints and knuckles. Purifies blood.

VITAMIN C with Bioflavonoids--Strengthens the capillary walls in the joints preventing them from collapsing and causing pain and swelling. Helps to eliminate uric acid in the blood. Helps to maintain the health of collagen or "glue" that holds us together. Prevents infection. Helps reduce resistance to stress and infection.

CALCIUM--Essential for preventing arthritis. Essential for healthy muscles. Natural tranquilizer. Very helpful for pain.

CITRUS FRUIT--High in sodium. Good if fruit is picked tree ripened.

COD LIVER OIL--High in vitamins A and D. Necessary for lubricating the joints and cartilage.

CHAPARRAL--Adds life to the cells with mineral and oxygen-bearing properties; dissolves uric acid accumulations and acts as an antiseptic.

COMFREY--Cleans and purifies the system.

VITAMIN D--Builds the bones, works with calcium and phosphorus.

DANDELION and YELLOW DOCK--Works together to provide healthy blood and prevent anemia. Rich in vitamins and minerals. Arthritis can produce anemia.

DEVIL'S CLAW--Used in Europe for arthritis. Contains cleansing and pain-relieving properties.

VITAMIN E--Helps bring circulation to muscles and joints and helps to repair damaged body tissues.

EVENING PRIMROSE--Contains fatty acids, helps reduce inflammatory reaction.

FOOD ENZYMES DIGESTIVE AID--Helps assimilation of food and herbs for better digestion and utilization.

GREEN DRINKS--Contains chlorophyll which purifies the blood, eliminates build-up of uric acid in the blood. Destroys toxins in the body.

GOAT MILK--Rich in sodium, necessary to keep calcium in solution.

JERUSALEM ARTICHOKES--Eaten raw on salads or in soups, contain inulin.

JUICE DIETS--Fresh fruit and vegetable juices every few months will help remove toxic wastes.

KELP--Supplies minerals to the body, removes toxins from the veins.

LECITHIN--Dissolves cholesterol.

MEGAVITAMIN THERAPY (Chelated)--Vitamins and minerals work together in the enzyme system which controls our body's activities.

NICOTINAMIDE--Helps ease pain and helps loosen stiff joints.

OKRA--Can be purchased in powder form. High in sodium, helps keep calcium in solution.

PARSLEY--Helps eliminate excess water from the tissues. Rich in vitamin A and minerals.

PHOSPHORUS--Helps the metabolism of calcium, keeps it from settling in the joints and the tissues.

PROTEIN--Plant protein (alfalfa, herbs, seeds, nuts, grains). Lack of protein and calcium can produce osteoporosis or bone softening.

SPROUTS--Alfalfa, red clover, mung beans, buckwheat and wheat help decrease the toxic effects of cortisone.

WATERCRESS--Excellent preventive herb, very rich in vitamin E.

WHEY--Rich in sodium, helps keep calcium in solution and from settling in the joints.

YARROW--Helps regulate function of liver; blood cleanser.

YOGURT--Helps maintain intestinal bacteria or "flora".

YUCCA--Contains saponins which help clear the body of toxic waste. Precursor to synthetic cortisone.

ZINC--Helps joint swelling stiffness. Lack of zinc can cause slow
wound healing which contributes to arthritis which begins
because of injuries.

CANCER

Fifty-seven million Americans are destined to suffer from
cancer in one form or another. It hits the lives of two out of three
families. One out of three children born today will die of cancer, if the
trend continues as it has been doing.

The National Academy of Sciences validated what many
nutritionally-oriented physicians have been saying for years. The
United States government has found evidence that there is a strong
connection between diet and health, and now the American Cancer
Society says that diet is a major cause of cancer. We can no longer
deny the link between diet and cancer.

The type of harmful foods we eat gradually create a toxic
condition in the body. Lack of dietary fiber in the diet prolongs the
elimination of food residue from the lower bowel. The delay gives the
bacteria the opportunity to change certain chemicals in the stool residue
of bile into potent carcinogenic material. Bowel cancer is common in
the United States.

Dietary eating habits need to be changed, excluding meat
which is dead matter, cutting fats, and eliminating salt-cured, salt-
pickled and smoked foods such as sausage, bacon, ham, smoked fish,
bologna and hot dogs. We need to include more fresh fruits and
vegetables, whole grains, seeds, nuts, sprouts, beans and vegetables
such as cabbage, broccoli, cauliflower and Brussel sprouts.

It has been estimated that proper diet can help prevent cancer of
the pancreas, ovary, uterus, breast, prostate, and colon--to name a few.
We need to avoid fried and burnt foods that produce carcinogenic
benzopyrene. Stomach and esophageal cancer are found in populations
who use large amounts of smoked and salt-cured foods, especially meat.
Alcohol and cigarette smoking need to be eliminated.

Many doctors believe that the supplements of vitamins A, C,
and E and selenium, along with proper diet, can cut the risk of cancer
fifty percent. Supplements are necessary in our day and time. Our soil
is depleted of essential minerals, our food is tampered with additives,
milk is pasteurized (which destroys necessary enzymes, vitamins and
minerals), and meat is full of antibiotics and hormones. The air we
breathe is full of lead, carbon monoxide, herbicides, pesticides and
chemicals which find their way into our food supply and drinking water.

SPECIAL DIETARY HELPS

VITAMIN A--A protective vitamin. 50,000 IU a day has been used effectively as a cancer prevention. Especially useful for skin and the lungs.

ALMONDS--The protein in almonds help the pancreatic enzyme production. Best to eat 10 for breakfast and 10 for lunch. Protein of any kind should not be eaten after two p.m., for it is very hard to digest. Almonds help to rebuild healthy cells.

ALFALFA--Especially sprouts, contains chlorophyll to inhibit and fight infections. Alfalfa helps in assimilation of protein, calcium and other nutrients. The enzymes help to neutralize cancer in the system. Alfalfa contains B17 to help in the control of cancer.

APRICOT KERNELS--Contain natural B17. Himalayans use them as a staple in their diet, and incidence of cancer is relatively unknown.

BARLEY GREEN--It is the dried juice of the barley leaf. Rich in calcium, magnesium, vitamin C, vitamin B12, and iron. Also contains bioflavonoids, polysaccharides, polypeptides and enzymes which are helpful in the detoxification of poisons in the body. It contains SOD, an enzyme that has been found to be a cell protectant and a possible aging retardant.

BEANS--Dry, lima, kidney and pinto have properties to help inhibit cancer cells. All beans are good. Sprout before cooking to increase the nutrients and help to eliminate gas-causing properties. Cook at low temperature in the oven. Eating beans often helps the body to adjust to the gas-causing properties.

BEE POLLEN--Helps hormone balance, contains protein, vitamins and minerals.

BLACK WALNUT--Helps burn up excessive toxins and fatty materials. Rich in iodine. A good mineral balancer.

BREWERS YEAST--Helps build resistance to cancer and disease. Rich in selenium and an anti-cancer mineral. Very rich in amino acids, minerals, and B vitamins.

BURDOCK--A blood purifier, rich in vitamin C, high in protein for rebuilding healthy cells.

VITAMIN C--Antioxidant, destroys, neutralizes and protects against nitrates, nitrites and benzo(A)pyrene. Up to 5,000 mg a day. Strengthens collagen, the cement that holds normal cells together to help prevent cancer invasion. Builds the immune system. Helps to detoxify viruses and carcinogens which could cause cancer.

CHAPARRAL--Cleans the cells and tissues; antioxidant, anti-tumor, and antiseptic. Ointment made with chaparral, red clover and vitamin E may be of help in skin cancer.

CALCIUM--Helps build immunity to cancer and radiation. Helps in pain and the healing process.

CARROT JUICE--Raw juice helps in leukemia; high in calcium.

DANDELION--Liver cleanser; helps to keep liver activated to clean out toxic waste material that could cause cancer.

VITAMIN D--Helps the body to use calcium, phosphorus and vitamin A. Found in fish liver oils, oatmeal, egg yolk, brown rice and beans.

VITAMIN E--Free radical scavenger. Up to 1,220 IU daily has helped to protect against radiation; helps prevent skin tumors. Works synergistically with selenium.

EGG YOLKS--Used raw in drinks for full benefit of protein and vitamins.

ENZYMES--Food digestive aid; body's natural help for preventing and eliminating cancer. Helps the body to digest protein left in the body.

EVENING PRIMROSE OIL--The gamma linolenic acid content stimulates the immune system, and in test tube experiments reverts cancer cells back to normal. The use of vitamin C with evening Primrose oil enhances its value.

FIGS--Beneficial for constipation, rich in minerals easy to assimilate.

GARLIC--Antibacterial, rich in selenium, a cancer prevention mineral. Garlic contains 77.1 micrograms of selenium in 100 grams of raw garlic. Nature's antibiotic. Stimulates the lymphatic system to throw off waste material. Contains vitamins A and C.

GRAINS--Eat often, two large portions daily. Rich in amygdalin and dietary fiber, which reduces bowel transit time and reduces cholesterol.

KELP--Rich in iodine. Helps in breast cancer, helps to eliminate toxins from the body and very rich in iodine and other essential minerals.

JUICES--Fresh raw fruit and vegetables, cleanses and sustains the body while healing and cleansing.

LECITHIN--Helps in vitamin A and E assimilation. Brain food, cleanses veins.

LENTILS--Source of B17, iron and protein; very nourishing and easy to digest.

MILLET--Complete protein, easy to digest. An alkaline food to clean system, containing B17.

OLIVE OIL--Preferable to use for it does not cause the release of free radicals during the metabolic breakdown in the body.

PARSLEY--Rich in essential minerals and vitamins. Very rich in potassium, and cancer cells have a hard time multiplying when the body has sufficient potassium. Natural diuretic.

PAU D'ARCO--Powerful antibiotic; has virus-killing properties.

PROTEIN DIGESTIVE AID (HLC)--Helps break protein down so it can be easily assimilated.

RED CLOVER--Purifies the blood. It has been proven effective in cancer treatment.

SALADS--Eat all the fresh raw salads possible. Cooking destroys enzymes. Keeps the digestive track in proper working order.

SEEDS--Rich in easily digestible protein, calcium and vital minerals. Sunflower seeds, pumpkin seeds, sesame seeds and chia seeds.

SELENIUM--Protects against cancer in the breast and lungs. In the United States where the soil is low in selenium, there is an increasing incidence of breast and colon cancer. Selenium helps prevent damage to the DNA in the cells, which is the forerunner of the breakdown of tissues. Works with vitamin E in protecting cells of degradation.

SLIPPERY ELM--Nourishing, and is easily assimilated into the system.

SORGHUM--Contains nitrilosides and vitamin B17. Helps to inhibit cancer cells.

SPROUTS--Contains live enzymes. Eat raw for vitamin and mineral content. Easy to digest. Use alfalfa, red clover, fenugreek, buckwheat and wheat--to name a few.

STRESS--Severe emotional stress can trigger a deficient immune system. The body gives up because the emotional agony hurts. Need to check thymus gland activity. When it declines it makes the body vulnerable to organism invasions. This weakens the system and makes it less able to fight.

WATERCRESS--Purifies the blood; is rich in vitamins and minerals, especially A, C, D and E. It is considered a cancer prevention herb.

WHEAT GRASS--The juice. The chlorophyll molecule bears a striking resemblance to hemoglobin, the red pigment in human blood. It is a blood cleanser and builder.

WHEY POWDER--Concentrated, rich in natural lactic acid. It is valuable in the cancer diet. Contains antiseptic properties.

YARROW--Blood cleanser, absorbs different kinds of toxins, moves them out of the body. Contains A, C, E and F.

YELLOW DOCK--Excellent blood builder, it stimulates elimination, improving the flow of bile; nourishes the spleen and liver for better detoxificationn. Rich in easily assimilated iron, vitamins A and C.

ZINC--Very deficient in the American soil. It is essential for maintaining healthy T-cells which protect the body from cancer and disease.

COLON

The type of diet you eat will determine the nature of the bacteria in the intestine. The colon cannot be efficient in its proper function if the diet has consisted mostly of processed food, fried or overcooked food of white sugar, white flour products, and white rice, all of which take longer to travel through the colon than fibrous foods. This gives any cancer agent longer to act on the bowel wall. A diet high in animal protein promotes bacterial growth which changes harmless amino acids and transforms them into very strong and powerful toxins. After these toxins are formed they are absorbed into the blood stream. The liver doesn't always protect us from all the toxins. Many of these toxins pass through the liver almost entirely unchanged and then enter the bloodstream to find a weakened spot in the body to do its job. Fatigue, nervous irritability, intestinal problems, headaches and many others develop.

When these processed foods coat the inner walls of the colon they become encrusted. This accumulation of stagnant material coating the walls of the colon needs to be softened and loosened so it can be eliminated from the system. This material cannot be eliminated if the same diet is continued.

Autointoxication is the process whereby the body poisons itself by harboring a cesspool of decaying matter in its colon. It contains a high concentration of harmful bacteria. The toxins released by the decay process get into the bloodstream and go to all parts of the body and weaken the entire system. The weakest part of the body will suffer the most.

Before World War II it was typical for physicians to make statements about autointoxication as being the most important primary and contributing cause of many disorders and diseases of the human body. There were many articles written in medical journals about intestinal toxemia and autointoxication. This idea has been abandoned by the medical profession in favor of drugs and surgery. The typical American diet has deteriorated so badly that it breeds bacteria and causes intestinal toxemia.

A normal healthy colon has the function of proper absorption, assimilation and utilization of nutrients from the foods we eat as well as the elimination of waste material.

Colon cleansing will have a lasting effect on any ailment, sickness or disease.

COLONICS AND ENEMAS

Colonics are colon irrigations administered by a trained operator who uses many gallons of water in a very controlled atmosphere. It is very important that the person is a knowledgeable, trained operator and is with you during the whole procedure, which takes approximately thirty minutes. It is considered a very thorough and sophisticated enema.

If a person feels rotten and has built-up toxins as well as problems of the colon, then periodic colonics are an essential way to cleanse out the entire colon and bring it to its proper function again.

Colon cleansing works faster if you take herbs orally to loosen up the build-up material on the colon walls. Also, you use enemas or colonics to help remove old built-up toxins as soon as they are loosened. Just using herbs orally causes the material to be dissolved but can cause constipation if it isn't removed when it is loosened. It is very important to remember to remove all loosened material from the colon as quickly as possible, whether using herbs, liquids, enemas or colonics.

The reluctance to accept enemas is brought about by ignorance of the function and purpose. The enema helps to relieve stress, provides a clean colon, and gives a sense of well-being. The enema helps with the proper removal of toxins and debris from the colon so nutrients can be absorbed properly and to help diseases from taking hold of the body. Almost any ailment can be helped with cleansing the colon.

HOW TO TAKE AN ENEMA

Use a regular enema bag or a hospital disposable bag. The bag should not be over 18 inches higher than the body, since the enema solution would run into the colon too fast and cause discomfort. Lubricate the tube with vitamin E or lubricant jelly.

The knee-chest position is very efficient, and many people prefer this method. The head, shoulders and arms are on the floor with the buttocks elevated. Another position is lying on the left side, letting in about one cup of enema solution at a time. Massage gently on the left side of the abdomen, working down in the direction of the rectum. Massage the right side. Turn over on the back for about five minutes, then on the right side. Try to retain the enema for about 15 minutes or longer if you can, then it can be expelled. Remove the colon tube and stay on the left side for a few minutes.

Control the enema tube and allow as much as is comfortable. Expulsion is determined by cramping and also the urgency to expel.

The ability to hold more will come the more the colon is cleansed. Only use purified water.

TYPES OF ENEMAS

GARLIC ENEMA--Six garlic bulbs in three cups of pure water; blend and strain. Use 1/2 cup of this mixture in 2 quarts of water. Garlic is nature's antibiotic for it helps relieve stress and kills parasites while cleaning toxins from the colon.

CATNIP ENEMA--Steep 2 tablespoons of catnip in a quart of pure water; strain and add to enema bag with more pure water. Catnip is soothing to the colon and helps children in colic, fevers and childhood diseases.

SLIPPERY ELM--Use one quart pure water in blender with 2 tablespoons slippery elm powder. Strain, add to enema bag with more water. It neutralizes acidity and absorbs foul gas. Acts as a buffer against irritations in the colon. Good for colitis, diarrhea and hemorrhoids.

FLAXSEED TEA--Boil 1/4 cup flaxseed in one quart of pure water. Strain and add to the enema bag.

SPECIAL DIETARY HELPS

VITAMIN A--Important in maintaining strong, healthy cells. Needs a steady supply to strengthen and repair the tissues. Needed to support mucous membrance linings.

ACIDOPHILUS--Taken orally is beneficial in detoxifying the bowel as well as building the friendly bacteria. Very beneficial for healthy bowels.

AGAR AGAR--Is widely used as a thickener and emulsifier. It is very beneficial for constipation. It swells to many times its bulk when it reaches the intestines and helps increase the peristaltic action without causing painful gripping. Mixes with the food intake and moves it out.

ALFALFA--Very nourishing. Provides the bowels with bulk material which gets into the pockets of the bowels to keep it clean.

ALOE VERA--Very good for colon health. Use with ginger to prevent gripping.

APPLES--Good for constipation, with its fruit-acid salts which stimulate the digestive processes. The cellulose content helps soften the partly digested food in the intestines.

BENTONITE--(Hydrated) Absorbs and neutralizes toxins and bacteria found in the alimentary canal and detoxifies it.

BLACK WALNUT--Kills parasites in the colon and other areas of the body.

BRAN--Unprocessed bran increases stool weight and reduces transit times of food. It stabilizes intestinal regularity without irritating. Removes waste from the bowels. Always use with a large glass of water. Nourishes the colon.

BREWERS YEAST--Rich in the amino acids and all the B complex vitamins.

BUCKWHEAT--Provides bulk in the colon. Sprouted is best.

BUTTERMILK--Contains lactic acid for bowel tone. Is also soothing to the nervous system and the bowels.

VITAMIN C--Very important to control the sievability of the cells. Needed for healthy mucus membranes.

CALCIUM--Aids the body's utilization of iron, regulates the passage of nutrients in and out of the cell wall. The most abundant mineral in body. Good for nerves.

CHLOROPHYLL--Healing and cleansing for the colon. It helps stop growth of toxic bacteria in the bowels, and encourages normal growth of friendly bacteria.

COMFREY--Healing and soothing to the bowels.

ENZYMES--Taken at bedtime will help complete the digestion of food left in the colon.

EXERCISE--Lack can cause a lazy colon. Exercise strengthens the colon. Natural lactic acid is produced when you exercise.

FIGS--Prunes and raisins are all good for bowel health. Soak overnight in juice or pure water for best results. Figs are good especially when eaten fresh. High in natural sugar, the seeds have a natural laxative coating.

FLAXSEED--Used internally, it helps furnish bulk to the bowels. Used as tea for enemas. Relieves inflammation in the bowels, as well as cleanses toxins.

GINGER--Wonderful herb for nausea and stomach cramps and to prevent spasms and flatulence. Contains elements to destroy parasites in the colon.

HYDROCHLORIC ACID--Helps in protein assimilation as well as fats and carbohydrates.

IRON--A deficiency in iron may be related to toxins and poor elimination. Avoid inorganic iron, it oxidizes vitamin E and makes it ineffective.

LAXATIVES--Interfere with the proper absorption of important sodium and potassium balance in the large intestine. Potassium is lost when laxatives are taken.

LEMON and WATER--Taken first thing in the morning helps clean bowels and stomach.

LICORICE--Helps reduce flatulence and is soothing to the lining of the stomach and intestinal tract.

LYMPHATIC SYSTEM--The colon is the principal organ for the detoxification of the lymph glands. Rebound exercise helps remove toxins from the lymph glands. Echinacea, red clover and mullein are herbs that clean the lymphatics.

MAGNESIUM--Necessary in the digestion of food, tones muscles, helps in depression.

MEAT--Avoid meat for a healthy colon. Very strong putrefactive material. It spoils in the intestinal tract faster than any other food.

MILLET--High in protein, provides fiber for the colon; easily assimilated.

PANTOTHENIC ACID--Up to 50 mg daily has helped restore function in paralysis of the colon.

PAPAYA--Use often, especially if you eat meat. It will digest meat better than anything else.

POTASSIUM--Diarrhea, as well as stress, can cause loss. Potassium is needed to help balance body fluids.

SESAME SEEDS--Easily assimilated. Fiber for the colon.

PSYLLIUM HULLS--Provides bulk and lubrication for the bowels. It expands when taken with water to create bulk and removes intestinal putrefaction.

SPROUTING--Seeds and grains sprouted increase the nutrients.

STRESS--Can cause colon tightening, poor digestion and assimilation. Prolonged stress can cause constipation and leads to diarrhea and diverticulosis.

TOXINS--The brain suffers. Toxins also interfere with chemical balance of the body.

YOGURT--Provides friendly bacteria in the bowels, helps build immunity to disease.

ZINC--Large amounts have proved to be healing for the colon and for chronic ulceration of epithelial tissues. 15 to 30 mg daily, even larger at times.

FIBER FOODS

Alfalfa	Chia Seed	Oats--Steel Cut
Almonds	Corn, Grain	Pinto Beans
Barley	Flax Seeds	Rye
Blackeyed Peas	Garbanzo Beans	Soybeans
Bran	Lentils	Split Peas
Brown Rice	Mung Beans	Sunflower Seeds
Buckwheat	Millet	Whole Wheat
Carob		

SEED CEREAL FOR COLON

1 T. ground sesame seeds
1 T. ground sunflower seeds
1 T. ground almonds
1 tsp. chia seeds
1 tsp. flax seeds

Add two tablespoons of currants, raisins or chopped, dried apricots. Add raw apple juice or pineapple juice to cover. Set overnight in refrigerator. Ready to eat in the morning.

DIABETES

Ten million Americans have diabetes. Twice that number are pre-diabetic. During the last thirty years the United States has had one of the highest ratios of diabetic deaths in the world, as well as complications from the diseases. And it is steadily increasing. Researchers in other countries call it the American Candy Syndrome.

Diabetes is one of the ten most common causes of death and the third most common cause of blindness. Millions have genetic tendency to diabetes. Fifty percent of the cases of diabetes could be avoided or improved by changing eating habits, many people are finding help by changing their diets. Millions of children and youth are moving toward hypertension and diabetes. Children should avoid salted snacks, sugar, candy, soda pop, and all other sweets and salt that can lead to this crippling disease.

A diet of fruits, vegetables, nuts and seeds enables the acid condition of the body to become more alkaline to decrease a burden on the system. Avoid overeating, for this puts a load on digestion. It is far better to eat small meals.

SPECIAL DIETARY HELPS

VITAMIN A--Helps protect the eyes from damage. It is plentiful in fish liver oils. It is hard for diabetics to convert carotene into vitamin A. Carotene is the precursor of vitamin A found in carrots and many green vegetables.

ALL VITAMINS--Vitamins and minerals together are involved directly or indirectly in maintaining normal sugar metabolism.

ALLERGIES--Some doctors feel that about 50% of diabetics would benefit in testing food allergies. This can be done by fasting and testing one food per day while checking the blood sugar.

AVOCADOS--Rich in protein and fatty acids for easy digestion. Eat with fruits or green vegetables.

B COMPLEX VITAMINS--Helps to cut down on insulin intake, strenghtens and repairs the nerves.

BLACK WALNUT--Kills parasites, which have been found to cause some diabetes.

BRAN--Good for regularity, does not slow down absorption.

BREWERS YEAST--Rich in chromium, which has been shown to be a glucose-tolerance factor which allows the body to get by with less insulin. High processed carbohydrates cause chromium to be lost in the urine. Unless you eat whole grains daily you are deficient in chromium.

BROWN RICE--Rich in B vitamins, helps to create proper digestion, contains protein.

VITAMIN C with Bioflavonoids--This vitamin is essential for artery health and slows down the complication of cardiovascular diseases.

COMPLEX CARBOHYDRATES--Contains long chains of sugars hooked together by chemical bonds. The body absorbs complex carbohydrates more slowly than simple ones (sugar, white flour, white rice). Grains, brown rice, buckwheat and millet are better.

VITAMIN E--Necessary to help the body store sugar as glycogen. Helps iron to be absorbed by the thyroid and cuts down on artery complications.

DIGESTIVE ENZYMES--Helps to normalize digestion, breaks down protein left in the colon.

EXERCISE--Helps use up excess blood sugar. Twenty to thirty minutes of aerobic exercise a day benefits up to twelve hours later.

FIBER--May be able to repair faulty sugar metabolism by its complex effects on stomach and intestinal functioning. Grains, sprouts, beans.

GOLDEN SEAL--Stops internal bleeding. Acts as natural insulin, but you need to watch the tape test to determine amounts.

GRAINS--Natural carbohydrates are essential in the diet of diabetics. Slow-digesting foods such as buckwheat, brown rice, oats and millet are better.

HOPS--Has a beneficial effect on the nerves. Strengthens the nervous system.

IRON--Diabetics can develop iron deficiency anemia. Dandelion and yellow dock build the iron in the blood up faster than any other ingredients.

JUNIPER BERRIES--Natural herb that acts as a natural insulin. Can be used with golden seal.

KELP--Contains natural sugars, does not raise blood sugar levels. Cleanses the veins and nourishes the blood.

OBESITY--Raises the cholesterol and triglyceride levels. Extra fat cells cause the body to produce more and more excess insulin, trying to keep them nourished. Excess goes to the liver, which produces extra triglycerides that add further to the insulin resistance, becoming a vicious cycle. Eventually the pancreas can no longer keep pace with the demand for insulin. Blood sugar rises to dangerous levels, and obesity diabetes is born. Weight reduction improves sugar metabolism.

PROTEIN DIGESTIVE AID--It has been said that to bring about normal acidity it helps to restore natural secretion in insulin. Insulin can only function in an acid condition, so it aids the PH balance. Overacidity in diabetics is due to a lack of metabolism of fats and protein.

PUMPKIN SEEDS--Kills worms and parasites, which have been found to be one cause of diabetes.

PSYLLIUM HULLS--Causes the stomach to empty more slowly. Food is therefore absorbed from the intestines more gradually and does not release a sudden sugar load into damaged system.

RAW FOOD--Studies done on diabetics found that when they ate a diet consisting of 90% to 100% raw food they were able to discontinue medications.

SPROUTS--Live enzymes help to stimulate the pancreas, help increase the production of insulin. Natural hormones are essential for the pancreas to efficiently produce insulin. Alfalfa, mung beans, red clover, wheat, buckwheat.

ZINC--One of the main ingredients of insulin necessary for insulin activity and fat-tissue functions.

HEART

Heart disease, stroke and related disorders kill more Americans than all other causes of death combined. Heart attacks will strike and kill over 60,000 Americans this year.

A study comparing diet and deaths from heart disease in seven countries showed those eating animal foods had the highest rate of deaths. Other factors associated with heart disease include smoking, stress, lack of exercise, obesity, high blood pressure and high blood cholesterol levels.

Fat consumption has steadily increased in the average American diet. The consumption has been correlated with cancer and coronary heart disease. An increased intake of sugar and refined flour and other simple carbohydrates has been linked to an increased rate of deaths from heart attacks.

Reducing the intake of sugars and other refined carbohydrates, red meat, white flour products, combined with increased activity, such as walking and mini-trampoline, will help lower blood fat and cholesterol levels.

SPECIAL DIETARY HELPS

VITAMIN A--Builds the immune system and helps to recover from illness. Take along with vitamin D, which aids in assimilation. Taken with vitamin A and C it can help to prevent colds. Vitamin E intake enhances the use of vitamin A.

ALOE VERA JUICE--Has a beneficial effect on the health of the colon and stomach.

APPLES--Contains natural pectin for healthy arteries. Nourishing to the body.

ASPARAGUS--Beneficial for the heart; has diuretic properties.

B COMPLEX--Calming for the nerves as well as nourishment, the heart is extremely sensitive when the nerves are on edge. Pangamate (B15) prevents and helps in heart disease. It improves available oxygen to the blood. B15 and other B complex enhance the circulatory blood volume and lower arterial pressure. Found in apricot kernels, pumpkin and sesame seeds, brewers yeast, brown rice, whole grains and black walnut herb.

BEE POLLEN--Provides energy and strengthens the heart muscles.

BIOFLAVONOIDS--Provides protection against capillary fragility. Along with vitamin C. Makes vitamin C much more effective when using at the same time.

BANANAS--Rich in potassium, which is essential for a healthy heart.

BEANS--Helps to lower cholesterol and prevent heart disease. Soak the beans overnight and cook on slow heat to retain the vital nutrients.

BREWERS YEAST--Very rich in B vitamins, amino acids, both of which are very necessary for a healthy heart. Very beneficial for the nervous system.

BROWN RICE--Rich in B vitamins, dietary fiber; also a food to eat for nourishment as well as keeping the weight off.

BRAN--Natural fiber in the diet. Two tablespoons in eight ounces of tomato juice.

BUCKWHEAT--Rich in rutin for healthy capillaries, arteries. Cleans the vessels, provides nourishment and builds strong cell walls. Lowers blood pressure.

VITAMIN C--Antioxidant and helps prevent blood clotting, strengthens the heart. Helps prevent artery damage, eliminates fats and lowers the serum cholesterol level.

CALCIUM--Helps lower high blood pressure, reduces blood cholesterol and helps proper clotting of the blood to protect against strokes and hemorrhages.

CAYENNE--Cleans the circulatory system, regulates the heart and feeds the heart. One teaspoon in a glass of warm water has stopped heart attacks in some people.

CHELATION--Oral chelation therapy using vitamins, minerals, herbs, glandulars. Flushes away the calcified deposits from clogged arteries. Also keeps the plaque from forming and provides the body with essential nutrients.

CHLOROPHYLL--Helps to rebuild the heart, very rich in potassium. All green plant life is rich in potassium and other essential minerals.

CHROMIUM--Needed in small amounts, but essential for a healthy heart.

DIURETICS--Depletes the body of potassium and acts directly on the kidneys. Can also cause allergies, skin rashes, headache and weakness.

VITAMIN E--Improves oxygen utilization, circulation and muscle strength. D-alpha tocopherol is the natural and best to use.

EXERCISE--Leg muscles need exercise. Legs and feet help pump blood up to the heart and to the brain. Jumping on trampoline, walking a couple of miles a day. Always work up very gradually when starting to exercise.

FLAXSEEDS--Rich in linolenic acid and essential fatty acid (vitamin F). Essential for a healthy heart.

GRAINS--Provide vitamin E and B complex vitamins in their natural state. Wheat, buckwheat, rye, barley and millet.

HAWTHORNE BERRIES--Strengthens and feeds the heart. Helps in rapid and feeble heart action, heart valve defects, enlarged heart, angina pectoris and difficult breathing due to ineffective heart action and lack of oxygen in the blood.

INOSITOL and CHOLINE--Lowers cholesterol and is necessary for adequate production of dissolving agents. Prevents plaque build-up.

KELP, DULSE--Feed and nourish the blood. Supplies vital minerals to the body. Essential minerals to feed the heart as well as clean the arteries.

LECITHIN--Prevents fatty deposits in the arteries. Contains soap-like properties. Strong emulsifying agent, dissolves cholesterol deposits.

LICORICE--Food for the adrenal glands. Contains glycosides which can chemically purge excess fluid from the lungs, throat and body. It will supply necessary energy to the system. It has a stimulating action and helps counteract stress.

MAGNESIUM--Strengthens the heart muscles.

NERVOUS TENSION--Can upset the heart rhythm, which uses calcium, B vitamins and nervine herbs such as hops, scullcap, passion flower and valerian root.

NIACIN--Helps reduce cholesterol and normalizes blood clotting.

PARSLEY--Rich in vitamin A, has diuretic properties. Strengthens the heart, muscles and nerves.

POTASSIUM--Balances body fluids, calms the nerves, protects the cells from leaking and helps normalize the heart action. Potassium heals and cleans the blood. The more salt you eat the more potassium is necessary.

POTATOES--Baked and eaten with skins, very nourishing. Rich in potassium and protein.

SAFFRON--Helps to eliminate and neutralize the acids in the body.

SEEDS--Rich in calcium, fatty acids and protein to strengthen the heart. Sesame, sunflower and chia seeds.

SELENIUM--Protects the heart. Works closely with vitamins C and E. Eliminates cadmium from the body and helps lower cancer risks.

SCULLCAP--Has a tranquilizing effect on the central nervous system. Contains ingredients that have a positive influence on the heart.

TOFU--Easily assimilated protein, nourishes the heart.

VEGETABLES--Raw, easy to digest and assimilate. Celery, endive, cucumber, leaf lettuce, parsley, tomatoes, and watercress.

WHEY POWDER--Helps dissolve calcium deposits, and keeps calcium in circulation to be deposited where it is most needed.

YOGURT--Lowers cholesterol; helps keep the colon clean.

HYPERTENSION
(High Blood Pressure)

Twenty-five million Americans suffer high blood pressure. This could be reduced if over-consumption of certain foods were eliminated. Lack of exercise, obesity, poor eating habits and letting the problems of life put too much stress are all causes of high blood pressure. High blood pressure could be a symptom of body chemistry imbalance caused by the harmful effects of the wrong foods over a long period of time, such as too many refined carbohydrates such as white flour, pastries, white sugar, fat. If these types of food are consumed over a lifetime the blood vessels collect plaque and cause arteriosclerosis or atherosclerosis. Hypertension leads to heart attacks, strokes and kidney diseases.

SPECIAL DIETARY HELPS

VITAMIN A--Builds the immune system, maintains healthy arteries, and helps control high blood pressure.

ALMONDS--High in protein and calcium, necessary for healthy arteries. Rich in amino acids to strengthen vascular walls.

APPLES--Contains pectin, rich in malic acid, which helps to relax the body to control blood pressure.

B COMPLEX VITAMINS--High potency, calms the nerves, builds blood. B3 has a dilating effect on the arteries and reduces cholesterol levels. B6 calms nerves, natural diuretic.

BROMELAIN--Found in pineapple, an enzyme that repairs and heals arterial walls. Helps in digestion and provides better assimilation.

BROWN RICE DIET--Along with fresh fruits and vegetables, lowers blood pressure, cleans toxins from the blood stream, and provides protein, vitamins and minerals.

BUCKWHEAT--Rich in rutin, helps lower blood pressure.

VITAMIN C with Bioflavonoids--Strengthens the blood vessels and lowers cholesterol levels. A natural diuretic.

CADMIUM--A toxic metal that is linked in hypertension. Intake of zinc displaces cadmium.

CALCIUM--Necessary to control blood pressure, lack can cause high blood pressure. Herbal calcium, bone meal or oyster shells.

CHELATION THERAPY--Oral, using herbs, vitamins, minerals and amino acids. Cleans the arteries and improves circulation.

CHOLINE--Dissolves accumulation of fats to improve circulation.

VITAMIN E--Dilates the blood vessels; small amount to start; could temporarily elevate blood pressure.

GARLIC and ONIONS--Dilates the capillaries and arteries, reduces high blood pressure, helps the sodium balance of the cells. A natural diuretic.

EXERCISE--Strengthens the arteries. Regular exercise will lower high blood pressure.

HAWTHORNE BERRIES--An herb that nourishes and strengthens the heart.

INOSITOL--Helps in hypertension.

JUICE FASTING--Very effective in lowering high blood pressure.

LECITHIN--Helps to prevent build-up of plaque in the arteries; breaks up cholesterol; helps to repair arterial walls.

MAGNESIUM--Helps the nervous system. Magnesium is depleted by diuretics. Essential for a healthy heart.

PARSLEY--Natural diuretic, helps to eliminate excess water in the tissue.

POTASSIUM--Helps the body to eliminate too much sodium, essential for normal heart function and strengthens the nervous system.

SALADS--Raw; use with oil and lemon or sour whey.

SALT--Avoid excess salt, which interferes with metabolism and causes stress and water retention. Increases blood pressure and interrupts stomach acids.

SCULLCAP and VALERIAN--Help to stabilize blood pressure. Relaxation is essential to normalize blood pressure.

SELENIUM--Lowers blood pressure. Where it is low in the soil, blood pressure problems are more likely to occur. Protects artery walls.

SESAME SEEDS--Contain high amounts of calcium, protein.

TYROSINE--Amino acid; helps to lower high blood pressure.

WHOLE GRAINS--Barley, bran, brown rice, bulghur, wheat, millet, oats. These are natural carbohydrates which soothe the nerves and give energy to the body to help stabilize high blood pressure.

YOGURT--Rich in calcium, provides friendly bacteria for healthy bowels.

ZINC--Necessary for the utilization of vitamin A, necessary to control high levels of cadmium in the blood. High cadmium levels are often associated with high blood pressure.

HYPOGLYCEMIA
(Low Blood Sugar)

Many Americans suffer from low blood sugar. Even though it is a physical condition it causes mental and emotional changes in the body. Many doctors in the medical field claim it does not exist. It does exist and is increasing rapidly, and mainly because of the eating habits of the American people. The American diet is strongly overbalanced with refined foods, which damage the nervous system as well as the immune system, and starts the development of hypoglycemia. Some of the classic symptoms are weakness, hunger, fatigue, sweating, rapid beat of the heart, a feeling of anxiety or fear. Hypoglycemia has been attributed to addiction, alcoholism, allergies, arthritis, migraine headaches, stomach pains, and many other symptoms.

It is felt by some doctors that if hypoglycemia goes untreated for a long period of time it develops into diabetes. Some people can handle hypoglycemia, while others cannot because of the amount of stress they are confronted with. The glands suffer when we are under stress. We need to overcome the stress, learn to turn off what we have no control over, solve what we can, and learn to cope. Licorice root is a concentrated food that acts in the body like the cortin hormone and assists in helping the body handle stress.

The most effective way to control hypoglycemia is a natural food diet. Foods that are important are grains, nuts and seeds; vegetables, fruits and especially sprouts. Meals should be small, eaten about six times daily.

SPECIAL DIETARY HELPS

ALFALFA--Aids in the assimilation of protein, calcium and other nutrients. It gives vitality to the body since it is a rich source of chlorophyll, vitamins and minerals and protein.

ACIDOPHILUS--Improves nutritional utilization of enzymes, vitamins and minerals. Biotin deficiency is improved with acidophilus. Constipation is relieved, for calcium is more readily absorbed because of the acidic properties of acidophilus. Converts lactose in milk to lactic acid, and this supplements the hydrochloric acid in the stomach, easing digestion in a natural, drugless way.

AVOCADOS--Contains a special sugar which does not stimulate insulin production but suppresses it. Excellent food for hypoglycemics. Contains protein, fats, carbohydrates, minerals and vitamins.

B COMPLEX--Builds the adrenals, needed to help control hypoglycemia. Calms the nerves. B3 (niacin) can help regulate blood sugar level.

BEE POLLEN--Complete protein, packed with energy for the body in a natural and healthy way. Full of enzymes, vitamins and minerals.

BLACK COHOSH--Acts like the female estrogen hormone. It may be needed if hormones are out of balance.

BREWERS YEAST--Rich in phosphorus and low in calcium. Add more calcium when using brewers yeast. Use with sesame seeds or yogurt to help create a better mineral balance.

BUCKWHEAT--Complete protein. Digest slowly so the body can better utilize it. Contains B vitamins, iron, calcium, high in magnesium, manganese and zinc.

VITAMIN C--Can help prevent low blood sugar attacks. Needed for resistance to disease. Vitamin C is concentrated in the adrenal glands and has an affect in hypoglycemia. Plays a role in sugar metabolism.

CHAMOMILE TEA--Soothes the nerves and aids digestion. Contains calcium.

CHROMIUM--Essential to the utilization of glucose.

DANDELION--It contains all the nutritive salts that are required for the body to purify the blood. Excellent herb for low blood pressure; it builds energy and strengthens endurance. High in protein, increases activity of the pancreas and the spleen.

VITAMIN E--Helps to assure proper adrenal function. Acts to protect as an antioxidant to pollutants in the air. Aids in storing glycogen in the muscles and tissues.

ENZYMES--Necessary to provide energy. Sprouts contain live enzymes. Enzymes are necessary for proper digestion and assimilation of nutrients in the body. Lack can cause built-up toxins in the system.

EXERCISE--Helps burn off excess sugar in the blood.

FRUIT--Banana 1/2 at a time, one small apple, one slice of pineapple, 1/2 cup fresh berries, 1/2 grapefruit. Use with yogurt or kefir, raw nuts or seeds for energy.

GARLIC & ONIONS--Contain elements to help regulate sugar levels.

GINSENG--Contains the male hormone.

GREEN DRINKS--The chlorophyll in the drinks can help the body to combat hardening of the arteries. Ten drops of chlorophyll in pure water. See recipes for green drinks.

HAWTHORNE BERRIES--It has been known for centuries as a treatment of heart disease. Strengthens the heart muscles. It has been used in preventing arteriosclerosis.

JERUSALEM ARTICHOKES--Contain a starch that the pancreas can handle. Use raw in salads.

JUNIPER BERRIES--Nourish and regulate the pancreas.

KELP--Helps to normalize mineral balance and supply necessary trace elements which are involved in sugar metabolism.

LECITHIN--Helps to keep the veins clean and healthy.

LEMONS--Cleans and rebuilds the liver. The liver plays a role in keeping a proper sugar balance. Use with pure water.

LICORICE--Acts as a stimulant to the adrenal glands. Supplies necessary energy to the system. It gives a feeling of well-being. It acts in the body like certain hormones and assists in helping the body handle stress.

MAGNESIUM--Helps the nervous system, prevents depression, nourishes the heart, helps in conversion of blood sugar to energy.

MILLET--Cooked or sprouted to help break down the phytin and releases the minerals. Easily digested, acts as akaline in the body, a carbohydrate that has a beneficial effect on hypoglycemia.

NUTS--Almonds, as well as other nuts, rich in protein and calcium. Quick energy food, concentrated food, eat only 10 at a time and chew well or grind.

OLIVE OIL--When used in natural state (cold-pressed) contains essential fatty acids. Helps to balance hormone levels and could be important to proper sugar metabolism.

POTASSIUM--Protects the cells from leaking, balances body fluids, calms the nerves, and helps the body handle stress. Useful for hypoglycemia.

PROTEIN DIGESTIVE AID--The digestive system can be defective in hypoglycemia. With proper digestion the food is assimilated and utilized.

SAFFLOWER--Cleansing herb for the arteries, helps with cholesterol level in the blood.

SEEDS--Chia, very rich in protein, a wonderful energy food. Flax, high in fatty acids, linoleic acid and linolenic acids (vitamin F), high mucilaginous for a healthy alimentary canal and eliminative system. Sunflower seeds for energy, high in protein. Sesame seeds are rich in calcium.

SPIRULINA--Very rich in protein, chlorophyll, vitamins and minerals, as well as amino acids. Very rich in calcium. Contains some vitamin B12.

SPROUTS--All sprouts, seeds, grains and beans. They digest faster than cooked foods. They release sugar into the bloodstream gradually and at a slower pace. It is important that the body have evenly sustained sugar levels in the blood and that the assimilation of carbohydrates be as slow as possible.

STRESS--Avoid stress like the plague, for it is one of the main causes of adrenal fatigue. Watch diet to eliminate further stress on the body.

ZINC--Necessary for a healthy pancreas. Can have a healthy effect on the lining of the arteries.

IMMUNE SYSTEM

The immune system is made up of specific cells scattered throughout the body which have the wonderful power to recognize what could be a threat to survival and destroy them. The immune system tries to neutralize and destroy foreign substances or infections that invade the body. The key to prevention and treatment of disease is a healthy immune system. The immune system accumulates damage and can gradually become defective over many years or if we abuse our bodies to the extent that it cannot repair itself it can become damaged in a shorter period of time.

We are constantly coming in contact with internal and external agents that can create free radicals. Pollutants, cigarette smoke, lead, cadmium, sodium nitrite, sulfur dioxides, ozone, radiation and many of our so-called modern foods, especially if the food is rancid, especially oil. Toxic residues from exhaustion, illness and stress are also factors in free radicals forming.

A free radical is a toxic chemical which is out of control and is capable of putting a hole (chemical hole) in any tissue of the body. It could destroy a gene or cause a cell wall to leak. When it causes damage to the cell it liberates more free radicals and more toxins to damage other cells. In our youth, we produce enzymes that destroy free radicals, but as we age enzyme production declines, making the body vulnerable. Also long term nutritional deficiencies--malnutrition brings on genetic weakness through chemical imbalance along with poor elimination which leads to an environment that invites unfriendly bacteria, which thrive on dead tissues and cause toxins and free radicals to multiply.

Fat intake creates abnormalities in metabolism and initiates drastic changes in immunity. These abnormalities are created into free-radicals with excessive ingestion of rancid oils, found in many commercial products (salad dressings, fried foods, rancid butter, potato chips, french fries and doughnuts as well as any deep fried foods).

There are supplements which have been proven effective in preventing free-radical accumulation as well as promoting health and protection against disease. These supplements help to promote a youthful body to prevent premature aging and strengthen the immune system. The body needs a reserve of nutrients to build up a healthy immune system to protect us from invaders.

IMMUNE SYSTEM DESTROYERS

AGENE (nitrogen trichloride) is a flour bleach which can cause epileptic-like fits and ataxia (failure of muscle coordination).

GLUTAMIC ACID, found in monosodium glutamate, affects the central nervous system. It can cause depression, gloomy fantasies and rage as long as two weeks after eating foods with MSG.

SODIUM NITRITE is found in many foods as a preservative. It is capable of producing seemingly permanent epileptic changes in brain activity and damage to the central nervous system.

FOOD DYES, FLAVORINGS and ANTIOXIDANTS have been found to be a potent factor in behavioral problems such as learning disabilities and hyperkinesis in children and adults.

SWEETS, CHOCOLATE and WHITE FLOUR can cause an imbalance in metabolism which lowers the immunity and resistance to depression and diseases.

SPECIAL DIETARY HELPS

VITAMIN A--Contains anti-viral properties. Use with zinc and protein (sunflower seeds). Increases immunity, especially against air pollution. Beta-carotene converts into vitamin A inside the body. The liver stores vitamin A and when stress or disease develop and increase the need for vitamin A, the liver will release enough stored vitamin A to keep the blood levels up.

ACIDOPHILUS--Helps to eliminate intestinal putrefaction; provides better digestion and assimilation.

ALCOHOL--Creates a lot of hard work for the detoxifying organs-- liver, kidneys and the pancreas. Depletes the body of B complex vitamins.

B COMPLEX VITAMINS--Needed to be replaced daily. Brewers yeast, bee pollen, rice polishing, grains.

BARLEY JUICE POWDER--Dried juice of the barley leaf. Contains SOD, an enzyme that has been found to be a cell protectant against free radicals. It helps in the detoxification of poisons in the body.

BEE POLLEN--Rich in amino acids. Works with vitamin A to build up the immune system.

BLACK WALNUT TINCTURE--High in organic iodine for killing germs; very healing.

BROWN RICE--A valuable and natural, balanced, nutritious food. Excellent source of the B complex vitamins. It retains the previous germ, vitamins, minerals, protein, fat, starch and fiber. It is an inexpensive source of fuel for the body. It is considered a protective food.

VITAMIN C--Helps the body to produce natural interferon (the molecule that helps to destroy viruses) to protect the immune system. Vitamin C is a potent antioxidant that protects us against cancer. It helps to block the formation of nitrite compounds that develop from the foods we eat.

CALCIUM--Healing to the body, prevents many disorders in the body, bone loss, nervous problems, works with magnesium, phosphorus. Vitamin D for absorption.

DEPRESSION--Avoid situations that cause depression, for depressed people have more viral infections, herpes and candida. There are higher cancer risks in the depressed. Depression lowers the immune system.

CLEANSING DIETS--Help build up the immune system when used periodically.

VITAMIN E--Helps to repair cell damage, builds up immunity along with selenium. Vitamin E prevents the oxidized state that cancer cells thrive in, and it deactivates the free radicals that promote cellular damage leading to malignancy.

ECHINACEA--Increases the immunity levels and contains properties which elevate the white blood count to absorb and eliminate harmful bacteria. Contains essential fatty acids which are involved in the proper function of the immune system.

EVENING PRIMROSE OIL--Stimulates the T-cells of the immune system. Experiments done in test tubes show that it reverts cancer cells back to normal cells. PGE is required for the T-cells of the immune system to attack cancer. T-cells are the main mechanism of the immune system to protect the body from foreign cells, viruses, bacteria, fungi and allergens. Evening primrose contains high amounts of PGE, a vitamin-like compound involved in proper function of the immune system. A shortage of PGE is believed to cause abnormal and harmful immune response.

FOLIC ACID--Along with B12 are involved in maintaining a healthy immune system. The B12 carries folic acid into the white cells of the immune system. They are both deficient in the typical American diet.

FOOD ENZYMES--Deficiency in enzymes can inhibit proper digestion and cause toxins to weaken the immune system. Enzymes help to digest food left in the colon.

GARLIC--Considered to be nature's penicillin. Contains antibiotic properties.

HIGH FAT DIETS--Prevent the body from producing the intrinsic factor necessary for B12 absorption, as well as many other enzyme reactions.

HOPS--Rich in B complex vitamins and calming for the nerves. Relaxes the body and builds up the nervous system to protect the immune system from damage.

IRON--Necessary for healthy blood. Yellow dock and dandelion together will build up the blood. They are both very rich in organic iron and other minerals.

JUNK FOOD--Puts a double stress on the body. When too much junk food is eaten the appetite for wholesome food is dulled. Caffeine puts stress on the body by weakening the heart, nervous system and respiratory tract. Caffeine is a potent diuretic for it washes the water soluble vitamins from the system. Vitamin C and the B complex vitamins are among the most important for combating stress.

LYSINE--An amino acid; helps calcium absorption; helps to control herpes infections, and along with the right diet, helps inhibit its growth.

MILLET--A very nourishing food to use often, it acts as an intestinal lubricant aiding elimination and absorption. It will not leach calcium from the tissues as red meat can. Complete protein, alkaline reaction in the body. Rich in lecithin, B complex vitamins, calcium, iron, phosphorus and others.

MYRRH--Strengthens and builds up the immune system; contains antiseptic properties to combat staph and other infections.

PAU D'ARCO--Contains anti-fungal properties. Strengthens the immune system. Need to simmer 30 minutes to steep out the active ingredients.

RED RASPBERRY--Contains anti-fungal properties, rich in calcium and other vital vitamins and minerals. A good herbal tea to build up the immune system.

SAGE--Contains anti-fungal properties.

SCULLCAP--A weakened immune system is related to stress and puts a strain on the nerves. Scullcap feeds and strengthens the nerves. It calms the nerves and helps in emotional problems.

SELENIUM--Strengthens the immune system and helps clean up free radicals before they cause harm. It improves antibody production and protects against cancer.

STRESS--Avoid stress for constant stress will cause the weakest part of the system to suffer first. Learning to control stress has a strong influence on the immune system.

SWEETS--Eating white sugar products, chocolate and white flour can cause an imbalance in metabolism that lowers the immunity and causes depression and disease.

THYME--Strengthens the immune system and has antiseptic and anti-fungal properties.

TRYPTOPHAN--An essential amino acid, soothing for the nerves. Taken at the first sign of an attack of herpes II has helped many people.

VEGETABLES--Eating lots of raw vegetables provides live enzymes, vitamins and minerals, as well as providing bulk for a healthy colon.

WATERCRESS--A prevention herb, rich in iodine, good for the thyroid and all the endocrine glands. By using it regularly, the body builds up resistance to disease, especially catarrhs and infectious disease. The wild-growing is superior to the cultivated one.

WHEATGRASS--Especially the wheatgrass juice builds the immune system. It has a nourishing and cleansing effect on the blood.

WHOLE GRAINS--Very nourishing especially when sprouted. Use buckwheat and wheat often.

YARROW--Contains tranquilizing properties, builds up the central nervous system. Contains vitamin C and bioflavonoids.

ZINC--Speeds up the healing process and helps balance minerals. Along with vitamin A, builds up the immune system and improves the body's ability to fight diseases. Seventy enzymes in the body depend on zinc.

LUNGS

Almost all of the body's vital functions depend upon oxygen, especially energy production in the muscle cells. Lack of oxygen quickly depletes the body of energy. Lungs are also one of the organs of elimination. Breathing properly is essential to cleanse the body of toxins, as well as help the body utilize the nutrients. Exercising in fresh air helps the lungs increase their ability to pump oxygen. The vessels and circulation are kept healthy by the blood vessels. The bone marrow is stimulated to produce more red cells, carbon dioxide and waste materials are removed from the cells, and metabolism in all of the body organs is stimulated.

Incomplete digestion and poor nutrition, along with free radicals and rancid fats, can result in particles of matter which gradually close the "pores". The lungs then lose their elasticity.

SPECIAL DIETARY HELPS

VITAMIN A--Releases an enzyme called proteolytic which tends to soften the matrix of the cell tissues. Strengthens the lungs, protects against infections and toxins. At the beginning of a cold, some people respond by taking large amounts for about five days.

B COMPLEX--Strengthens the lungs, nourishing and healing.

B6--Reduces the severity of asthma and lung problems.

BIOTIN--Helps to prevent lung infections.

VITAMIN C with Bioflavonoids--Needed every day, helps to rebuild the capillaries and cells of the lungs. Also builds up the immunity against lung diseases.

BARLEY WATER--Cook barley in pure water, strain, drink liquid with lemon. Contains hordenine which relieves bronchial spasms.

CAYENNE--Useful to add to soups to loosen up mucous.

CALCIUM--Necessary for healthy lungs.

CHLOROPHYLL--Liquid or green drink, blood purifier, rich in vitamins and especially iron. Necessary for healthy lungs.

COMFREY--Soothes and heals the lungs, removes mucus, heals inflamed tissues.

CRANBERRY JUICE CONCENTRATE--One teaspoon at a time in water. Contains natural citric, malic and benzoic acids, acting as intestinal antiseptic and aids in digestion.

DANDELION--Blood cleanser and purifier, strengthens the lungs and expels phlegm.

ESSENTIAL FATTY ACIDS--Increases the oxygen-carrying capacity of the blood, thus reducing the need for oxygen.

EXERCISE--Deep breathing fresh air has a vital effect on all parts of the body.

VITAMIN E--Antioxidant that guards against toxins. Enough vitamin E in the body can utilize more available oxygen. Vital in protecting the lungs against air pollution.

ELECAMPANE--Expectorant, good for chest colds. Helps lungs and bronchi.

FENUGREEK--Dissolves mucus, contains natural dehydrating properties, cleanses the kidneys.

FLAXSEED--Cleans mucus from bronchial tubes; cleans bowels.

GARLIC--Clears congestion and mucus from the nose and chest. Cut cloves in water and heat, add fresh lemon juice.

GOLDEN SEAL--Expectorant, soothes inflamed mucous membranes. Good for infections of nose, sinuses and throat.

HORSERADISH--Used with lemon juice very good for the lungs.

IRON--An essential nutrient to lung tissues; use natural because inorganic iron oxidizes or burns up vitamin E.

JERUSALEM ARTICHOKES--Contain vitamins A, B, B2 and C. Feed the lungs and help to relieve lung conditions; best to use grated, raw in salads and soups.

KELP--Rich in iodine and is needed for healthy lungs. Contains all the essential minerals for healthy lungs.

LICORICE--Builds the body's resistance to allergies. Aids adrenal functioning.

MARSHMALLOW HERB--Soothes irritated tissues of lungs, removes hardened phlegm and relaxes bronchial tubes.

MULLEIN--Calms nerves, relieves pain and is rich in potassium whose lack can cause asthma.

ONIONS--Sliced, with garlic and honey and soaked overnight, use this honey morning and night to strengthen the lungs.

PAPAYA--Aids in digestion for better assimilation.

PINEAPPLE JUICE--Fresh, sip slowly for sore throat.

RED CLOVER--Builds the body's resistance to allergies.

ROSE HIPS--Supplies the body with easily assimilated source of vitamin C.

SUNFLOWER SEEDS--Easily assimilated protein.

VEGETABLES--Especially green leafy, contain vitamin A, necessary to maintain elasticity in lung membranes. Contain both vitamin E and iron.

WHEY--Mineral food, high in calcium and natural phosphorus. Aids digestion, stops intestinal fermentation, holds calcium in solution for limber joints.

YOGURT--High in protein and easy to digest. Replaces enzymes that are destroyed by air pollution and antibiotics.

Sodium chloride (table salt) and starch are toxic to persons with lung problems. It would be better to eliminate those from the diet as well as milk, eggs, chocolate, sugar and white flour. Too much animal phosphorus foods can damage the lungs and kidneys. The kidneys and lungs have the job of expelling the largest percentage of built-up phosphorus. If too much phosphorus is consumed over a long period of time the lungs and kidneys can lose their efficiency. The oxidation in the blood and tissues is upset when our bodies have toxic by-products of phosphorous.

COMPLETE MEAL SALAD

2 C. leaf lettuce	4 green onions
1 C. alfalfa sprouts	2 small tomatoes
1/2 C. fenugreek sprouts	1/4 C. sunflower seeds,
1/2 C. red clover sprouts	ground
1 small cucumber	2 T. sesame seeds,
1/2 C. zucchini	ground

Mix all together. Serve with clove crushed garlic, olive oil and fresh lemons. Add kelp, paprika and dash of cayenne.

OBESITY

Overweight is a very serious problem, and we as a nation are fatter than we were twenty years ago. Overweight predisposes you to heart disease, hardening of the arteries, hypertension, strokes, heart attacks, diabetes, bladder disease and cancer. One third of all Americans are overweight. Osteoarthritis is another problem (from increased strain on the joints). There is an increased susceptibility to infectious diseases and very serious personality problems.

The immune system becomes more defective as we gain unwanted weight. The metabolism of fat cells destroys substances in the bloodstream that protect the body from heart disease. Too much fat increases the risk of diseases.

Eating junk food stimulates the appetite, and since it does not satisfy the nutritional needs of the body, the brain tells the body to eat more, that it is hungry and tries to get you to give it some nourishing food. The body needs nourishing food and supplements to meet its nutritional needs.

SPECIAL DIETARY HELPS

ALFALFA--Very good for digestion; supplies vitamins and minerals to the body. Helps protein and calcium to digest.

VITAMIN A--While losing weight the liver is called on to do extra detoxifying. Vitamin A protects the liver from damage.

ALLERGIES--Food allergies can make you fat. You have strong urges for certain food and cannot satisfy your craving unless you eat that certain food, such as chocolate, potato chips, cheese, ice cream, coffee, dairy products, wheat. Food sensitivities could cause allergic persons to crave these foods to which they are allergic. Removal of an offending food will usually result in a rapid water loss of five to ten pounds within a week.

BEE POLLEN--Provides stamina to the body. Contains all of the amino acids. Goes directly into the bloodstream, consuming fat, burning calories and speeding up the burning of fat. When taken alone, seems to help in fat metabolism.

BLACK WALNUT--Rich in iodine, helps to correct thyroid which stimulates weight loss and a sense of well being.

BRAN--Using a few teaspoons in a large glass of pure water before each meal will not only give bulk to the bowels but will help depress the appetite, to help cut down on the amount of calories.

VITAMIN C--Large amounts of vitamin C helps check the craving for sugar.

CHICKWEED--Helps to dissolve the plaque out of the blood vessels as well as the fatty substances in the system.

COMFREY and PEPSIN--Comfrey helps promote the secretion of pepsin and is a general aid to digestion. It has a beneficial effect on all parts of the body, being an over-all tonic. Pepsin helps clean up the stomach and colon to provide a healthy atmosphere for proper food and nourishment.

DANDELION--Provides vitamins and minerals, cleans the liver. Congestion of the liver can cause obesity.

VITAMIN E--Protects the liver from the fat which will flood into the blood stream when reducing weight.

EVENING PRIMROSE OIL--Contains GLA (gamma-linoleic acid) a natural nutritional supplement to help restore the body's ability to process calories and generate brown fat activity. 4-8 capsules per day.

EXERCISE--Helps reduce overweight, increases energy, cleans the brain and helps towards better disposition. Lowers blood pressure and cholesterol levels, strengthens the heart, helps prevent premature aging, improves lung capacity, helps prevent calcium loss from bones and helps prevent depression.

FLAXSEEDS--Soaked in apple juice or pure water overnight and eaten before meals helps stop excessive food cravings.

GLUCOMANNAN--Helps lose or maintain weight by helping to control hunger pangs, it provides dietary fiber to help maintain regularity and healthy bowels. It has a water-binding, gel-forming capacity.

KELP--Contains iodine, the thyroid needs iodine to produce thyroxin. Lack of it will store fat and cholesterol. Iodine makes the metabolic system burn the fuel the way it should. Kelp promotes balanced absorption, assimilation and distribution of vital nutrients.

LECITHIN--Helps control fat deposits, natural diuretic, helps remove fat out of the body.

PANTOTHENIC ACID--Promotes proper digestion so that food won't go to fat. It also helps avoid food allergies.

POTASSIUM--Diets usually deplete potassium and leave sodium in the body to retain water in the tissues.

SARSAPARILLA--Purifies the blood and glands, for proper elimination of unwanted fat.

SUGAR--Excessive sugar and starch creates an abnormal appetite. They affect the body chemically like alcohol. The more they are used the craving is set in orbit. Sugar and starch are a dangerous combination. Sugar hastens decay or fermentation and acid is rapidly produced.

ZINC--Is excreted fast from the body and is needed for many enzyme functions in the body.

THESE FOODS INTERFERE WITH THE PITUITARY GLAND AND HINDER THE ABILITY OF THE HORMONES TO METABOLIZE FATS. THEY STICK TO YOUR INTESTINAL TRACT AND PROMOTE WEIGHT GAIN:

White Flour	White Sugar Products
Bakery Products	Ice Cream
Soft Drinks	Bread
Creamed Vegetables	Crackers
Candy	Potato Chips
Sweet Wines	Sweetened Canned Fruit
Waffles and Pancakes	Processed Cereal
Pasta	Doughnuts and Cookies
Jams and Jellies	Biscuits and Rolls
	Beer

FOODS THAT ARE EASIER TO DIGEST AND HELP FEED AND SUPPORT THE ENERGY NEEDS OF THE BODY WITHOUT ADDING FAT:

Whole Grain Cereals
Brown Rice
Red Clover
Fresh Fruits
Fresh Vegetable Juices
Raw Vegetables

Steamed Vegetables (lightly)
Alfalfa Sprouts
Fenugreek
Herbs
Rice Flour
Bean Sprouts

ANTI-FAT SALAD

1 C. leaf lettuce
1 C. alfalfa sprouts
1/2 C. grated red cabbage
1/2 C. grated carrots
2 stalks celery

1 raw grated beet
6 radishes
6 green onions
2 chopped tomatoes
Kelp to taste

Mix with olive oil and lemon juice.

PREGNANCY

It is essential to gain knowledge of the importance of nutrients in the body before you decide to get pregnant. Whatever you take into the body has an effect on the fetus. The food you eat is what creates the substance of the baby. Too much sugar puts stress on the pancreas of the mother as well as on the pancreas of the baby. (Excess sugar robs the body of vitamins and minerals essential for the development of the baby, especially the B vitamins. Excess sugar can cause hypoglycemia in the baby.)

Pregnancy can be a very happy experience if the mother's body is free from toxins. Toxins can cause nausea and hormonal imbalances. Cleansing the colon and the liver will help to avoid any undue nausea during pregnancy.

SPECIAL DIETARY HELPS

VITAMIN A--Builds resistance to disease, promotes growth, protects against toxins. Aids in the growth of strong bones, along with calcium and vitamin C.

ALCOHOL--Avoid during pregnancy. Alcohol passes freely through the placenta. It becomes toxic when used in quantities in excess of the organism's ability to metabolize it. It can cause fetal alcohol syndrome and small stature, small head, narrow eye slits, flattened nasal bridge, receding chin, mental retardation and cardial defects. Drinking can affect the baby even before conception.

ALFALFA--Very rich in calcium and magnesium balance. Excellent food for mothers-to-be as well as nursing mothers to promote rich milk for the baby. High in vitamin K which clots the blood and prevents hemorrhages, contains enzymes to help assimilation and digestion of food.

ALMONDS--Raw almonds are an excellent source of protein. Help promote normal bowel function. Almond milk is good for inflamed stomach and intestines. Rich in calcium. *Almond Milk*: Soak one cup of almonds overnight. Put the almonds in blender with 4 cups of pure water, blend until it looks like milk, about three minutes. Add a little honey or pure maple syrup. Use on cereals, granola and in sauces instead of milk.

ANEMIA--It is very common during pregnancy. If there are problems with the the assimilation and digestion, the iron may not be utilized. Digestion will be helped if papaya, alfalfa, enzymes tablets are taken along with the iron herbs, dandelion and yellow dock.

B-COMPLEX VITAMINS--Essential to build up the immune system. Helps to avoid infections of the vagina. The B vitamins help protect the body form exhaustion and irritability. Extra B6 helps keep down swelling and prevents nausea. 300 mg. in the morning and 300 mg. at night has been helpful for some people. Extra B6 provides more energy. Builds the body against allergies, strengthens the brain and heart, and helps in enzymatic function.

BROWN RICE--Provides the B vitamins; provides energy.

BEANS--Pinto helps to leach out toxic metals; sprout before cooking.

VITAMIN C COMPLEX (C with Bioflavonoids)--Helps enhance contractions, minimize stretch marks along with zinc. Helps to keep viruses under control during pregnancy. Will protect the growing embryo from virus particles in the mother's tissues. Massive doses of C have been successful in treating acute attacks of viral diseases. 1,000 to 15,000 daily with bioflavonoids, will help prevent bacterial infections, and help the liver to detoxify the system.

CALCIUM--Pregnant women require more calcium. Deficiency is caused by high-protein diet, especially meat. Calcium protects against toxic environment. Calcium and iron are very deficient minerals in women's diets, so it is essential to add natural supplements during pregnancy. Calcium provides proper development of the bones in the fetus.

CHEMICALS--Avoid especially during pregnancy. Preservatives, additives, food coloring, pesticides, and any unnatural substances like MSG; read labels. Wash fruits and vegetables before eating. Chemicals overwork the liver, which is already stressed because of pregnancy.

CHLOROPHYLL--Obtained through green drinks, sprouts, wheat grass juice or liquid, chlorophyll is very beneficial during pregnancy. Builds blood. Anaerobic bacteria, a disease-producing microorganism living within many human bodies, cannot live in the presence of oxygen or oxygen-producing agents such as chlorophyll. It is considered a protection to the body. Chlorophyll possesses the properties to break down poisonous carbon dioxide as well as releases free oxygen. Chlorophyll was discovered to be similar to that of hemoglobin (red cells) in human blood.

CONSTIPATION--Common during pregnancy because the same hormone that maintains your pregnancy also makes your intestines less active. In order to increase absorption of nutrients for the growing baby, drink pure water.

VITAMIN D--Essential to help calcium to absorb. Very vital to bones and teeth development. Helps development of jaw bones so that the teeth have room for proper growth.

DRUGS--Should be avoided at all times, but especially during the first three months of pregnancy. *Aspirin* interferes with the clotting of blood, so bleeding could develop. It also interferes with uterine contractions and could delay labor. *Antibiotics* interfere with the production of RNA and protein, and could cause damage to the fetus. Drugs can cause problems in the newborn baby, such as jaundice, respiratory problems, deformed limbs, mental retardation, loss of appetite. DES given to pregnant women to prevent miscarriages showed up in the child after they were grown. The daughters are showing high risks of miscarriages, tubal pregnancy, stillbirth and premature births. *Caffeine* passes the placental barrier and into the baby's blood, interfering with the growth and development. It can also interfere with DNA repair, delays labor and inhibits uterine contractions. *Heavy Drugs* such as heroin and cocaine when taken during pregnancy expose unborn babies to serious harm. The infants can be born addicted, which is a very pitiful sight.

EXERCISE--Helps for easier delivery. Helps the lymph glands to clean the system.

VITAMIN E--800 units a day has been recommended by nutritionists. It reduces the body's need for oxygen, provides more available oxygen for mother and baby. Strengthens the circulatory system and helps to prevent miscarriage. D-alpha is natural. Synthetic does not work, d-alpha tocopheral is synthetic.

FIBER FOOD--Bran, whole grain, nuts and seeds (sunflower, sesame, chia, flax), barley, brown rice, buckwheat, corn, millet, oats, and rye.

FLUIDS--Herb teas (red raspberry). Pure water. Helps the liver to detoxify, and helps prevent constipation.

FRUIT--Eat lots of frest fruit during pregnancy. Apples are a cleanser of the body, for they help to eliminate toxins. Bananas are high in potassium, but use very ripe. Best to use the fruit when it is in season. Organically grown if possible.

GRAINS--When using grains be sure to eat a lot of fresh green vegetables. This prevents the calcium in the body from leaching out. Buckwheat is rich in magnesium, protein, providing the synthesis for oxidation of carbohydrates. Magnesium helps to prevent toxemia in pregnancy; red meat can cause toxemia, so it would be better to substitute grains for meat. Whole grains include the bran and the germ which are full of nutrients. Contain B vitamins, vitamin E and iron. Helps eliminate constipation.

HEARTBURN--Papaya, mint tea, ginger, alfalfa. Eat more food with B vitamins such as wheat germ and yogurt. Eat papaya tablets with meals. Eat smaller meals and eat slowly.

IRON--Builds the blood, essential for building the baby's liver. Eat cooked cereals, grains, raisins, apricots, prunes, molasses, brewers yeast, sunflower seeds, sesame seeds, kelp, egg yolks, dulse and dry beans. Extra rich iron is found in dandelion and yellow dock, alfalfa and liquid chlorophyll.

LENTILS--Sprout before cooking, increases the nutrients.

MINERALS--Very essential during pregnancy. Aluminum can leach out zinc. Even one mineral lacking in the body can cause birth defects.

MILLET--Rich in protein, easy to digest. Use with vegetables, sesame and sunflower seeds.

NAUSEA--Eat smaller more frequent meals for this prevents the blood sugar level from fluctuating. Eat protein before bed--sunflower seeds, ginger, papaya and mint help in nausea. Low magnesium levels have been associated with nausea and vomiting. Blend papaya powder in milk for better assimilation. Severe nausea--use vitamin E oil in rectum.

PROTEIN--Very important, vegetable source is best. Use brown rice, buckwheat, millet, beans, grains, seeds and nuts.

PUMPKIN SEEDS--Rich in zinc and iron. The zinc can help prevent stretch marks.

SESAME SEEDS--Rich source of methianine and other amino acids which are usually lacking in vegetables and grains. Use sesame seed milk.

SMOKING--Avoid at all times, especially during pregnancy. The carbon monoxide prevents the intake of oxygen in the fetus and could cause birth defects. Increases the risk of miscarriage, fetal death or death soon after birth. Can cause stunted growth and birth weight and hyperactivity in children.

SPROUTS--When using pure water to sprout it is one of the most uncontaminated, untreated foods that are available. Sprouting enhances the high nutritional value. The vitamins and minerals in sprouts are utilized more efficiently in the body. Mung and lentil sprouts provide balanced amino acids. Alfalfa, high calcium to phosphorus balance.

STRESS--Pregnant women need a calm environment and emotional support. Studies have shown that emotional stress in pregnancy during the first trimester is capable of causing damage to the biological quality of the body. It alters the chemistry of the body. Exercise helps in stress, it helps use up the adrenalin that has accumulated during stress. Walking is good, relaxation is essential, at least a half hour of quiet time during the day. During stress high doses of vitamin C, 5,000 milligrams per day. Protein is used up during stress. Use plant protein, for meat will put more stress on the body. B vitamins should double under stress. Alfalfa, brewers yeast, and wheat germ are effective foods. When using brewers yeast, it should be used with added calcium and magnesium.

SUGAR--Excess absorbs quickly into the bloodstream and can affect the proper growth of the fetus. Sugar robs the body of nutrients.

SWEET POTATOES--Bake in the oven, and when craving sweets use instead of white sugar products. Rich in vitamin A and C and minerals.

VEGETABLES--Eat a lot, for the more you eat the better. As much raw foods as possible. Use a lot of green leafy vegetables such as watercress and leaf lettuce.

ZINC--Essential for vitamin A to be released from the liver. Necessary for proper growth of baby. Heals stretch marks and cuts.

PREMENSTRUAL SYNDROME

Premenstrual Syndrome (PMS) is not the silent malady it once was. Women used to receive indifference when they exposed their feelings and fears about what was going on in their bodies and minds.

They were usually told that it was all in their heads. The doctors listened to the complaints of women but could not understand or recognize the symptoms and didn't know the treatments so they thought that PMS was incurable. They would tell the women to go home to bed and take aspirin, or for more serious cases they wrote millions of prescriptions for tranquilizers.

There are at least one hundred and fifty symptoms that have been diagnosed as the cause of PMS. For some women the pain is severe, tension builds up, migraine headaches and mood swings so severe and drastic that it leads to violence. When an illness becomes so debilitating that lawyers can use PMS successfully as a mitigating circumstance in defending women accused of crimes then something must be done. It has been used as an excuse for murder, suicide, child beating and car accidents. It disrupts growing families, husband and wife relationships and the work force.

Although PMS is not a disease or a neurosis it has the symptoms of both. Some doctors consider it a monthly endocrine disorder, and feel that it is essential to feed and stimulate the glands with proper nutrients as well as the circulatory, nervous and the digestive systems.

SOME SYMPTOMS OF PMS

Hot flashes	Delusions	Easy bruising
Pelvic pain	Indecisiveness	Migraines
Headaches	Dizziness	Backaches
Irritability	Nervousness	Graying of the hair
Lethargy	Anxiety	Peeling of fingers
Physical pains	Swelling of breasts	Puffiness
Bloating	Feet swelling	Frequent colds
Depression	Abdomen swelling	Vertigo
Faintness	Hoarseness	Allergies
Restlessness	Constipation	Diarrhea
Sluggishness	Bowel changes	Appetite changes
Crabbiness	Hemorrhoids	Fatigue
Impatience	Skin eruptions	Insomnia

1/ HORMONAL IMBALANCE--Tests have shown that the flow of estrogen through the liver can be be turned off or on by providing B complex vitamins in the diet. When excess estrogen builds up and the liver is unable to detoxify it there is havoc created in the body, from water retention to severe mental anguish. Excess estrogen has a strong effect on women in various ways. Changes in hormone levels are noticeable anywhere from four days to two weeks before the period begins and definite drops in the pituitary and ovarian hormones have been measured, which may be the reason for the emotional reaction during this time.

2/ MALNUTRITION AND CONSTIPATION--Proper nutrients are not being assimilated into the bloodstream. Blood is the life of the body. It needs to be kept clean and pure so it can carry nutrients to the system and carry off all waste material. Constipation puts pressure on the uterus and causes pain. Change the diet and clean the bowels before menstruation. Herbal laxatives are very useful. They rebuild the bowels and provide proper function for the whole system.

3/ STRESS--We are confronted with all kinds of stress. Stress affects our immune system. Stress depletes nutrients from our system. We need to replace nutrients to strengthen our immune system so we can properly handle stress. Vitamins A and C with bioflavonoids should be used daily. The nervine herbs will build and feed the nervous system. The body craves and demands food to nourish it and if it isn't satisfied this puts more stress upon the body. This can cause irritability and emotional problems as well as disease.

4/ CALCIUM DEPLETION--Blood calcium drops ten days prior to menstruation. It occurs when ovaries are least active and continues steadily until even after the onset of bleeding. Steady calcium decrease causes tension, headaches, nervousness, insomnia and depression. The body needs adequate calcium, vitamin D and magnesium.

5/ HYPOGLYCEMIA AND OTHER AILMENTS--Increases the severity of PMS. It seems to suppress the immune system and trigger more illnesses. Many women have experienced allergies, food or chemical sensitivities, migraine headaches, flu and other illness just before their period when their immunity level was down.

SPECIAL DIETARY HELPS

VITAMIN A--Helps to regulate normal cycle, protects the glands. Helps monthly skin problems. Protects the body from disease, and rebuilds the cells.

ACETAMINOPHEN (Tylenol, Datril, Bromo-Seltzer, Allerest, Anacin 3)--Can cause nausea, upset stomach, vomiting, liver damage hepatitis, reduces white blood cell count, diarrhea, loss of appetite, cramps and stomach pains.

ALFALFA--Used in capsule or tablet form is very good for digesting food and supplements. Rich in vitamins, minerals and enzymes. Rich in magnesium and calcium.

ASPIRIN--Suppresses the proper function of hormones, causes stomach irritation and bleeding. It can interfere indirectly with the immunological response to infection. Leads to vitamin C deficiency, can cause kidney impairment.

ANEMIA--A very serious cause of depression and fatigue. Eat iron rich foods, B12, up to 50 Mcg to 200 Mcg. Dong Quai helps in menstrual anemia. Dandelion and yellow dock are two herbal foods to build rich, red blood.

B COMPLEX VITAMINS--Essential to combat fatigue, helps to reduce sugar cravings, weight fluctuation and bloating. B complex vitamins are necessary to provide the liver material to detoxify excess estrogen in the body and prevent hormonal imbalance. B6 helps in treating tension, aggression, depression and irritability. It also acts as a natural diuretic. It also restores the balance between progesterone and estrogene. Daily supplements of 40 to 100 mg have been used with success, and sometimes 500 mg were given in severe cases for short periods. B2--needed during stress, lack of can cause depression hysteria, trembling, and fatigue. B12--lack of can cause depression, fatigue, loss of appetite and irritability. It is needed daily.

BIRTH CONTROL PILLS--Deplete B complex vitamins, C, especially B12. B6 is needed daily for complete metabolism of tryptophan (amino acid). There is a risk of inducing cervical and breast cancer when using over a long period.

BLACK COHOSH--Contains estrogenic-like properties, helps in delayed flow, cramping, childbirth and menopause. Contains potassium and magnesium which act as a nerve sedative. It has a built in safety valve, it will cause a brief sharp headache if too much estrogenic stimulant. Very easy to determine the amount to take.

BLOATING--B6 (50 to 100 mg) natural diuretic. Alfalfa, parsley, dandelion, fennel, horsetail are natural herbal diuretics.

BRAN--It is the outer layer of the wheat and it contains the hormones like estrogen, vitamins and minerals that are needed in our bodies. Contains the B vitamins.

BROMELAINE--An enzyme, found in pineapple, very useful for its anti-inflammatory effect. It promotes the biosynthesis of prostaglandin and PGE factor.

VITAMIN C with BIOFLAVONOIDS--Repairs cells, relieves stress, builds immune system. Natural diuretic, helps when menstrual flow is too heavy. Helps to fight infections, bruises and allergies. The bioflavonoids helps in cell regeneration, strengthens capillaries, and feeds the thyroid gland, and helps menstrual irregularity.

CALCIUM and MAGNESIUM--Deficiency may be the cause of headaches, nervous symptoms, and fluid retention. About 10 days before menstruation calcium levels drop and remain that low until the period is over. Relieves cramps, calms, blood clotting agent. Use with vitamin D to help absorb calcium. Prevents cramps in uterus walls, leg muscles, irritability and depression. Magnesium suppresses the craving for chocolate. Increases B complex absorption, relieves cramps, soothes nerves and corrects deficiencies of this mineral that is noticeable in PMS.

CHAMOMILE--Used as a tea or in capsule form is calming for the nerves and relieves stomach cramps. Very good for menstrual pains. It contains high amounts of calcium and magnesium. It contains tryptophan which acts like a sedative.

CHLORINATED WATER--Is an antagonist to Vitamin E and disturbs hormones.

CRAMPS--Green drinks (pineapple or raw apple juice in blender with alfalfa, comfrey, parsley and watercress) have an antiseptic effect on the body, and will help to relieve cramps. Calcium (1,000 mg with magnesium 500 mg). Chamomile, hops, scullcap, and ginger. Red clover helps to relieve cramps.

VITAMIN D--Essential for calcium absorption. Important for the nerves, helps in insomnia.

DIURETICS--Contain aspirin and/or ammonium chloride. Draw off water along with trace minerals, especially potassium and magnesium causing cramps in legs, feet, toes and even hands and fingers. Causes trembling and twitching, weak muscles, irritability, nervousness, depression, confusion and insomnia.

DONG QUAI--Chinese herbs, helps to balance female hormones. Need to use at least five days before onset of menstruation, before the body reaches its estrogen-progesterone low. It feeds the nerves and brain. It nourishes the female glands as well as strengthens.

VITAMIN E--Helps to ease the symptoms of PMS. Relieves pain, helps in cramps, blood circulation, inhibits breast tenderness. Increases body's resistance to stress. Important both to the adequate production and to the proper metabolism of the sex hormones.

EVENING PRIMROSE OIL--Rich in gamma-linolenic acid (GLA), about 9% GLA is essential to good health. It is needed in order for the body to make a family of hormone-like compounds that control every organ of the body. The body could manufacture its own GLA from linolenic acid, but is not being adequately formed because of too much fat in the diet.

EXCESSIVE BLEEDING--Raw vegetables, fruit, nuts, seeds, sprouts and green drinks. Comfrey, cayenne, raspberry, yarrow, ginger, vitamins A, B, C, D, and K. Mineral supplement.

EXERCISE--Strenous exercise leads to the release of endorphins, of natural pain killers, found in the brain. One half hour twice a day would bring relief in PMS.

HERBS--Are considered natural foods that do not have side effects. They rebuild the areas that are not functioning properly, keep the organs healthy so they are able to supply the proper amounts of estrogen and progesetrone. The following herbs help to stimulate hormone balance and action. Black cohosh, sarsaparilla, ginseng, blessed thistle, licorice, false unicorn, squaw vine, dong quai, red raspberry, queen of the meadow and uva ursi.

HYPOGLYCEMIC DIET--This has been used successfully to help regulate and nourish hormone imbalance. Foods such as nuts, seeds, chicken, fish, grains, beans, split peas, lentils, green leafy vegetables, raw fruits and vegetables.

IODINE--Thyroxin is necessary for the breakdown of estrogen. Too little thyroxine means too much estrogen. This can bring intense and poorly timed menstrual periods, water retention and even blood clotting. Kelp is an herb high in natural iodine and is able to help regulate the iodine the body needs, as well as other important minerals needed by the body.

JUNK FOOD--Avoid coffee, chocolate, sugar, salt and alcohol. They increase irritability and interfere with the metabolism of nutrients to the body.

L-LYSINE--An amino acid, strengthens the immune system, and regulates the cells.

LICORICE--Contains estrogen like steroids. It is good for female problems. It also gives the body energy it needs for depression.

PANTOTHENIC ACID--Supports the adrenals, calms the central nervous system.

SELENIUM--A very essential mineral that protects the immune system. It also helps in menstrual cramps and breast tenderness.

SUGAR--Has the ability to attract calcium and washes it out of the tissues. If sugar is consumed constantly calcium is leached from the body and can cause severe depression and deprives the bone structure, teeth and natural immunity of vital nutrients.

YEAST INFECTIONS--History of antibiotics, recurrent vaginitis, chemical imbalance can be one reason PMS is so severe.

YOGURT--Plain and natural, eaten daily along with calcium and magnesium will help in all female problems. Add vitamin A and D for better absorption.

ZINC--Very important for the release of DGLA from its storage place. It helps in hormone balance, improves skin and reduces cramping.

HERBAL PMS HELP

GLANDS--Burdock, echinacea, sarsaparilla, black walnut, chapparral, golden seal, red clover, licorice, yellow dock, barberry, dandelion, peach, Oregon grape, yucca, chickweed and watercress.

CIRCULATION--Capsicum, ginger, Siberian ginseng, garlic, hawthorne, rosemary and watercress.

NERVOUS SYSTEM--Black cohosh, hops, scullcap, ho shou-wu, wood betony, passion flower and valerian root.

DIGESTION--Alfalfa, kelp, comfrey, pepsin, ginger, chamomile, wild yam, papaya and peppermint, catnip, spearmint and fennel.

PREMATURE AGING

Aging cannot be avoided, but we can prevent disease, in some cases, which are common with old age. It is disease that destroys us, not our age. I believe most of us would be interested in extending our vital health, mental alertness, and productive life helping others. Premature aging can be corrected by altering our lifestyle and diet. A nutritional program, with supplements, exercise and eliminating undue stress, could lead to one answer in prolonging our lives.

Thomas Edison predicted, "the doctor of the future will give no medicine, but will interest his patients in the care of the human frame, in diet, and in care and prevention of disease." Modern medicine has not adopted this as yet, so it is up to us to help ourselves.

The following supplements can help in the nutritional needs of the body cells and tissues. One vitamin, mineral or herb alone does not extend life span, but a complete nutritional program with supplements and diet will help. Most diseases are caused by a damaged immune system. Refer also to the information in this book on the immune system. Supplements and diet help to protect the immune system, and the immune system is connected with premature aging.

SPECIAL DIETARY HELPS

ALFALFA--Contains all essential amino acids, helps digestion of food, and helps in the absorption of calcium. Full of essential vitamins and minerals.

AGRININE--An amino acid that strengthens the immune system against bacteria, viruses and tumor cells. Enhances the liver to protect against physical and mental fatigue.

ALUMINUM and LEAD--Can produce early senility. Alzheimer's disease is increasing and is almost epidemic in proportion. It is fatal and runs its course. Aluminum deposits have been found in the brain, many times more than what is normal.

VITAMIN A--Protects and strengthens the respiratory tract which is so susceptible to tissue damage from smog, air pollutants, especially nitrogen dioxide. Helps to increase lifespan and reduce cancer risk, one of the leading causes of death in the aged. Retards the formation of free radicals.

B COMPLEX VITAMINS--Needs to be supplied every day, chelated and natural, and high potency. B1 helps supply oxygen absorption by the blood, increases mental alertness and ability to concentrate and learn. B2 increases life expectancy, promotes general health, provides extra stamina and vitality. It builds immunity and helps DNA. B3 helps reverse senility and inlarges blood vessels to increase blood supply. B5 prevents the onset of premature aging, wrinkly skin and baldness. Protects the body against cellular damage. B6 is essential for the production of antibodies. Helps prevent arteriosclerosis, feeds the adrenal glands and helps produce the hormone adrenalin, which is used up under stress. B12 is essential for the normal functioning of all body cells. Increases concentration and memories. It is manufactured in the lower intestines when eating natural, living foods such as sprouts. Laxatives can deplete the B12 reserves as well as other nutrients. B15 supplies oxygen to the muscles, provides endurance and reduces fatigue.

BEE POLLEN--Food to provide the RNA and DNA factors.

BRAN--Provides bulk to keep the colon clean and active. Provides B vitamins.

BREWERS YEAST--Rich in B complex, amino acids and nucleic acid.

BLACKSTRAP MOLASSES--Supplies minerals to activate the enzyme produced.

BUCKWHEAT--Contains rutin for healthy arteries; also has ingredients to help leach out toxic metals. Provides proteins. Nourishing when sprouted.

VITAMIN C--Anti-stress nutrient. Protects against viruses and bacterial infections. Helps retard free radicals. Along with bioflavonoids it helps keep the arteries from clogging. Helps the calcium assimilation and absorption and hold it in the bone matrix. Helps reduce the buildup of heavy metals.

CALCIUM--Along with hydrochloric acid for assimilation. Calcium absorption can be a problem long before aging. Calms nerves and strengthens bones. Natural herbal calcium: comfrey, alfalfa, oat straw, Irish moss and horsetail.

CHOLINE--Builds resistance to bacterial infection, strengthens the immune system.

CHELATION--Oral, using vitamins, minerals, glandular extracts, amino acids and herbs. Chelation comes from the Greek "chele" meaning to clasp or bind. These elements bind with heavy metals, such as lead, aluminum, plaque, deposits, and carry them out of the body.

COMFREY and PEPSIN--Aid digestion and absorption of food.

VITAMIN D--Enhances the immune system. We need 6 times more than what was previously thought. Retards formation of free radicals. Retards the aging process by inhibiting harmful pollution, better assimilation of nutrients. It helps protect tissue cells against aging by oxidization. Protects genetic weakness. Oxygen to the cells can be increased 40% when sufficient vitamin E is increased in the diet.

ECHINACEA--Strengthens the immune system, to help resist infections. It stimulates lymphatic filtration and drainage, and helps remove toxins from the blood. Non-toxic way of cleaning the system.

EVENING PRIMROSE--The PGE in the gamma-linolenic acid found in evening Primrose oil stimulates the T-cells of the immune system and helps protect it. Genetic mutations can be kept in check and sometimes reversed by PGE.

EYEBRIGHT--Strengthens all parts of the eye and provides an elasticity to the nerves and optic devices responsible for sight. It is used as a remedy for eye problems, such as failing vision, eye inflammations, conjunctivitis, ulcers and even eye strain.

EXERCISE--Lack of can cause bone and muscle loss, and inhibit food assimilation. Exercise produces natural lactic acid. It increases the metabolic rate and reduces body fat, helping to prevent obesity, which is the cause of many degenerative diseases. Exercise improves heart function and circulation to help get more blood to the brain. Prevents stiffening, lack of energy and fatigue. It helps remove toxins from the body. Inactivity accelerates calcium loss. Trampoline jumping is a good way to stimulate heart action, lymph circulation and better breathing habits. Proper nutrition and exercise work together helping the nutritional elements to enter all the body's tissues and cells.

FATS--Reduce the overall intake in the diet. Fats increase the toxins in the tissues, as well as put on weight. It also inhibits absorption of food and especially B12.

FOOD--Decrease the over-all food intake. It has been proven that too much food, and especially the wrong kind, decreases life.

FOOD ENZYMES--Provide proper digestion and eliminate toxins in the body that weaken the immune system.

GINSENG--Increases endurance and slows down the aging process. It inhibits free radicals, which are believed to produce disturbances in the body that lead to internal stress, cancer, aging and other destructive processes.

GOTU KOLA--Food for the brain, to help in senility and mental fatigue. Helps to keep the mind young and provide clean thinking.

HONEY--Predigested sweetener for better assimilation. A nourishing substitute for white sugar. It increases calcium retention. Provides vitamins, minerals and enzymes. It is soothing to the stomach.

IRON--Is needed at all ages to improve quality of blood, and increase resistance to stress and disease. Dandelion and yellow dock have easily assimilated iron.

KELP--A natural chelating herb, providing easily assimilated vitamins and minerals essential for health. Strengthens the tissues in the brain and heart, cleans toxic substances from the colon.

L-CYSTEIN--Protects the body against bacteria, viruses, chemicals and radiation damage. It neutralizes the effects of harmful chemicals and smog, which can lead to wrinkles, emphysema and lung cancer.

LECITHIN--Dissolves cholesterol. It supplies choline and inositol which form brain transmitters to send nerve impulses from one neuron to another. Cleans the arteries for better nourishment of cells to the brain.

LICORICE--Acts as a detoxified of the blood, mild laxative, stimulates the adrenal and lymph glands, and provides strength and energy to the body.

MAGNESIUM--Essential to convert vitamin D into usable form and prevent crystals from forming into kidney stones.

PAPAYA--One of the fruits to help increase the immune system, help in digestion; rich in vitamins and minerals.

PINTO BEANS--Use often, contains ingredients to help leach out toxic materials.

PROTEIN--High protein diets, especially red meat, are very taxing to the system. It produces uric acid which leads to arthritis, gout and other diseases. It also leads to loss of calcium.

RADIATION--Avoid; damages the body by creating masses of free radicals. Vitamins C, E and selenium protect against free radicals.

ROYAL JELLY--It is a mixture of pollen and honey with a special nectar the young bees secrete from glands on the tops of their heads. It contains protein, lipids, glucides, vitamins, hormones, enzymes, minerals and vital elements that act as biocatalysts in cell regeneration processes in the body. It helps to reverse the aging process.

SALT--Avoid salt (table salt, sodium chloride). It makes the heart work harder. It robs calcium from the body and harms the mucous lining of the intestinal tract. It irritates the nervous system. It cannot be digested, assimilated or utilized. It produces toxic acids. It holds water in the tissues of the body, and can cause lumps and cysts, high blood pressure, arteriosclerosis, arthritis and heart problems. It is also very harmful to the kidneys.

SARDINES--High in sources of DNA without heavy metal pollution; improves memory.

SARSAPARILLA--Contains saponins which act as cleansing agents in removing the accumulated toxins and calcification from around the joints and also from the system.

SELENIUM--Considered an anti-cancer mineral. Slows down the aging process. Builds the immune system, retards formation of free radicals, helps oxidation of cells. Found in garlic, kelp and red clover.

SILICON--Helps keep a youthful appearance. It is essential for all connective tissues. It is rich in oat straw, horsetail. Also found in kelp, cornsilk, eyebright, ginseng, hawthorne and parsley.

SPIRULINA--Supplies 65 to 70 percent pure protein, provides all essential amino acids in the correct proportions. Contains high amounts of B12. Rich in chelated minerals and trace elements, including potassium, magnesium, selenium, zinc, iron, phosphorus, calcium and manganese. A rich source of vitamin E as well as vitamin A. Contains B complex vitamins. It is easily digested and assimilated. Contains phenylalanine and tyrosine, two amino acids that are readily converted into basic brain compounds that affect mood. It provided proper nutrients which help curb appetite. It accelerates metabolic rate, suppresses allergy symptoms, and promotes a feeling of strength and stamina.

SULPHUR--Slows down the aging process. Natural sulphur is found in many herbs such as alfalfa, catnip, comfrey, dandelion, garlic, kelp, mullein, parsley and sarsaparilla.

WHEY--Rich in organic sodium, and is good for acid indigestion; builds the blood. It contains calcium, helps joints remain limber and prevents calcium deposits.

YUCCA--Helps in joint inflammations for arthritic and rheumatism. It helps to clean and purify the blood.

ZINC--Essential for maintaining T-cells in the immune system. Essential for vitamin A to be released from the liver. Zinc is often lacking in the diets of the elderly. The brain and central nervous system need zinc.

ULCERS

A change in dietary habits could bring a reduction in the incidence of ulcers. Ulcers are open sores or lesions of the mucous membranes of the lining of the stomach. Nutritionists call stomach and gastric ulcers a deficiency disease caused by unhealthy tissues as a result of eating incompatible combinations of food, leaving fermentation and putrefaction as the end-product. Wrong foods will increase the flow of digestive juices, causing an irritation to the lining of the stomach.

Avoid heated vegetable oils for they may be one cause of ulcers. Avoid eating food or drinks too hot or cold. Avoid eating when under stress. Emotional stress and anxiety are the main causes for the formation of gastric ulcers.

Cimetidine (tagamet) is widely prescribed. It works well to control the ulcer pains, but does not promise to cure them. It has been found that the long use of cimetidine may be associated with an increased risk of gastric cancer and may even mask the cancer. Long term use by male patients have found to have reduced levels of male sex hormones in their blood stream (read Health Shock by Martin Weitz). It could even cause sterility. Cimetidine works by reducing the amount of acid secreted into the stomach, which causes unwanted higher levels of strong cancer-causing chemicals in the stomach called nitrosamines.

Antacids which contain magnesium and aluminum can accumulate in the brain and cause a dementia or increase bone aluminum concentration and demineralized bones. Antacids can upset the metabolic balance of the body.

SPECIAL DIETARY HELPS

VITAMIN A--Protects the stomach acid from irritating the sores. A and E together form a protection against development of ulcers when caused by stress as well as a healing effect on ulcers.

ALMOND MILK--Helps to neutralize excess acids in the stomach and supplies high quality protein and calcium.

ALOE VERA JUICE--Helps to relieve ulcers from acidic irritation by restricting the flow of gastric juices. It contains antibiotic, astringent and coagulating agents. It will help heal scar tissue of ulcers lesions.

BARLEY--Helps to rebuild the lining of the stomach and soothes stomach ulcers with its B1 and B2 content.

BEE POLLEN--Helps corrects digestive problems. Will not ferment or "sour" in the digestive tract. Helps contribute to a healthy digestive system.

VITAMIN C with Bioflavonoids--Large amounts will heal ulcers.

CABBAGE JUICE--Contains healing vitamin U, controls acidity, heals ulcers.

CARROT JUICE with Celery Juice--Soothing and healing to ulcers; provides vitamin A to rebuild destroyed cells of the stomach lining. Use with celery juice. Also, a carrot soup is very nourishing and healing.

CHLOROPHYLL--Cleanses the blood, heals ulcers.

COMFREY and PEPSIN--Heal ulcers and help soothe the digestive tract and dissolve mucus from the walls of the intestines.

CONSTIPATION--Could be one cause of ulcers. When the lower colon is clogged and delays the passage of food, that causes fermentation and acid conditions which irritate the stomach walls.

VITAMIN E--Helps in the healing of scar tissue.

FLAXSEED TEA--Coats the digestive tract and works as a soothing agent. Simmer two tablespoons in a pint of water for about 3 to 4 minutes.

GOAT MILK--Help to heal ulcers. Soothing and easily digestible.

GREEN DRINK--Very healing and nourishing for ulcers. Add cayenne for faster healing.

IRON--Builds rich blood, gives energy to the body. Dandelion and yellow dock are natural iron.

VITAMIN K--Helps in blood clotting and prevents excess bleeding.

LICORICE ROOT--Helps to relieve ulcer conditions and inflammation of the stomach and colon. Supplies energy to the system.

OKRA POWDER--Demulcent food for its protective coating to stop irritation of membranes.

PAPAYA--Eat often, contains enzymes which improves digestion powers, helps heal the stomach lining and helps digest protein.

PERSIMMONS--High energy food. Will promote healing of ulcers by soothing the mucous membranes in the digestive tract.

PROPOLIS--Heals ulcers. Contains antibiotic properties. Contains vitamins, amino acids, minerals, rich in bioflavonoids.

SLIPPERY ELM--Soothing and nourishing to the stomach.

SPROUTS--Contain live enzymes for proper digestion. Also contain
vitamins and minerals.

SWEET POTATOES--Soothing.

WHEY POWDER--Contains natural sodium, healing to the stomach
lining.

YOGURT--Richest source of enzymes. Soothing and healing to the
stomach.

ZINC--Can speed up the healing of gastric ulcers.

SPROUTING FOR HEALTH

SPROUTING

Seeds have total food value, for the seed is life itself. The life-giving elements in seeds have a condensed germinating energy. The forces in the seeds lie dormant until combined with water, air, and sunshine. They contain all the elements a plant needs for life and growth. The sprouts alone are able to sustain life. They contain all the nutrients necessary for reproduction and healthy growth.

The endosperm of the seed is the storehouse of carbohydrates, protein and oil. When the seed sprouts, the predigested amino acids and natural sugars of this life force we eat are filled with energy and nutrients capable of generating cells of the body and supplying us with life and vitality. It helps to retard the aging process, contains good amounts of hormones and is very rich in vitamins.

Sprouts grown at home and in pure water, using untreated seeds, are the safest food we can use in today's world. Sprouts when left in the light for a day are rich in chlorophyll, which is the life blood of plants and which is similar to human blood. Only a few atoms of chemicals keep it from being perfect blood.

Scientists know that sprouting seeds increases the vitamin content, but they do not know how. Some vitamins are found in sprouts that are not present in the unsprouted seeds. Minerals found in small quantities in the seeds are increased when sprouted. In some sprouted seeds the calcium has been transmuted into magnesium, which is deemed impossible by some.

HOW TO SPROUT

SEEDS	SOAK HOURS	RINSE TIME EACH DAY	HARVEST TIME--DAYS
ALFALFA	5-8	2-3	5-6
BUCKWHEAT	8	3	2-3
FENUGREEK	8	3	2-3
GARBANZO	8	3	3-4
LENTILS	8	3	2-4
MUNG BEANS	8	3	3-4
PINTO BEANS	16-24	4-5	3-4
RADISH	8	3	3-4
RED CLOVER	8	3	3-5
RYE	8	3	2-3
SOYBEANS	24	3	3-5
TRITICALE	8	3	1-2
WHEAT	8	3	3

KINDS OF SPROUTS

ALFALFA--Use alfalfa sprouts in salads, sandwiches, soups and green
   drinks. Best when eaten raw, used in tacos, as a garnish, in
   jellied salads or omelets. Alfalfa sprouts are high in protein
   and chlorophyll and are good sources of vitamins D, E, K, and
   U. Minerals are iron, calcium, potassium, and many others.

BUCKWHEAT--(Remove the remaining husks after they are sprouted.)
   Use in soups, salads, pancakes, muffins, vegetable loaves.
   Buckwheat sprouts are 12% protein. Contains phosphorus,
   potassium, iron, niacin, calcium and high in rutin.

FENUGREEK--Use fenugreek sprouts in salads, sandwiches, soups (do
   not cook), curry dishes, sauces and dips. Fenugreek sprouts
   are high in protein, vitamin A, iron and choline.

GARBANZO (Chick Peas)--Use the sprouts in soups, salads,
   vegetables, casseroles, vegetable loaves. Garbanzo sprouts are
   20% protein, high in vitamins A, C and iron. They can be
   roasted slowly in the oven and used as a substitute for nuts in
   recipes (cooked beans).

LENTILS--The lentil sprouts need to be cooked before using in
   uncooked dishes. Use in salads, soups, and vegetable
   casseroles. Lentil sprouts are 24% protein; high in vitamins
   C, E, and iron phosphorus and potassium. The small brown
   are best for sprouting. They have a tangy, peppery taste and
   are delicious for green salads.

MUNG BEANS--Change the water several times during the soaking.
   They are good in salads, omelets, soups, stir-fry vegetables,
   potato salads, jellied salads, fried rice and dips. Mung beans
   are 24% protein, good sources of choline, calcium, iron and
   vitamins A and E. Remove hulls if they are bitter.

PINTO BEANS--Change water every 24 hours. Pinto beans have to be
   cooked until tender before using. Grind and add to vegetable
   loaves or patties. Chill and add to salads, mash and use in
   bean loaves. Add to soups and casseroles, baked beans and
   tamale pies. Cook at low heat under 120°F. for 4 to 5 hours
   or until tender. Pinto beans are very high in protein.

RADISH--Radish sprouts can be used in sandwiches, salads, soups (add
   before serving), cottage cheese or yogurt. The sprouts are high
   in vitamins A and C, calcium and potassium.

RED CLOVER--Red clover sprouts are best eaten raw. Use as you
   would alfalfa sprouts in sandwiches, salads, soups, and tacos.

RYE--Rye sprouts can be ground and used in breads, granola, soups,
   cereal, casseroles, grain loaves and rice dishes. Rye sprouts are

12% protein. Rich in iron, potassium, phosphorus, manganese and vitamin E. Similar to wheat sprouts.

SOYBEANS--Change soaking water every 8 hours. Use in casseroles, stir-fry vegetables, salads. Soybean sprouts are 35%-40% protein. Use as meat substitutes. Rich in B vitamins, lecithin, vitamins A, E and C. 1/2 cup equals 6 glasses of orange juice. High in iron and calcium. Grind and add to casseroles, stuffings, stews, chili, oriental dishes, soups. Oven roast slowly and grind and substitute for nuts.

TRITICALE--Triticale sprouts are used to make bread, granola, hot cakes, soups, salads, casseroles. Grind and use in loaves. Triticale is a cross between rye and wheat. 14% protein. Rich in B vitamins, vitamins C and E, minerals.

WHEAT--Wheat sprouts are ground and used in bread. Use in granola, pancakes, chili, salads, stews, grain loaves, patties. Wheat sprouts are 12% protein, high in vitamins E, C and niacin and other vitamins and minerals.

VITAMINS AND MINERALS

VITAMIN A

FUNCTIONS--Builds immunity to fight infection, especially of the respiratory tract. Essential for pregnancy and lactation. Necessary to prevent night blindness and weak eyesight. Helps to maintain and repair healthy tissue, especially skin. Protects body from toxins in air pollution.

COMPLIMENTARY NUTRIENTS--Protein (plants such as sunflower seed), B complex, choline, C, D, E, F, calcium and zinc.

NUTRIENT DESTROYERS--Air pollutants, alcohol, coffee, cortisone, excessive iron, mineral oil, vitamin D deficiency.

DEFICIENCY--Retarded growth, increased susceptibility to infections, night blindness, dry and scaly skin, lack of appetite and poor digestion, lack of vigor, sinus trouble, tooth or gum decay.

SOURCES--Fish liver oils, butter, yellow vegetables, green vegetables, egg yolks, whole milk, yellow fruits, hot red peppers, liver, parsley, alfalfa, bee pollen, capsicum, comfrey, dandelion, papaya, paprika, yellow dock.

VITAMIN B1 (THIAMINE)

FUNCTIONS--Helps to maintain a healthy nervous system, aids growth and digestion, builds muscles and heart. Helps the metabolism of carbohydrates and heightens learning capacity.

COMPLEMENTARY NUTRIENTS--B complex, B2, folic acid, niacin, C, E, manganese, sulphur.

NUTRIENT DESTROYERS--Alcohol, coffee, fever, raw clams, excess sugar, stress, surgery, tobacco, heat.

DEFICIENCY--Can cause irritability, nerves on edge constantly, feeling of persecution, memory loss, no appetite, constipation, mental depression, fatigue, and digestive disturbances.

SOURCES--Brewers yeast, rice polishings, whole grains, peanuts, wheat bran, wheat germ, nuts, egg yolks, blackstrap molasses, brown rice, potatoes, green leafy vegetables, alfalfa, dandelion, fenugreek, ginger, kelp, okra, papaya, red clover, red raspberry, hawthorne, marshmallow and mullein.

VITAMIN B2 (RIBOFLAVIN)

FUNCTIONS--Helps in metabolism of fats, carbohydrates, and proteins. Essential for growth and general health. Promotes healthy eyes, skin, nails and hair. Promotes antibody and red cells for motion; cell respiration.

COMPLEMENTARY NUTRIENTS--B complex, B6, niacin, C and phosphorus.

NUTRIENT DESTROYERS--Alcohol, coffee, sugar, tobacco, caffeine, oral contraceptives and ultraviolet lights.

DEFICIENCY--Can cause depression, lack of energy, hysteria, hypochondria, bloodshot eyes, cracking of lips and corners of mouth, itching and burning of eyes, poor digestion and dizziness.

SOURCES--Egg yolk, milk, cheese, brewers yeast, blackstrap molasses, wheat germ, whole grains, almonds, sunflower seeds, liver and leafy vegetables. Alfalfa, dandelion, dulse, eyebright, fenugreek, ginger, hawthorne, hops, kelp, licorice, marshmallow, mullein, papaya, red clover, saffron, wild rose hips.

VITAMIN B3 (NIACIN)

FUNCTIONS--Necessary for healthy skin conditions and nervous system. Improves circulation, helps in metabolism of carbohydrates and normal function of gastro-intestinal tract. May prevent migraine headaches and schizophrenia.

COMPLEMENTARY NUTRIENTS--B complex, C, and phosphorus.

NUTRIENT DESTROYERS--Sugar, caffeine, antibiotics, alcohol, excessive starches, sleeping pills and estrogen.

DEFICIENCY--May result in coated tongue, canker sores, irritability, nervousness, diarrhea, memory loss, headache, insomnia, anemia, digestive disorders and skin lesions.

SOURCES--Brewers yeast, wheat germ, rice bran and polishings, nuts, sunflower seeds, whole grains, green vegetables, liver. Beans, milk, fish, poultry, whole wheat and desicated liver. Alfalfa, burdock, capsicum, catnip, chickweed, dandelion, eyebright, fenugreek, ginger, hops, kelp, licorice, marshmallow, mullein, papaya, red clover and rose hips.

VITAMIN B5 (PANTOTHENIC ACID)

FUNCTIONS--Assists in building of body cells, utilization of vitamins, healthy skin, normal digestion, helps cope with stress, both mental and physical. Aids normal development of the central nervous system. Protects against damage from radiation.

COMPLEMENTARY NUTRIENTS--B complex, B6, B12, biotin, folic acid and C.

NUTRIENT DESTROYERS--Alcohol, coffee, sugar, caffeine, heat, antibiotics, sleeping pills, estrogen and stress.

DEFICIENCY--Hypoglycemia, digestive problems, bloated feeling, constipation, gloom, unexplained personality alteration, retarded growth, burning feet, dizziness, allergies, chronic fatigue and skin disorders.

SOURCES--Brewers yeast, wheat germ, bran, royal jelly, whole grain, green vegetables, peas, beans, peanuts, blackstrap molasses, egg yolk, liver, soybean, rice polishings, salmon, legumes, alfalfa, burdock, capsicum, cascara sagrada, catnip, chickweed, dandelion, eyebright, fenugreek, ginger, golden seal, hawthorne, hops, horsetail, kelp, licorice, marshmallow, mullein, papaya and red clover.

VITAMIN B6 (PYRIDOXINE)

FUNCTIONS--Aids in digestion and food assimilation, weight control, production of red blood cells, prevents nausea.

COMPLEMENTARY NUTRIENTS--B complex, B1, B2, pantothenic acid, C, magnesium, potassium, linoleic acid and sodium.

NUTRIENT DESTROYERS--Alcohol, birth control pills, coffee, radiation, tobacco, sugar, caffeine, antibiotics, anticonvulsants, cortisone, DES, isoniazid, oral contraceptives, estrogen, cooking.

DEFICIENCY--Slow brain function, nervousness, loss of muscle control, skin problems, insomnia, anemia, irritability, hair loss, acne, depression, slow learning, general weakness, decreased immunity.

SOURCES--Brewers yeast, bananas, avocados, wheat germ, bran, soybean, nuts, blackstrap molasses, egg yolk, liver, green leafy vegetables, green peppers, carrots, milk, legumes, cantaloupe, cabbage, alfalfa, burdock, chickweed, dandelion, eyebright, fenugreek, ginger, hawthorne, hops, kelp, licorice, marshmallow, mullein, papaya, red clover.

VITAMIN B9 (FOLIC ACID)

FUNCTIONS--Essential for cellular growth and synthesis of DNA and RNA. Important for protein metabolism and production of antibodies that prevent and heal infections.

COMPLEMENTARY NUTRIENTS--B complex, B12, biotin, pantothenic acid, vitamin C.

NUTRIENT DESTROYERS--Stress, alcohol, caffeine, tobacco, anticonvulsants, barbituates, dilantin, sulfa drugs, sunlight, food processing and heat, oral contraceptives and sleeping pills.

DEFICIENCY--Can cause anemia, mental illness, intestinal disturbances, metabolic disturbances, reproductive disorders, retarded growth and graying and loss of hair.

SOURCES--Broccoli, dark green leafy vegetables, asparagus, lima beans, Irish potatoes, leaf lettuce, brewers yeast, nuts mushrooms, wheat germ and liver.

VITAMIN H (BIOTIN)

FUNCTIONS--Involved in protein and fat metabolism and in body growth. Helps in healthy skin, hair and muscle development. Aids in vitamin B utilization.

COMPLEMENTARY NUTRIENTS--B complex, B12, folic acid, pantothenic acid, vitamin C and sulphur.

NUTRIENT DESTROYERS--Alcohol, coffee, raw egg white, sugar, sulfa drugs, estrogen and food processing.

DEFICIENCY--Can cause depression, exhaustion, muscle pain, dermatitis, a grayish pallor of the skin and mucous membrane, appetite loss.

SOURCES--Brewers yeast, rice polishings, soybeans, liver, egg yolk, wheat germ, oats, nuts, chicken, brown rice, beans, cheese and milk.

VITAMIN B12 (COBALAMIN)

FUNCTIONS--Metabolism of foods, appetite, blood cell formation, cell longevity, healthy nervous system, growth in children.

COMPLEMENTARY NUTRIENTS--B complex, B6, choline, inositol, C, potassium and sodium.

NUTRIENT DESTROYERS--Alcohol, antibiotics, aspirin, diuretics, antacids, tobacco, caffeine, laxatives, estrogen, sleeping pills and birth control pills.

DEFICIENCY--Anemia, lack of concentration, walking and speaking difficulties, depression, tired of school, work and life. Dizziness, fatigue, brain damage, growth failure in children.

SOURCES--Egg yolk, milk, cheese, liver, brewers yeast, sunflower seeds, bananas, nuts, Concord grapes, wheat germ, bee pollen, alfalfa, comfrey, burdock, capsicum, catnip, chickweed, dandelion, dong quai, eyebright, fenugreek, ginger, ginseng, golden seal, hawthorne, hops, kelp, licorice, marshmallow, mullein, papaya, red clover, white oak bark.

VITAMIN B15 (PANGAMIC ACID)

FUNCTIONS--Increases oxygen levels in the blood, muscles and tissues to help extend cell life. Stimulates the glandular and nervous systems. Increases circulation and prevents premature aging. Protects against carbon monoxide poisoning.
COMPLEMENTARY NUTRIENTS--B complex, choline, inositol, C, potassium and sodium.
NUTRIENT DESTROYERS--Alcohol, caffeine, most laxatives, water and sunlight.
DEFICIENCY--Could lead to atherosclerosis and conditions affected by lack of oxygen--heart disease and nervous and glandular problems.
SOURCES--Apricot kernels, pumpkin and sesame seeds, brewers yeast, brown rice and whole grain. Black walnut.

VITAMIN B17 (LAETRILE)

FUNCTIONS--Used in 17 countries in the control and prevention of cancer; not legal in the United States.
COMPLEMENTARY NUTRIENTS--B complex
NUTRIENT DESTROYERS--Alcohol, caffeine.
DEFICIENCY--May be connected with an increased susceptibility to cancer.
SOURCES--Apricot kernels, found in the whole kernel of fruits of apples, peaches, plums, nectarines, raspberries, cranberries, blackberries and blueberries, mung beans, garbanzos, millet, buckwheat and flaxseed.

VITAMIN C (ASCORBIC ACID)

FUNCTIONS--An important factor in maintaining sound health and vigor, needed daily. Helps prevent infection. Strengthens connective tissue, healthy teeth, gums, bones. Promotes healing, maintains integrity of capillaries. Aids in the absorption of collagen and interferon production.
COMPLEMENTARY NUTRIENTS--Bioflavonoids, calcium, magnesium, and all vitamins and minerals.
NUTRIENT DESTROYERS--Antibiotics, aspirin, cortisone, high fever, stress, tobacco, diuretics, barbiturates, pain killers, heat in cooking, alcohol.

DEFICIENCY--Scurvy, bleeding gums, tooth and gum decay, capillary weakness, hemorrhages, general weakness, increased susceptibility to infection, loss of appetite. Fatigue, restlessness.

SOURCES--Citrus fruits, tomatoes, green peppers, strawberries, kale, alfalfa, sprouts, papaya, broccoli, hot red peppers, parsley, rose hips, barberry, bayberry, bee pollen, burdock, catnip, chickweed, comfrey, dandelion, echinacea, eyebright, fennel, garlic, ginger, golden seal, hawthorne, juniper, kelp, red clover, papaya, thyme, yarrow, yellow dock.

VITAMIN D

FUNCTIONS--Ultraviolet rays from the sun change the ergosterol (an oily substance) on the skin into this vitamin. Regulates the use of calcium and phosphorus in the body and is therefore essential for the proper formation of teeth and bones--thyroid function, skin, blood clotting.

COMPLEMENTARY NUTRIENTS--Vitamin A, C, F, choline, calcium and phosphorus, magnesium and sodium.

NUTRIENT DESTROYERS--Mineral oil, smog, barbiturates, primidone, anticonvulsants, dilantin, doriden, sleeping pills and cortisone.

DEFICIENCY--Insomnia, myopia, nervousness, poor metabolism, softening of bones and teeth--rickets, tooth decay, lack of vigor, muscular weakness, increased susceptibility to infection, loss of appetite, inability to center thoughts.

SOURCES--Sunshine, butter, milk, fish liver oils, egg yolk, bone meal, sardines, salmon, alfalfa, bee pollen, chickweed, eyebright, fenugreek, mullein, papaya, red raspberry, rose hips.

VITAMIN E

FUNCTIONS--Antioxidant; improves circulation, promotes longevity, prevents blood clots, strengthens capillary walls, helps prevent sterility. Protects the lungs against air pollution, helps prevent miscarriages, still births, menopause, symptoms and disorders of the reproductive glands.

COMPLEMENTARY NUTRIENTS--Vitamin A, B complex, B1, inositol, vitamins C and F, manganese, selenium, phosphorus. Vitamin E helps the magnesium and selenium to be absorbed.

NUTRIENT DESTROYERS--Birth control pills, chlorine, mineral oil, rancid fat and oil and heat.

DEFICIENCY--Heart disease, impotency, miscarriages, sterility, dry, dull or falling hair, enlarged prostate gland, strokes, tiredness, general weakness, PMS (pre-menstrual syndrome).

SOURCES--Wheat germ and wheat germ oil, nuts, egg yolks, leafy greens, nut and seed oils, whole wheat and oatmeal, alfalfa, bee pollen, blue cohosh, burdock, comfrey, dandelion, dong quai, echinacea, eyebright, ginseng, golden seal, kelp, licorice, papaya, red raspberry, rose hips, scullcap, slippery elm, watercress.

VITAMIN F (ESSENTIAL FATTY ACIDS)

FUNCTIONS--Helps prevent hardening of the arteries, promotes growth, healthy hair and skin; normal glandular activity prevents cholesterol build-up and vital organ respiration.

COMPLEMENTARY NUTRIENTS--Vitamins A, C, D and E, phosphorus and calcium.

NUTRIENT DESTROYERS--Radiation, X-rays, saturated fats, rancid oils, heat, oxygen.

DEFICIENCY--Acne, dandruff, dry hair, diarrhea, eczema, weak nails, varicose veins, gallstones.

SOURCES--Butter, wheat germ, safflower oil, sunflower oil and seeds, corn oil, almonds, avocados, pecans, walnuts. Evening Primrose oil, red raspberry, slippery elm, yarrow.

VITAMIN K

FUNCTIONS--Promotes growth, proper blood clotting, healthy liver function, longevity and vitality.

COMPLEMENTARY NUTRIENTS--B complex, E, A and C.

NUTRIENT DESTROYERS--Aspirin, mineral oil, rancid oils, radiation, X-rays.

DEFICIENCY--Nose bleed, hemorrhaging due to improper clotting, miscarriage, diarrhea, poor intestinal absorption.

SOURCES--Egg yolks, fish liver oils, soybeans, leafy green vegetables, blackstrap molasses, yogurt, alfalfa, gotu kola, kelp, papaya, safflower, slippery elm, yarrow.

VITAMIN P (BIOFLAVONOIDS)

FUNCTIONS--Prevents bruising, strengthens capillaries and blood vessel walls, colds and flu prevention. Increases effectiveness of vitamin C, builds the immune system, hypertension.

COMPLEMENTARY NUTRIENTS--Vitamin C, calcium, magnesium.

NUTRIENT DESTROYERS--Aspirin, alcohol, antibiotics, cortisone, high fevers, stress, tobacco, diuretics, barbiturates, pain killers, heat in cooking.

DEFICIENCY--Scurvy, bleeding gums, tooth and gum decay, capillary weakness, hemorrhages, general weakness, increased susceptibility to infection, loss of appetite, fatigue, restlessness.

SOURCES--Buckwheat, white skin of citrus fruits, apricots, cherries, grapes, papaya, tomatoes, burdock, cayenne, dandelion, paprika, red clover, rose hips, slippery elm.

CALCIUM

FUNCTION--Health of teeth and bones (any age), blood clotting, strengthens nervous system, heart rhythm, aids in muscle contraction, normalizes metabolism.

COMPLEMENTARY NUTRIENTS--Vitamins A, C, D and F, iron, magnesium, manganese and phosphorus.

NUTRIENT DESTROYERS--Aspirin, chocolate, stress, lack of exercise, lack of magnesium, lack of hydrochloric acid, mineral oil, oxalic acid, phytic acid, tetracyclines.

DEFICIENCY--Insomnia, muscle cramps, nervousness, arms and leg numbness, tooth decay, brooding, constant complaining about little things, difficulties in concentrating.

SOURCES--Milk, cheese, yogurt, carrot juice, leafy green vegetables, millet, kelp, blackstrap molasses, bone meal, dolomite, almonds, sesame seeds, alfalfa, aloe, black walnut, camomile, comfrey, dandelion, garlic, ginger, horsetail, kelp, marshmallow, papaya, parsley, red clover, red raspberry, rose hips, slippery elm.

CHOLINE

FUNCTIONS--Helps fat metabolism, nervous system, healthy liver, healthy thymus gland and hair.

COMPLEMENTARY NUTRIENTS--Vitamins A, B complex, B12, folic acid, inositol and linoleic acid.

NUTRIENT DESTROYERS--Alcohol, coffee, sugar estrogen, food processing, sulfa drugs, water.

DEFICIENCY--Growth problems, bleeding stomach ulcers, heart trouble, high blood pressure, intolerance to fats, liver and kidney malfunction, high cholesterol level, hardening of arteries.

SOURCES--Wheat germ, nuts, soybeans, lecithin, brewers yeast, fish, egg yolk, green leafy vegetables, legumes, alfalfa, anise, blue cohosh, burdock, capsicum, cascara sagrada, catnip, chickweed, dandelion, eyebright, fenugreek, ginger, golden seal, hawthorne, hops, kelp, licorice, marshmallow, mullein, papaya, red clover.

CHROMIUM

FUNCTIONS--Healthy blood circulation, glucose tolerance (energy), increased insulin effectiveness, synthesis of fatty acids, cholesterol and protein.

COMPLEMENTARY NUTRIENTS--Zinc, vitamin C.

NUTRIENT DESTROYERS--Sugar refined grains, refined carbohydrates.

DEFICIENCY--Arteriosclerosis, hypoglycemia, glucose intolerance in diabetics.

SOURCES--Brewers yeast, whole grains, clams, corn oil, shellfish, chicken, potatoes with skins, fresh vegetables, jojoba, kelp, licorice, nettle, spirulina.

COBALT

FUNCTIONS--Aids in the assimilation and synthesis of vitamin B12; prevents anemia; helps build healthy red blood cell production, body cell maintenance and function.

COMPLEMENTARY NUTRIENTS--Folic acid, vitamin B12, copper, iron.

NUTRIENT DESTROYERS--Acids, sunlight, alcohol, estrogen, sleeping pills.

DEFICIENCY--Pernicious anemia.

SOURCES--Meat, organ meats, haddock, tuna, eggs, Swiss cheese, cottage cheese, white meat of chicken, turkey, Cheddar cheese, yogurt. Dandelion, horsetail, juniper, kelp, lobelia, parsley, red clover, spirulina.

COPPER

FUNCTIONS--Healing process of body, necessary for production of RNA. Aids in protein metabolism and in bone development, brain cells, nerves, and connective tissue. Helps retain the natural color of hair. Necessary for the absorption of iron.

COMPLEMENTARY NUTRIENTS--Cobalt, iron, zinc.

NUTRIENT DESTROYERS--High intake of zinc.

DEFICIENCY--General weakness, skin sores, impaired respiration.

SOURCES--Mushrooms, raisins, nuts, legumes, whole grains, seafood, organ meats, blackstrap molasses, bone meal, birch, burdock, caraway, chickweed, comfrey, dandelion, echinacea, eyebright, garlic, golden seal, horsetail, juniper, kelp, lobelia, red clover, slippery elm, spirulina, valerian, yarrow.

FLUORINE

FUNCTIONS--Strengthens bones, helps prevent tooth decay, protection against infections. Internal antiseptic.
COMPLEMENTARY NUTRIENTS--Calcium.
NUTRIENT DESTROYERS--Aluminum salts of fluoride. Sugar destroys mineral balance.
DEFICIENCY--Tooth decay.
SOURCES--Apples, brown rice, beef liver, soybeans, wheat germ, oats, sunflower seeds, milk, cheese, carrots, garlic, beet tops, leafy green vegetables, almonds, sea water, hard water, alfalfa, black walnut, hops, kelp, spirulina.

INOSITOL (B COMPLEX VITAMIN)

FUNCTIONS--Vital for hair growth and healthy heart muscle. Health of vital organs, metabolism of fats and cholesterol.
COMPLEMENTARY NUTRIENTS--B complex, B12, choline and linoleic acid.
NUTRIENT DESTROYERS--Alcohol, coffee, sugar, water, estrogen, food processing, antibiotics.
DEFICIENCY--High blood cholesterol, constipation, eczema, eye problems, hair loss.
SOURCES--Brewers yeast, wheat germ, lecithin, whole grains (oatmeal and corn), nuts, milk, blackstrap molasses, citrus fruits, liver, beans, raisins, brown rice, cabbage, cantaloupe, alfalfa, black cohosh, burdock, capsicum, cascara sagrada, catnip, chickweed, dandelion, eyebright, fenugreek, ginger, gentian, golden seal, hawthorne, hops, kelp, licorice, marshmallow, mullein, papaya, peppermint, red clover.

IODINE

FUNCTIONS--Regulates metabolism, stimulates circulation, healthy thyroid, energy production, physical and mental development, healthy hair and skin, nails and teeth.
COMPLEMENTARY NUTRIENTS--Calcium, iron magnesium, phosphorus, potassium, vitamins E and F (fatty acids).

NUTRIENT DESTROYERS--Food processing, soaking in water, heat and cooking.

DEFICIENCY--Thyroid disorders, obesity, goiter, irritability, nervousness, dry hair, cold hands and feet. Slow thinking, lack of energy. Can cause loss of interest in living.

SOURCES--Haddock, halibut, salmon, sardines, eggs, tomatoes, cottage cheese, raw milk, brewers yeast, seafood, mushrooms, black walnut, burdock, echinacea, eyebright, hops, horsetail, kelp, dulse, agar, Irish moss, licorice, mistletoe, spirulina, slippery elm, sarsaparilla, watercress, white oak bark, yarrow.

IRON

FUNCTIONS--Aids in the formation of hemoglobin, which carries the oxygen from the lungs to every cell of the body; resistance to disease, provides energy.

COMPLEMENTARY NUTRIENTS--B12, folic acid, vitamin E, calcium, cobalt, copper, phosphorus.

NUTRIENT DESTROYERS--Coffee, excess phosphorus, tea, excess zinc, food additives, tetracyclines.

DEFICIENCY--Fatigue, anemia, paleness, brittle nails, constipation, difficulty in breathing, low immunity to disease, persistent headache, impossible to please, continually finding fault with everything.

SOURCES--Rice bran, blackstrap molasses, apricots, peaches, raisins, wheat germ, sunflower seeds, liver, egg yolks, fish, poultry, alfalfa, aloe, burdock, capsicum, chamomile, comfrey, dandelion, garlic, kelp, mullein, parsley, red clover, red raspberry, rose hips, skullcap, taheebo, yellow dock.

MAGNESIUM

FUNCTIONS--Acid/alkaline balance in the body, blood sugar metabolism (energy). Metabolism of calcium and vitamin C. Natural tranquilizer. Function of nerves and muscles, arteries, bones, heart and teeth, utilization of fats.

COMPLEMENTARY NUTRIENTS--Vitamins B6, C, and D, calcium, phosphorus.

NUTRIENT DESTROYERS--High protein diet can cause magnesium deficiency, alcohol, diuretics, sugar, refined flour, food processing.

DEFICIENCY--Severe diarrhea can lead to magnesium deficiency leading to mental confusion, irritability, depression, tremors, filled with grief, apprehension and disorientation.

SOURCES--Almonds, apples, bran, brown rice, yellow corn, sesame, wheat germ, leafy greens, cashews, soybeans, honey, bone meal, seafood, alfalfa, aloe, kelp, black walnut, dandelion, garlic, gotu kola, hops, mullein, papaya, parsley, red clover, wood betony.

MANGANESE

FUNCTIONS--Digestion of fats, sex hormone production, reproduction and growth, enzyme activation, tissue respiration, metabolism of vitamin B1, and vitamin E utilization.

COMPLEMENTARY NUTRIENTS--B complex and vitamin E, zinc, calcium.

NUTRIENT DESTROYERS--Excess of calcium and phosphorus intake.

DEFICIENCY--Lack can cause fainting and crying spells, urgency to be left alone, find excuses to fight over everything, possible sterility, growth retardation, digestive problems, abnormal bone development, respiratory disorders, male impotence, dizziness, loss of hearing.

SOURCES--Bananas, chives, parsley, celery, cucumbers, carrots, beets, green leafy vegetables, oranges, grapefruits, apricots, outer coating of nuts and grains, peas, wheat germ, egg yolks, sweet potatoes. Aloe, barberry, black walnut, cascara sagrada, catnip, camomile, chickweed, garlic, golden seal, hops, horsetail, kelp, licorice, red clover, red raspberry, sarsaparilla, wood betony, yarrow, yellow dock.

MOLYBDENUM

FUNCTIONS--Carries oxygen to the body cells, involved with proper carbohydrate metabolism. Integral part of certain enzymes. Promotes well being.

COMPLEMENTARY NUTRIENTS--Iron.

NUTRIENT DESTROYERS--Poor soil depleted, refined food.

DEFICIENCY--Not known.

SOURCES--Dark green vegetables, whole grains, meat and beans, peas.

PABA

FUNCTIONS--Aids health of skin, natural sunscreen, promotes growth and formation of blood cells, healthy intestinal flora, assists in protein metabolism.

COMPLEMENTARY NUTRIENTS--Vitamin B complex, folic acid, vitamin C.

NUTRIENT DESTROYERS--Alcohol, coffee, sulfa drugs, estrogen, food processing.

DEFICIENCY--Can cause extreme fatigue, irritability, depression, nervousness, headache, constipation and digestive disorders, anemia, loss of hair color and skin pigmentation.

SOURCES--Wheat germ, brewers yeast, yogurt, milk, eggs, organ meats, rice bran, blackstrap molasses, leafy green vegetables, alfalfa, boneset, burdock, capsicum, cascara sagrada, catnip, chickweed, cornsilk, hawthorne, hops, horsetail, kelp, licorice, marshmallow, mullein, papaya and red clover.

PHOSPHORUS

FUNCTIONS--Proper growth of bones and teeth, works with calcium to aid in the metabolism of fat and carbohydrates, growth and repair of cells, nerves and muscle activity, heart muscle contraction and essential for maintaining an appropriate acid/alkaline balance.

COMPLEMENTARY NUTRIENTS--Vitamin B12, calcium, vitamin D, iron, niacin, vitamins E and F, magnesium.

NUTRIENT DESTROYERS--Sugar, excessive intake of magnesium, aluminum and iron.

DEFICIENCY--Lack of can cause a fear of tomorrow, fearful of anything new, growing dislike of the opposite sex. Loss of appetite, phorrhea, fatigue, weakness, poor formation of bones and teeth. Nervous disorders.

SOURCES--Rice bran, dark green leafy vegetables, wheat bran, pumpkin seeds, wheat germ, nuts, seeds, cheese, egg yolks, poultry, meat, legumes. Alfalfa, barberry, black cohosh, black walnut, capsicum, catnip, chickweed, comfrey, dandelion, garlic, ginger, golden seal, hawthorne, kelp, licorice, papaya, parsley, red raspberry, sage, slippery elm, white oak bark, wood betony.

POTASSIUM

FUNCTIONS--Maintains proper acid/alkaline balance in blood and tissues, and in maintaining intercellular fluid balance. Helps kidneys in detoxification of blood. Stimulates endocrine hormone production. Regulates heart beat.

COMPLEMENTARY NUTRIENTS--Vitamins B6 and B12, sodium.

NUTRIENT DESTROYERS--Sugar, caffeine, most diuretics, stress, most laxatives, alcohol, cortisone, excess salt.

DEFICIENCY---Acne, continuous thirst, dry skin, constipation, general weakness, insomnia, muscle damage, excessive accumulation of sodium (table salt), high blood pressure, cardiac arrest, nervous disorders and low blood sugar.

SOURCES--Apples, carrots, celery, seaweed, leafy green vegetables, bananas, apricots, blackstrap molasses, figs, wheat germ, raisins, seafood, legumes, whole grains, sunflower seeds, potatoes, kelp, parsley watercress. Alfalfa, aloe, black walnut, capsicum, cascara sagrada, camomile, chaparral, comfrey, dandelion, echinacea, fennel, garlic, ginger, golden seal, mullein, papaya, peppermint, rose hips, slippery elm, valerian, white oak bark, yarrow.

SELENIUM

FUNCTIONS--Works with vitamin E, has an antioxidant effect similar to vitamin E. Counteracts and protects the body from toxin damage by mercury poisoning. Preserves tissue elasticity, promotes healthy function of testicles.

COMPLEMENTARY NUTRIENTS--Vitamin E, zinc.

NUTRIENT DESTROYERS--High fat intake, food poisoning, stress.

DEFICIENCY--Premature aging, impired male sexual function, skin problems, possible cancer and tumors.

SOURCES--Brewers yeast, bran, egg yolks, milk, mushrooms, onions, broccoli, tuna, wheat germ, most vegetables, whole grain, sea water, garlic, kelp, lobelia, red clover, slippery elm.

SODIUM

FUNCTIONS--Works with potassium and chlorine, helps control and maintain cellular osmotic pressure and water balance, nerve and muscle function, helps in hydrochloric acid production in the stomach.

COMPLEMENTARY NUTRIENTS--Vitamin B complex, chlorine, potassium.

NUTRIENT DESTROYERS--Diarrhea, exercise, hot climate, excess sweating, excess vomiting.

DEFICIENCY--Chronic diarrhea, over-consumption of sodium chloride is the problem. It can cause water retention, high blood pressure, stomach ulcers, hardening of the arteries and heart disease.

SOURCES--(Organic Sodium) Beet greens, celery, kale, carrots, raisins, radishes, dried fruit, romaine lettuce, asparagus and watermelon. Alfalfa, aloe, catnip, chaparral, chickweed, dandelion, fennel, ginger, hawthorne, horsetail, kelp, lobelia, marshmallow, papaya, parsley, rose hips, rosemary, sage, sarsaparilla, slippery elm.

SULPHUR

FUNCTIONS--Aids digestion, counteracts acidosis, helps to maintain healthy hair, skin and nails. Purifies the blood and stops fermentation.

COMPLEMENTARY NUTRIENTS--Vitamin B complex, biotin, pantothenic acid.

NUTRIENT DESTROYERS--None

DEFICIENCY--Lack of can cause catatonic facial appearance, stupor, unresponsiveness, slow in getting over colds, coughs and flu, difficulty in talking, menstrual cycles thrown off balance.

SOURCES--Onion, radishes, garlic, soybeans, turnips, celery, string beans, raspberries, lettuce, fish, eggs, dried beans, nuts, Brussel sprouts, wheat germ, beef, alfalfa, burdock, capsicum, catnip, chaparral, comfrey, dandelion, echinacea, fennel, garlic, juniper, kelp, lobelia, mullein, parsley, sarsaparilla, watercress.

ZINC

FUNCTIONS--Aids in healing of wounds and burns protein and carbohydrate metabolism, prostate gland function, healthy reproductive organs, essential for the formation of RNA and DNA.

COMPLEMENTARY NUTRIENTS--Vitamins A, E and B complex.

NUTRIENT DESTROYERS--Stress (physical and emotional), depleted soil, food processing, alcohol, oral contraceptives, excessive calcium, phosphorus deficiency.

DEFICIENCY--Fatigue, hair loss, enlarged prostate, delayed sexual maturity, sterility, poor wound healing.

SOURCES--Wheat germ, wheat bran, sesame seeds, pumpkin seeds and sunflower seeds. Brewers yeast, egg yolks, onion, green leafy vegetables, sprouted seeds, milk, mushrooms, seafood, liver.

SUPER FOODS TO KNOW

ACEROLA CHERRY

Acerola cherry is a tropical fruit and extremely high in vitamin C. It is usually combined with rose hips for natural vitamin C supplement. Acerola cherry is very good to add to juices for infants and children and older people who cannot swallow pills. It can be used for liquid or powder in juices to supplement the necessary daily supply of vitamin C.

ACIDOPHILUS

Acidophilus is a cultured milk into which the bacteria of acidophilus has been introduced. Acidophilus milk aids the growth of healthful intestinal flora and also inhibits the growth of unfriendly bacteria. Works like yogurt except it is stronger. It converts lactose in milk to lactic acid and this supplements the hydrochloric acid in the stomach, easing digestion in a natural, drugless way. It remains in the stomach to provide protection even after it has been eaten and digested.

Acidophilus will speed the intestinal recovery from antibiotics, which destroy the small intestinal flora responsible for proper digestion and B vitamins production. Acidophilus is good for reducing the amount of histamine liberated by putrefactive bacteria in the intestine. Biotin deficiency is improved with acidophilus. Constipation is relieved and calcium is more readily absorbed because of the acidic properties of acidophilus.

AGAR-AGAR

Agar-Agar is a seaweed used as a thickener and emulsifier. Vegetarians use this to replace common gelatin (which is made from animal protein). It is excellent for thickening soups, and also used in molded salads and desserts. This is excellent for jams and jellies. When using agar-agar you need less sweetening. Just warm to jell.

Agar-Agar is useful for constipation as it increases peristaltic action of the bowels. It is also used as a jelling agent in salads, soups, and desserts in place of animal gelatin or pectin. Recipe is as follows:

3-1/2 C. liquid to 2 T. flakes
3-1/2 C. liquid to 1 T. granulated

FRUIT JELL

2 C. apple juice (orange juice)
2 C. pure water
1 T. agar-agar

Bring the juice and water to a boil. Add agar-agar. Stir until dissolved and simmer for 10 minutes.

ALFALFA

Alfalfa is one of the most valuable herbs given to mankind. It contains valuable vitamins such as D, E, G, K and U. Alfalfa contains the cell building amino acids, such as arginine, lysine, threonine and tryptophan. Alfalfa is also rich in minerals such as phosphorus, chlorine, iron, silicon, calcium, magnesium, sulphur, sodium and potassium. It is rich in chlorophyll, which is healing, good for the stomach and sweetens the breath. It is also an infection fighter and breaks down poisonous carbon dioxide.

Alfalfa helps in the assimilation of protein, calcium and other necessary nutrients. It has health building properties for all ailments. It is an excellent spring tonic to use in green drinks. It is a natural diuretic and helps neutralize cancer in the system. It has been used successfully in the treatment of recuperative cases of narcotic and alcohol addiction.

Alfalfa sprouts are easy to grow, and when sprouted with pure water are the most nutritious, pure, and free from chemicals of any greens you can buy. They can be ground and used in raw soups, salads and nut loaves. They can be used in sandwiches, and children love to eat them by the handsful. The herb can be used in an alfalfa mint tea for colds and flu. The seeds are about 35% protein and can be ground into alfalfa meal to use in many ways. Sprouting increases its value up to 10 times.

Alfalfa is a blood purifier. It is beneficial in anemia, bladder, kidney, and prostate problems. Good for arthritis, diabetes, toxemia, jaundice, tuberculosis, rheumatism, bright's disease, nerves, constipation, hardening of the arteries, dropsy, skin eruptions and poor circulation.

ALMONDS

Raw almonds are an excellent source of protein. They contain all the essential amino acids and are rich in linoleic acid. They are also high in B complex vitamins, calcium, potassium, magnesium, iron and phosphorus. The nutrients in almonds are compared to animal foods. Almonds are high in fat but are much more easily digested than meat, lard or butter.

Almonds are called "king" of the nuts. They are the highest alkaline nut. They are nourishing food and are considered a muscle and body builder. The calcium content makes them a valuable food for the teeth and bones.

They can be ground and added to cereals, fruit and nut casseroles and grain loaves. They can be made into a nourishing and digestible drink for infants and children. Almonds have been used in diets to nourish and feed cancer victims. (One Answer to Cancer by Dr. W.D. Kelley.)

ALMOND BUTTER

Blanch 1/2 cup almonds, roast lightly in oven and grind into butter with a nut and seed grinder.

To Blanch Almonds: Pour boiling water over them and let them soak for about 5 minutes. The skin will become loose and is easily pinched off by pressing the nut with your fingers. You can dry almonds by putting them in a moderate oven for a few minutes.

ARROWROOT STARCH

This is used as a tropical perennial herb. It has a mild vanilla flavor. Arrowroot starch helps in the acid and alkaline balance in the body. It is nutritious and more easily digested than corn starch or flour as a thickener. It agrees with babies and the sickly.

Arrowroot starch is used to thicken sauces, gravies, soups, ice cream, puddings, and fruit compotes. It thickens when combined with water and heated. It is rich in calcium and other trace minerals.

Basic proportions consist of this: 1 cup water and 1-1/2 tablespoons arrowroot.

BAKING POWDER

Most baking powder contains aluminum compounds as well as high amounts of sodium. You can purchase low sodium, aluminum-free brands in the health stores.

HOMEMADE BAKING POWDER

Two parts Cream of Tartar
Two parts arrowroot powder
One part potassium bicarbonate (at pharmacy)

Sift together and use it in recipes calling for double-acting baking powder. Avoid baking soda, for it is irritating to the stomach.

BARLEY

Barley is a very nourishing grain. The darker the barley the more nutritious. It nourishes and cleans the lymph glands as well as the colon. It supplies calcium in an easily digestible form for the weak and sick and for babies. It is rich in the B vitamins. It contains sulphur to promote healthy skin, hair and nails. It also contains potassium, phosphorus, iron. It is nourishing for good bones, teeth, muscles, nerves and the heart. It contains hordenine, which relieves bronchial spasms.

Barley water is excellent to use for babies with diarrhea or the sick and elderly with delicate stomachs. Good also to use for high fevers. Makes an excellent tonic for cleansing and building up the entire system. It is hard to cook unhulled barley.

BARLEY WATER

Boil 1/2 cup barley in 2 quarts of pure water. Simmer for one hour. Strain barley from water and save barley for soups. Add lemon juice to water for colds and flu. Add licorice for coughs, and figs for laxative.

BEANS, DRIED

Beans are an excellent meat substitute. They are rich in protein, niacin, vitamins B1 and B2, iron, magnesium, sodium and calcium. Beans are very delicious and nutritious and can be added to soups and stews and casseroles. They can be puréed and used as a base for soups or added to salads. They can be sprouted. Sprouting helps inhibit the formation of gas and converts starches to sugar.

The basic cause of gas in the system is the absence of enzymes in our systems which break down the tri-saccharides (raffinase and stachyose). They remain in the tract to come in contact with certain bacteria which react to break them down into carbon dioxide and hydrogen, which causes gastrointestinal gas.

METHODS FOR ELIMINATING GAS

Soak the beans overnight with two capsules of ginger. Wash the beans and throw away the soaking water. Cook the beans with another two capsules of ginger. This does not alter the flavor of the beans when you add your own flavoring.

Another method is to use apple cider vinegar along with flavorings and cook the last thirty minutes of the cooking time.

Another method is to pre-soak the beans in water overnight. Throw away the soaking water. Add boiling water to cover and cook for about thirty minutes. Discard this water and add fresh water and resume cooking until tender.

SEASONINGS FOR BEANS

Basil	Coriander	Sage
Bay Leaf	Garlic	Savory
Cayenne Pepper	Marjoram	Thyme
Chili Pepper	Oregano	
Cumin	Rosemary	

COOKING DRIED BEANS

Above 2,500 feet pressure cookers are life-savers. Beans are especially hard to cook since water boils at a lower temperature. Beans can take a long time to cook or never really become tender.

Pressure Cooking: Place beans, water and oil in pressure cooker (after you have pre-soaked overnight and boiled the beans for 30 minutes). Bring to desired pressure. When cooked the desired time remove from heat immediately and let pressure reduce naturally.

Add all other ingredients to beans. Bring to pressure and cook for 5 minutes. Let cool for 5 minutes and reduce pressure quickly by placing under the cold water tap.

ADZUKI BEANS

Adzuki are a small red bean from Japan and China. They are excellent for sprouting, similar to mung beans. They will turn bitter if pressure-cooked. It is an easier bean to digest than most beans. They can be used alone or mixed with brown rice or other grains.

SPROUTING

1/2 C. dry beans makes 2 C. sprouts

Rinse 4 times during the day. They take four days to sprout and should be one inch long when ready to use.

BLACK BEANS

Black beans are very rich in protein: three times as much as eggs, and eleven times more than milk. They also contain more calcium than milk and are very rich in lecithin. They are used in Mexican and Spanish foods. They are very good flavored with bay leaves, cumin, garlic, onions and tomatoes.

CHICK PEAS (Garbanzo)

They are high in protein, calcium, iron, B vitamins and potassium. They can be used in soups, salads, vegetable loaves, and party dip sauce.

HUMUS

1 C. cooked garbanzo beans
1/4 C. olive oil
1/4 C. fresh lemon juice

2 cloves garlic, finely
chopped
1/4 C. sesame Tahini
Flavoring to taste (such
as Sesame Kelp Salt

Put all ingredients in the blender except garbanzo beans. Blend well, then add the beans gradually and blend to a smooth paste. Delicious as a dip.

FAVA BEANS

Fava beans are used in Italian recipes. They are high in protein, also phosphorus, iron, sodium, potassium, vitamins A, B1, B2, C and niacin. They look like extra large lima beans.

GREAT NORTHERN BEANS

A large white bean. Delicious in soups and vegetables and very good for mixing with other beans.

KIDNEY BEANS

A red kidney-shaped bean. Used in chili recipes, salads and soups. Excellent as bean stew cooked with onions, celery, green peppers, garlic and herbs for seasonings. Mexican chili powder adds to the flavor of the beans. Tamari, garlic, onion, and blackstrap molasses also adds to the flavor of kidney beans. Add wheat flakes to the chili about the last 15 minutes before serving. This helps thicken the dish and adds to make a complete protein for those concerned about complete proteins at each meal. Excellent cooked with onions, garlic, olive oil and seasonings and served over brown rice.

LIMA BEANS

They are the large limas, baby limas and butter beans. Serve them with nut cream and butter. Make succotash with corn. Served with mushrooms, carrots and green beans. Use alone, in casseroles or in salads.

LIMA BEAN SOUP

1-1/2 C. dry large lima beans
4 C. pure water

Soak for 5 hours. Bring to a boil and add:

1 C. celery   *1 small onion*
1 pint tomatoes   *1 tsp. mineral balanced*
                       salt

Cook until tender. The last 10 minutes add 2 cloves of minced garlic.

NAVY BEANS

A good all-around bean to use in baked beans, casseroles and stews.

NAVY BEAN SOUP

1 C. nvy beans
4 C. pure water
1 medium onion

4 stalks of celery
1/4 C. grated carrots
1 C. tomatoes

Soak beans overnight. Bring water to a boil and add the beans. Cover and cook with all the other ingredients on simmer until done. Add bran water to thin. When beans are done add two tablespoons of olive oil. Add seasoning broth to taste.

PINTO BEANS

Pinto beans have the highest protein content of any other dried bean. It is a very versatile bean and can be used in many ways: in soups, stews, chili beans, bean loaves, burritos, and refried beans. They have a natural sweet flavor.

PINTO BEAN LOAF

2 C. cooked pinto beans,
    mashed
1 tsp. Italian seasoning
1/2 C. tomato sauce
1/4 C. chopped onions

1 tsp. vegetable seasoning
1/2 C. whole wheat bread
    bread crumbs or
    wheat germ
1 tsp. kelp

Combine all ingredients and pour into a greased loaf pan. Baste occasionally with olive oil. Bake at 350° for 45 minutes.

SOYBEANS

Soybeans are the most nutritious of all the beans. They are an excellent source of high-quality, inexpensive protein. Rich in the B vitamins, minerals and unsaturated fatty acids in the form of lecithin, which is essential to help the body emulsify cholesterol, soybeans have a bland flavor which makes it an excellent food to blend into a large number of dishes. Soybeans can be eaten as plain beans, as well as made into soy cheese, tofu, soy milk, flour, oil, tamari, miso, imitation meat, soy grits, flakes, and soy nuts. Since the soybeans are the most acid of the beans and high in protein and oil, it is recommended that they be eaten only occasionally as a separate side dish. The best way to eat soybeans is in the tofu, tempeh, miso and tamari.

COOKED SOYBEANS

1 cup soybeans soaked overnight in 3 cups of water. Bring water to a boil , skim off the foam. Reduce the heat and simmer for 2 to 3 hours or until beans are tender. Add flavorings at the end of the cooking time. Use the cooked soybeans in soups or with other beans. They can be mashed and used as soyburgers or in bean loaves.

SOY MILK

Soak soybeans in water overnight. Grind the beans or use a mortar and pestle to crush them. Put the beans into a pot and pour boiling over them to cover. Add a little cold water, stir and let sit for 5 minutes. Squeeze through a cloth bag. Pour hot water over the remaining beans, only use 1/2 as much water. Stir, let set 5 minutes and squeeze again through the cloth. The soy milk should be heated until it starts to boil.

Soy milk is a nutritional substitute for infants and children who are allergic to cow's milk. It is very nourishing to use in cooking.

SOY MILK

1 C. soy flour   *4 C. pure water*

Mix the soy flour in water. Let stand at room temperature for a few hours. Cook soy milk in a double boiler for about 45 minutes. It can be cooked in a large pan, stirring continually. It is best strained through cheesecloth for a smoother milk. Chill in refrigerator.

BRAN

Bran is the rich outer layer of the wheat grain. It is a natural plant fiber that is essential for the human body. Fiber has the ability to absorb large amounts of water which gives the food bulk it needs to pass along the bowel. This fiber absorbs toxins in the body and eliminates them. Toxic materials such as chemical waste, air pollution, pesticides and additives in the colon can be removed with the help of bran. Bran also builds immunity.

Bran has a natural laxative effect and is essential in preventing constipation. The unprocessed bran helps increase stool weight and reduces the transit time of waste out of the bowels.

It has the highest fiber content of any food. It is rich in B conplex vitamins. It also contains protein, iron, calcium, phosphorus and potassium.

Bran can be used as a laxative by using 1 tablespoon in 8 oz. of pure water. Use in granolas, breads, and add to soups just before serving.

BRAN WATER

To one quart of pure water add two cups of bran, soak overnight and strain through cheesecloth or a fine sieve. Use with juices or use in soups.

BRAZIL NUT

Brazil nuts are a good source of protein. They are high in saturated fats. They tend to become rancid quickly and should be checked over very carefully when purchasing.

They are rich in potassium, calcium, and phosphorus, which aid bones and teeth. They also contain small amounts of vitamins B, A and C. It is a rich food to build muscles. It is nourishing when made into peanut butter. The nut should be chewed thoroughly so as not to irritate the intestinal lining and so that proper digestion takes place.

NUT BUTTER

Grind equal parts of Brazil nuts and cashew nuts. Keep refrigerated. They can be used in salads, cookies, mixed with raw cereals and dried fruit.

BREWERS YEAST

Brewers yeast was originally a by-product of the brewing process. It is now grown especially for human consumption. It is an excellent source for all the B vitamins and is rich in protein. Good food for quick energy. It is excellent for helping in weight reduction, for it contains little fat, carbohydrates or sugar and will help give you energy for encouragement to eat less.

If there is a deficiency in the B vitamins, the yeast may cause gas at first, so it should be eaten in small amounts at first and gradually increased. It is one of the best and cheapest sources of B vitamins, minerals and protein. If the B vitamins are undersupplied, grooves will start to appear on the tongue. A healthy tongue should be pink and smooth around the edges. A large tongue indicates a need for pantothenic acid. a sore red tongue indicates the need for niacin. A magenta color can indicate a B2 (riboflavin) deficiency. Other symptoms of B vitamin deficiency include depressionn, irritability, fatigue, skin irritations, mouth sores and palpitatioins. It is a wonderful food for mental illness.

Brewers yeast contains sixteen of the twenty amino acids and all of the B complex vitamins. It is rich in phosphorus, iron and calcium and two vital trace elements: chromium and selenium.

Other good sources of B complex vitamins are wheat germ, rice polish and liver. B vitamins cannot be stored in the body and need to be replaced each day.

Brewers yeast can be added to soups, stews, bread and health drinks. It can be used in juices. My favorite is with tomato juice.

BROWN RICE

Brown rice is considered a valuable and naturally balanced nutritious food. It retains the precious germ, vitamins, minerals, protein, fat, starch and fiber. It is an inexpensive source of fuel for the body. It is easily digested as well as delicious. The short grain is a little more nutritious than the long grain. It takes longer to cook than the white rice. It is best cooked on a very low heat to preserve the lecithin, vitamin E and other nutrients. It contains the B complex vitamins, calcium, phosphorus, iron, copper and niacin.

Brown rice has a nutty, tasty flavor. It is excellent used in soups, stews, rice and nut loaves and cooked plain and served with vegetables.

BROWN RICE

1 C. brown rice   *1 T. oil*
2-1/2 C. boiling water   *1/2 tsp. kelp*

Pour boiling water over the rice. Steam or simmer for about one hour. For a better taste, set off stove for about 10 minutes before serving.

BUCKWHEAT

Buckwheat is considered the "king" of the grass cereals. It is an alkaline grain which neutralizes acids in the body. Buckwheat needs to be utilized more, for it is a hardy grain that is almost blightfree and does not need the insecticides that most grains do. It is considered a valuable and natural balanced food for humans. It is lower in calories than wheat, rice, corn or meat and richer in high quality protein which contains all the food value of meat. It is a good winter food for warmth and energy and is considered to be food for the muscles.

It is rich in rutin, which has a powerful effect on the arteries and capillaries and reduces recurrent hemmorrhage that goes along with it. It is high in potassium and phosphorus. It is rich in iron and contains almost all B complex vitamins. Also contains calcium.

Buckwheat can be used in muffins, pancakes and casseroles. The buckwheat groats, or Kasha, can be served as a breakfast cereal, used as a stuffing, or served as a rice substitute. It is excellent sprouted for a live food diet. Valuable for constipation, liver problems, dysentery, skin problems, anemia and nerves.

KASHA

1 C. groats
1 C. yellow corn meal
1/2 C. brown rice
1/4 C. ground sesame seeds

6 C. spring water
Sea salt or kelp to taste
Tamari to taste
1 clove garlic, pressed

Boil all ingredients but the sesame seeds and turn heat and simmer for about 30 minutes.

BULGHUR

Bulghur is cracked wheat that has the nutritional bran and germ of the grain still intact. It is nutritional and has an excellent taste in prepared dishes. It is an ancient wheat product that is still used in Europe today.

Bulghur is high in protein and B complex vitamins. It is rich in phosphorus and potassium and also contains calcium and iron.

BULGHUR

Cook 1 C. of wheat in 2 C. of pure water for one hour. Drain off the liquid, spread on a cookie sheet and cook at 225°F. until the wheat is completely dry, which takes about one hour. After wheat is cool, blend in blender or grinder. Do not grind too finely.

BULGHUR SALAD

Soak 3/4 C. bulghur in 1 C. boiling water for about 45 minutes or until water is absorbed. Drain and mix in chopped ingredients. Add kelp oil and lemon juices before serving.

1 C. fresh chopped parsley　　　*3 ripe tomatoes, chopped*
1 clove garlic, chopped finely　*Kelp to taste*
1/4 C. green onion, chopped　　*1/2 C. cold pressed oil*
　　　　　　　　　　　　　　　　1/2 C. lemon juice

CAROB

Carob is also called St. Johns bread or honey bread. The dark brown pods resemble cocoa but do not contain the caffeine or oxalic acid that chocolate does. (These substances interfere with the body's ability to assimilate calcium, as well as cause digestive problems.) Chocolate robs calcium, while carob provides calcium. Carob is low in fat and rich in vitamins and minerals. Carob is also rich in protein and natural carbohydrates. It contains a high amount of the detoxifying substance called pectin, which helps to normalize loose bowels. Carob is naturally sweet, containing one-third the calories that baking chocolate does. It contains B vitamins, vitamins F and A, and the minerals calcium, potassium, phosphorus, magnesium, silicon and niacin.

CAROB SYRUP

1 C. carob powder　　*1/4 C. honey*
1 T. arrowroot　　　　*1-1/2 C. water*
2 tsp. pure vanilla

Combine carob and arrowroot and gradually add water and honey, bringing to boil and simmer for five minutes. Remove from heat and cool. When cool add vanilla. Use on ice cream, puddings, or add to nut milks.

CASHEW NUTS

Cashew nuts are high in protein but also high in calories. They are good body builders. They are best when eaten raw and much easier to digest. They are high in phosphorus and B complex; good amounts of magnesium, sodium and calcium. Good for vitality, teeth and gums.

Cashew milk may be used to replace whole dairy milk in the same proportions for almost all recipes. It can be made into paste to be used in cream soups, milk nuts and nut butter.

CASHEW MILK

1 C. pure water
1/3 C. cashew nuts (raw)

1-2 drops vanilla (pure)
1/2 tsp. pure maple syrup

Grind nuts and blend with other ingredients. Blend. Strain off the nut meats.

CHESTNUTS

Chestnuts are low in calories and protein but high in carbohydrates. They are rich in potassium and magnesium, which are beneficial for heart problems and high blood pressure. They are also rich in sodium and contain calcium, iron and phosphorus. They should always be eaten cooked because of their tannic acid content. They are good eaten roasted. Chestnuts and sweet potatoes are good cooked together.

CHESTNUT STUFFING

2 C. cooked chestnuts
1 C. cooked millet
1 C. whole wheat bread
  crumbs
1/2 C. chopped onions
1/2 C. chopped celery

1/4 C. almond or cashew
  butter
3 T. butter or ghee
Sesame kelp salt for
  flavoring
1/2 tsp. sage

Saute´ onion and celery in butter. Add all other ingredients. For a moist stuffing add hot water.

CHIA SEEDS

Chia seeds are a tiny power house of nutrition and energy-giving properties. They are seeds the Indians and Mexicans have used for hundreds of years. The American Indians made use of the potent seeds to help sustain them on long journeys. One tablespoon of chia seeds was sufficient to sustain an Indian on a twenty-four hour march.

Chia seeds are very mucilaginous and when using, whole seeds should be soaked for a few hours to make them easier to digest. They are delicious soaked in apple juice. They were used to lower fevers by the mission fathers. Mexicans use chia seeds in citrus drinks to enhance its thirst-quenching properties.

Chia seeds are very high in protein, B complex. Also contains PABA, biotin, choline, inositol, pantothenic acid; also vitamins D and E.

The seeds can be finely ground and used in granola, peanut butter, cottage cheese and bread.

CHICKPEAS   (Garbanzos)

Chickpeas are a rich source of body building nutrients and a good source of protein for vegetarians. It is an easily digestible food for those with weak stomachs and for the sick. Controls diarrhea for children who need protein weight gain. Garbanzo flour is useful for those who are allergic to wheat products.

Chickpeas contain calcium, iron, B vitamins, vitamins A and C. Also contain phosphorus, potassium and sulphur. It is beneficial for hair, skin and nails. For those who are worried about obtaining complete protein with each meal, when chickpeas are combined with sesame seeds or sunflower seeds, you will have a complete source of protein.

HUMUS

A Middle East speciality. Use with flat bread and scoop up the humus for a complete meal.

2 C. cooked chickpeas *1/4 tsp. kelp*
1/2 C. tahini *Dash cayenne pepper*
Juice of one lemon *1 tsp. olive oil*
Paprika and parsley for
*   seasoning*

Mash chickpeas in a blender and add all other ingredients.

CHLOROPHYLL

Liquid chlorophyll is an all-around food beneficial for tissue repair. It is easy to absorb and assimilate. It goes directly to the bloodstream without having to be digested and it saves energy. It contains the greatest amount of minerals of any land plant.

Chlorophyll is the green pigment that plants use to carry out the process of photosynthesis. This process absorbs the light energy for the reduction of carbon dioxide to sugars and other plant material. The liquid chlorophyll helps to neutralize some of the pollution that we eat and breathe. It strengthens the body so that it can fight pollution. Chlorophyll helps to keep calcium and other minerals in the body.

Chlorophyll is also a natural deodorizer. Use 1 teaspoon in a glass of water in the morning. Gargle with one part chlorophyll to nine parts water for sore throat, laryngitis and tonsillitis every few hours. Rinse mouth after teeth extraction. It helps purify the liver, soothes ulcers, helps catarrhal problems, helps build high blood count and feeds the organs iron and essential nutrients. It clears bowel toxins and helps in lung conditions. Increases milk production in nursing mothers and heals sores quickly, purifies body odors, helps nasal drip, soothing to hemorrhoids and many other conditions of the body.

CORNMEAL, YELLOW

Cornmeal is a laxative starch and is high in magnesium that is useful in constipation. Will not produce catarrh. It can be used if colon problems exist. Yellow corn meal is very nourishinng. It contains vitamin A, B complex, calcium, phosphorus, iron, potassium, magnesium and silicon. When you grind your own corn it contains 25% more niacin, twice the vitamin A, and four times as much calcium and magnesium.

CORNMEAL

1 C. cornmeal to 4 C. water

Boil water, add cornmeal gradually to boiling water, reduce heat, cover and cook for about 40 minutes. Use over Mexican casseroles.

FILBERTS

Filberts are also called hazelnuts. They are high in comp'ete protein and low in carbohydrates. They are an acid-forming nu should be used sparingly. They are also a body building food.

They can be used in breakfast cereal such as granola, muesli, nut loaves and casseroles.

Filberts are rich in phosphorus and calcium. They contain B complex and small amounts of vitamin C and iron. Also some linoleic acid, magnesium, niacin, potassium and all the essential amino acids.

They are an excellent energy food for hormone production, energy and for burning fats.

Filberts help in anemia, brittle hair and nails, water retention, flabby muscles, low blood pressure and low blood sugar. They are rich in calcium and, therefore, good for nerves, bones and teeth. Along with phosphorus and potassium, they are good for muscular reaction and essential for converting sugar to energy. B1 is present to build heart muscles and aid circulation. Niacin for irritability and depression. Linoleic acid is essential for growth, for maintaining proper weight, for energy output, for intestinal bacteria which produces B vitamin. Magnesium for healthy heart, and aiding in lowering blood cholesterol.

FLAXSEEDS

Flaxseed is the best natural source of essential fatty acids such as linoleic and linolenic acids or vitamin F factor. These are also found in nuts, avocado, fertile eggs, cod liver oil, evening Primrose and mother's milk. Flaxseed contains all the essential amino acids, which makes it a complete protein and an excellent mucilagenous food so very beneficial for a healthy alimentary canal.

Flaxseeds are an excellent food to help regulate bowels and eliminate constipation. They help increase calcium metabolism, reduce cholesterol and improve heart action.

FLAXSEED LAXATIVE

1 T. whole flaxseeds   *1 T. raw bran*

Mix into a large glass of pure water. Soak overnight, drink in the morning. Add to granola, cereals, yogurt, cottage cheese. Excellent food for healthy, shiny and thick hair.

FLAXSEED TEA

This tea is useful for bronchial problems.

Steep 1 tablespoon flaxseeds in 2 cups boiling water for 15 minutes. When cool add comfrey, fenugreek and a little licorice root. It makes an excellent remedy to break up congestion.

FRUIT

The ideal food for man is fruit. When tree-ripened, the nutrients in fruit are very rich. It takes time, sun, water, soil and air to produce an ideal energy-filled food. The sugar in fruits, along with minerals and vitamins, is a great source of energy for the body. Fruit is easily assimilated and digested and provides alkalinity for the blood. The average American diet is lacking in fresh fruit. Use a lot when in season.

APPLES

Apples aid in digestion and stimulate all body secretions. They are very good for constipation. They contain fruit-acid salts which stimulate the digestive processes and cellulose content which soften the partly digested food in the intestines. They are beneficial for almost every ailment. "An apple a day keeps the doctor away" may be wise advice to follow.

Apples are good for the teeth for they help remove food and stimulate the gums. Very good for asthma, high blood pressure, insomnia, catarrh, gout, jaundice. They help skin disease, arthritis, indigestion. The peel of the apple contains pectin which helps to prevent protein matter in the intestines from rotting, acting as a natural germicide. It contains malic acid and glucose, an excellent food for the nervous system. An excellent blood purifier.

Apples contain vitamin A, some B complex, and vitamin C. Rich in potassium, apples contain some calcium, iron and phosphorus. Apples help to maintain a potassium-sodium balance. Apples stimulate the growth of healthy tissues.

Raw apple juice is delicious, or apples can be eaten raw, grated in salads or made into raw applesauce. They do not combine well with bread, pastry or potatoes. They are very good with yogurt.

FRESH APPLESAUCE

4 ripe apples, tart or delicious	*Raw apple juice*
	1 tsp. honey
1 tsp. lemon juice (keeps apples white)	*1/2 tsp. cinnamon*

Peel apples, especially if they have been waxed and sprayed. Put in blender with a little apple juice at a time. Add honey and cinnamon. For babies leave out the honey and cinnamon.

APRICOTS

Apricots are an excellent source of vitamin A in the form of carotene, which is readily available for use by the body. Vitamin A helps with healthy skin, eyesight, energy and growth and aids resistance to infections. Apricots are a good source of iron, which makes them beneficial for anemia, asthma, bronchitis, catarrh and blood impurities. Good for cleansing the liver and pancreas of toxins. Good for constipation and intestinal worms. The apricot kernels contain potassium, phosphorus, magnesium, vitamins C, B1, B3 and B17. Dried apricots are excellent soaked and used in cereals for breakfast, as a dessert or in fruit salads. They are best eaten in their natural form and tree ripened.

APRICOT BUTTER

2 C. dried apricots
2 C. pure water
Juice of 1 lemon

Dash of cinnamon
1/2 C. honey
1 tsp. arrowroot

Soak unsulphured apricots in pure water overnight. Blend apricots with water in blender, add lemon juice. Add honey and mix well. Soak 1 tsp. arrowroot in a little water, then add to mixture and heat until the mixture thickens.

AVOCADO

Avocados are rich in potassium, with some sodium fluorine and iodine. A good source of protein and rich in oil, vitamin A and some B1, B2, niacin, as well as vitamin C. Avocados stimulate the appetite and help in constipation. It is a soothing food for inflamed conditions of the mucous membranes, especially of the small intestines and the colon. It is also good for insomnia and the nerves. It is a body building food, for weak stomachs, ulcers, colitis, and hemorrhoids.

The magnesium content is useful for the nerves and muscles. The magnesium helps aid in the use of calcium, vitamin B6 and vitamin C. It is also helpful in preventing a high fat level in the blood after too much eating.

Avocados can be served with both fruit and vegetables. It is delicious cut in half, with the seed taken out and stuffed with ground seeds, celery, onions and tomatoes and topped with lemon and herbs. After cutting, brush with lemon juice to prevent discoloration and loss of vitamin C. It adds interest and a tasty treat addition to salads and other dishes.

AVOCADO MILLET

One large avocado, halved for each person. Fill each half with warm cooked millet. Top each avocado with chopped red onions, ortega chili, chopped raw tomatoes, grated mild cheese and alfalfa sprouts.

BANANAS

Bananas are a nutritious fruit when eaten ripe, with the skin darker and speckled with dark spots. It acts as a natural laxative when very ripe. They are a good source of energy. The vitamin content helps to maintain healthy skin and hair. The calcium and magnesium help the muscles and nerves. It is an excellent source of vitamins A, B, G and riboflavin. The minerals potassium, sodium, chlorine, phosphorus and calcium are also found in bananas. It is a very nutritious and valuable fruit, soothing for ulcers, colitis, diarrhea, and an excellent energy food for children.

BANANA SHAKE

1 banana	*2 heaping T. plain yogurt*
1 C. fruit and berry juice	*1 T. whey powder*
or apple juice	*4 ice cubes*
1 T. protein powder	*Fresh strawberries*

Combine banana, juice, protein powder, yogurt, whey powder, and strawberries and mix in blender. Add ice cubes to make it thick like a milk shake.

BERRIES

Blackberries

Blackberries are a sub-acid fruit. They have an alkaline reaction in the body. The unripe fruit has an astringent effect, and along with the root has been used for dysentery, as well as a gargle for sore throat. Blackberries are important as a blood cleanser as well as a tonic to the system.

Blackberries contain vitamins A and C, vitamin B complex, along with calcium, iron, phosphorus, potassium, niacin and magnesium. Good fruit for a healthy colon. Contain a natural sugar for energy.

Blackberries are best eaten uncooked. They are tasty in fruit salads. They are also used to make pies, cobblers and jams.

BLACKBERRY SALAD

1 C. fresh blackberries	*2 bananas*
2 peaches	*1/4 C. almonds, ground*

Slice peaches and bananas in a bowl. Top with fresh blackberries or frozen and ground almonds.

Blueberries

Blueberries are a good blood purifier and antiseptic. They contain myrtillin which fights bad bacteria in the intestinal tract. Berry tea is good for mouth and throat infections. Cook 1/2 cup of berries in a quart of pure water boiled down to one pint. Excellent for skin problems.

Contains vitamins A and C and some B complex, calcium, phosphorus, iron and potassium. A very nourishing fruit when eaten in its natural state.

BLUEBERRY MILLET SALAD

2 C. millet, cooked
2 C. blueberries, fresh
1/2 C. walnuts, ground

1/2 C. coconut, unsweetened toasted
1/4 C. maple syrup, pure
Nut cream

Mix millet, blueberries, walnuts and mix in nut cream and pure maple syrup. Top with toasted coconut.

Cranberries

Cranberries are high in vitamins A and C and calcium. They also contain phosphorus, iron, sodium, potassium and B complex. They are beneficial in cases of skin disorder, such as skin disease and pimples. It is useful in high blood pressure, constipation, obesity, poor appetite and fevers. Cranberries are high in acid, especially tannic and oxalic acids. When they are overcooked or when sugar is added to cranberries they are very acid-forming and should be avoided.

CRANBERRY RELISH

2 C. cranberries
1 sweet orange
1/4 C. honey

1 large sweet apple
1/2 C. pecans

Combine cranberries, orange and apple in blender. Add honey and pecans.

CITRUS FRUIT

Grapefruit

Grapefruit is a very valuable fruit containing organic salicylic acid, which helps in dissolving inorganic calcium in the body. Inorganic calcium can form in the cartilage of the joints, causing arthritis. It is a good fruit for cleansing the liver, good for fevers, poor digestion, obesity, colds, catarrh, and high blood pressure. It is also a natural antiseptic, which can be used for external wounds.

Grapefruit contains vitamins, B complex, calcium, phosphorus and some iron, sodium and potassium.

They are best eaten fresh, juiced or in fruit salads.

Lemons

They are very effective liver cleansers and rebuilders. They are a natural antiseptic that stimulates, decongests and cleanses the liver of toxins. It is a natural blood purifier. It is excellent for fevers and strengthens the gums. Use the white of lemons to rub on the gums. It can be used for dandruff by applying lemon juice to the scalp and shampoo. A lemon rinse helps to remove soap from the hair. It is good for itching from insect bites or poison oak and ivy.

Lemons are rich in potassium which strengthens the heart. Very high in vitamin C, A bioflavonoids and calcium.

Oranges

They are beneficial for many ailments, such as asthma, bronchitis, pneumonia, rheumatism, arthritis and high blood pressure. Citrus fruit, and especially oranges, helps to clear mucus secretions from the nose and head. Good for sinus infections.

Oranges are high in vitamins C and A and calcium. Also potassium and phosphorus. They are also a very good liver cleanser.

CITRUS FRUIT SALAD

1 C. grapefruit chunks
1 C. orange chunks
1 C. green seedless grapes,
    sliced

1 C. bananas, sliced
1 C. strawberries, sliced

Combine all ingredients together and chill. Fold in dressing made from 2 ozs. cream cheese, 2 T. lemon juice and 1 T. honey. Use more honey if needed.

CHERRIES

Cherries are considered an excellent spring cleanser. It is both a cleanser and a blood builder. The dark cherries are richest in magnesium and iron as well as silicon. They are effective as cleansers of the liver and kidneys. They stimulate digestion. Cherries are good for gout, arthritis, arteriosclerosis, liver, gallstone and kidney stones, intestinal problems and constipation.

Cherries are high in vitamins A and C, calcium, phosphorus, potassium, iron, sodium and vitamin B complex.

CHERRY DELIGHT

1 C. cherries, dark or red
1 C. seedless grapes, cut
4 T. yogurt

1 banana, sliced
1 C. pineapple
1 T. honey (more if needed)

Pit the cherries and cut in half. Cut grapes in half, slice banana. Add all fruit together and fold in yogurt and honey. Sprinkle the top with ground sunflower seeds.

COCONUT

Coconut is rich in enzymes and high in protein. It provides energy and minerals to the body. When mixed with almonds and cashew milk it makes a perfect food for the baby after weaning. It is considered a complete food and contains easily assimilated natural amino acids.

It is a food that is used for constipation and gas on the stomach. It is valuable for destroying tapeworms, which are contracted by eating infected meat. It also contains organic iodine and helps prevent thyroid gland problems.

Coconut is rich in the minerals calcium, iron, potassium, phosphorus and magnesium. It also contains vitamins A, B and G.

Coconut can be grated and sprinkled on fruit, salads, cottage cheese and natural candies. It is a body building food, good for the nerves, indigestion, colitis, ulcers, constipation and liver problems.

COCONUT MILK

2 C. boiling pure water   *1 C. fresh grated coconut*

Pour boiling water over the coconut. Beat and work together for about ten minutes. Put through a clean cheese cloth.

DRIED FRUIT

Dried fruit is concentrated food, and it only takes small amounts to give the body energy. They are easy to store and do not spoil. They are rich in natural sugars and easy to assimilate. Very rich in concentrated minerals. Dried fruit contain most of the B complex vitamins but will lose some vitamin A and C. Most of the fruit still retains its rich minerals such as potassium, iron, phosphorus, sulphur, sodium and silicon. It also contains calcium and some protein.

Unsulphured fruit is dried without sulphur dioxide. The residues of the sulphur dioxide could cause problems to some people. It would be better for your body to use the natural dried fruit. Sulphur dioxide has been known to cause wheezing, loss of breath, chest constriction and fainting.

Dried fruit is delicious when stored in pure water in the refrigerator. It can be used on cereals for breakfast, on cottage cheese for lunch, or in fruit salads. Be sure and drink the liquid you soak the fruit in. It will give you a boost as well as provide minerals.

DRIED FRUIT TREAT

1 C. dates
1 C. apricots
1 C. white figs

Soak fruit overnight in pure water. Next day chop fine. Mix the following ingredients together with the soaked, dried fruit. If more moisture is needed, use the liquid from the soaked fruit. Form into 2 logs and wrap in wax paper and store in freezer to get firm. Cut in circles.

1/2 C. sunflower seeds, ground
1/4 C. sesame seeds, ground
1/2 C. almonds, ground
2-3 T. lemon peel, grated

1-2 T. nutmeg, fresh grated
1 tsp. cardamom
1/2 C. pecans, chopped

GRAPES

Grapes are called the "queen" of fruits. They contain internal cleansing properties, they build up the blood and are a source of quick energy. They are easily assimilated and are good for constipation, gout, rheumatism, skin and liver problems. They should be eaten in abundance when they are in season.

The grape is an alkaline fruit and helps counteract the acidity of uric acid and eliminate it from the system. It contains potassium for activating enzymes for muscle contraction, water retention, and helps to change sugar to energy. Contains some vitamin A and C, phosphorus and calcium. They are a good source of the B complex vitamins, necessary for energy and the health of the nervous system.

Grapes make a wholesome snack for children, a pick-me-up food. Grape juice is an excellent food for those recovering from sickness.

GRAPE SALAD

1 C. red grapes (seeds removed)
1 C. apples, sliced (skins on)

1 C. bananas, sliced
1/2 C. pineapple chunks
1/4 C. pecans, chopped

Combine all ingredients together and toss with 2 ounces softened cream cheese mixed with 3 T. pineapple juice. You may add a little honey or pure maple syrup to sweeten.

MELONS

CANTALOUPE
CASABA

MUSKMELON
WATERMELON

HONEYDEW

Melons are better eaten alone. They are high in water and can interfere with digestion. Water dilutes the digestive juices, which pass from the stomach in a few minutes and take the juice with it. This leaves the food without adequate juice for proper digestion. Melons are a cleansing food. Watermelons contain cicurbocitrin that helps to lower blood pressure. It also produces a sedative effect. Melons are good for kidney and bladder problems.

MELON SALAD

One-half cantaloupe per person. Fill the cantaloupe with melon balls, cantaloupe, watermelon and honeydew. Add some seedless grapes and top with sliced strawberries.

PAPAYA

A delicious, tropical melon-like fruit known to be an excellent digestive aid. Papaya contains all vitamins in nourishing amounts. It has the ability to stimulate all vitamins into greater activity. It helps reduce the work of the digestive system. When combined with peppermint it strengthens the properties.

Papaya is an excellent source of easily digestible protein. Contains papain, an enzyme that breaks down protein into usable amino acids and an easily digestible state.

Papaya is rich in pectin, a substance which soothes the intestinal tract. It is cleansing to the digestive tract. It has been a beneficial aid in relieving infections in the colon and has a tendency to eliminate pus and mucus. Contains vitamins A, C, D, E and K.

PAPAYA SALAD

1 large papaya
4 apricots, fresh

1 C. strawberries, sliced
3/4 C. cashews, ground

Peel and slice papaya, cut apricots and strawberries and mix all together. Add nuts and serve plain or with whipping cream sweetened with honey, fructose or malt sweetener. Makes 2 servings.

PEACHES

Peaches are high in vitamin A and are a valuable food for anemia, asthma, bronchitis, skin diseases and constipation. They have been helpful in removal of worms from the intestinal tract. Peaches contain B complex, vitamin C, protein, calcium, iron, phosphorus and potassium.

They are wonderful eaten fresh or used in fruit salads along with apricots, apples, bananas, pineapple and pears.

PEACHES AND YOGURT

2 large ripe peaches
2 T. honey

2 heaping tsp. yogurt
Dash of cardamom

Peel the peaches. Slice the peaches in dessert dishes. Mix honey, yogurt and cardamom. Spoon over peaches. Serves 2.

PEARS

Pears are low in calories, about 75 calories each. It is a very smart way to satisfy a sweet tooth. They are good for indigestion, high blood pressure, colitis, catarrh and skin problems.

Serve in fruit salads, topped with cottage cheese or grated cheese. Also excellent diced and topped with muesli.

PEAR SALAD

2 C. pears, fresh diced	*1 C. grapes, halved*
1 C. pineapple, fresh diced	*2 oz. cream cheese,*
	blended with
	pineapple juice

Combine fruit and fold in softened cream cheese blended with pineapple juice.

PERSIMMONS

Persimmons are an excellent natural energy food. It is a very soothing food for the intestinal tract. It makes a soothing drink for sore throats. Pour pure hot water over cut fruit and mix in blender. They are high in vitamin A, some vitamin C, B complex vitamins, calcium, iron, phosphorus and potassium.

Persimmons are good in fruit salads and whipped desserts.

PERSIMMON WHIP

2 C. ripe persimmons, whipped
1 C. whipped cream
1/4 C. pecans, ground

Combine whipped persimmons and whipped cream. Put in dessert dishes and top with ground pecans.

PINEAPPLE

Pineapples contain pepsin, which aids digestion and helps to regulate the glands. Contain natural chlorine valuable for digestion of proteins. Pineapples contain vitamins A and C and B complex. Contain calcium, iron, phosphorus and potassium. Fresh pineapple juice has been used for expelling intestinal worms. Pineapples are good for lung problems, catarrh, high blood pressure and tumors.

The most beneficial way to use pineapple is to eat the fruit in its natural state. It is used in salads, bread, cookies, as well as in pies and puddings.

PINEAPPLE DRINK

4 C. pure water
2 C. pineapple, fresh
2/3 C. lemon or lime juice

2/3 C. honey
4 sprigs spearmint

Blend all ingredients in a blender. Add crushed ice, and it's ready to drink.

POMEGRANATE

Pomegranates are a very cleansing fruit for the system. They have been used as a good blood purifier. It is a popular fruit for expelling worms from the system.

Pomegranates can be juiced and added to apple or pineapple juice. It is fun to eat it fresh, but is excellent used in fruit salads.

POMEGRANATE SALAD

2 grapefruit, peeled and
sectioned
3 oranges, peeled

1 pomegranate, seeded
Juice of 1 lemon
3 T. honey

Mix all fruit together and drizzle the lemon and honey over it. Makes a nice breakfast dish.

TOMATOES

Tomatoes are excellent for removing toxins from the system because of their natural antiseptic properties. They also protect against infection. They contain nicotinic acid to help reduce cholesterol in the blood.

Tomatoes are high in vitamin C, B1 and B2. They are rich in potassium, calcium, magnesium and iron. Contain vitamin K which helps to prevent hemorrhages. They are good for gout, skin problems, sinus problems, liver congestion and rheumatism.

STUFFED TOMATOES

1 large mashed ripe
avocado
2 T. finely minced onion
1/4 tsp. kelp
1 tsp. lemon juice

1/3 C. seeded, minced
cucumber
6 medium ripe tomatoes
Sour cream and paprika

Mix all ingredients except tomatoes, sour cream and paprika. Cut off the top and core of each tomato. Slice each tomato from the top to within 1/2 inch of the bottom. Slice to make 8 sections. Press apart to make flower petal effect. Spoon the guacamole into the center of each tomato. Top with sour cream and decorate with paprika.

GHEE
(Clarified Butter)

Ghee will not spoil and helps to preserve food. It helps the nutrients to be assimilated in the system. Excellent for cooking herbs and spices before vegetables are added. Can be heated to higher temperatures without burning. Use to flavor potatoes and vegetables.

HOW TO MAKE

One pound unsalted butter put in a saucepan. Heat until it boils over medium temperature. Foam will accumulate on top. Start skimming when it begins to thicken while it is boiling. This removes the milky portion of the butter.

Do not stir the bottom and do not scorch. Solids remain on the bottom and should only brown slightly. It will be ready when all the water boils out and the oily clear part remains. Turn off the heat and let it settle for a minute. Pour off the Ghee into an earthenware or metal utensil. Use a cheesecloth to strain.

GARLIC

Garlic is a natural antibiotic and an excellent remedy for many ailments. It is a sulphur herb and is an excellent disinfectant for the lungs. It protects against glandular imbalance and many infections and purifies the blood stream. It is capable of dissolving the parasitory calcifications such as uric acid crystals found in arteriosclerosis. It prevents putrefactions and expels worms.

Garlic stimulates the appetite and digestion by increasing gastric secretions and the mobility of the stomach walls.

One way to utilize the benefits of garlic is to take one clove of garlic (you can work up to four) and put it in a glass of hot water, leave it to steep and dissolve overnight. The next morning strain the garlic and drink the water. Another way to use garlic is to add crushed garlic and parsley to pure olive oil. Use it to add to salad dressings or to lightly cooked vegetables. Garlic soaked in olive oil preserves and is handy in making cough syrups.

GARLIC SYRUP

1/2 C. garlic, sliced
1 C. onions, sliced
1 C. pure water

1/4 C. lemon juice, fresh
2 T. raw honey

Put garlic, onions and water into blender and liquify. Stir in lemon juice and honey. Put in a covered jar and leave at room temperature for several hours. A tablespoonful several times a day is good for respiratory ailments and infections.

GLUCOMANNAN

Glucomannan is a substance derived from the edible root of the tuber Konjac plant, the same family as the yam. It is used in various recipes for taste and as a healthful dietary fiber which cleans out the digestive tract. While in the stomach, glucomannan is believed to affect the rate and metabolism of absorption of dietary fat, carbohydrates and protein. The fiber gel surrounds the food, allowing minimum assimilation of calories through the digestive tract, retarding glucose and fat absorption.

It can help to lose or maintain weight by controlling hunger pangs. Glucomannan is a great way to help improve metabolism and food assimilation in a natural way. It also helps absorb toxic substances produced during digestion. Glucomannan helps bind toxic substances and eliminate them before they can be absorbed into the bloodstream.

HONEY

Honey is a natural, nourishing food. It is a predigested food, the sugars already converted into a form that is easily assimilated into the body. White sugar requires a complicated digestive process in the human stomach, but honey gives the body quicker energy, and is soothing to the stomach. Honey is a natural antiseptic and antibiotic.

It has a natural and gentle laxative effect, and a sedative value. It is easier for the kidneys to process honey than it is all the other sugars.

Honey contains several enzymes. Usually the darker the honey, the more minerals and vitamins present. Watch for natural raw honey from bees that have not been fed sugar. The honey is best used unfiltered and unheated. Honey contains B1, B2, B3 and B6, biotin and folic acid. It has, in some cases, contained large amounts of vitamin C. It contains iron, copper, sodium, potassium, manganese, calcium, magnesium and phosphorus.

WAYS TO USE HONEY

Honey is an excellent antiseptic, and when used on cuts or burns along with lemon juice there is no equal. It also works on bee stings and skin abrasions.

Two tablespoons of honey to a cup of whipped cream. When adding, use as a fine stream after the cream is whipped, then add the vanilla.

Dissolve 1/2 cup of honey in 2 cups hot water, add 2 tablespoons of fresh lemon juice, pour into trays and freeze. Use in juices and punch.

Chewing on a honeycomb is helpful to sinus and hayfever congestion.

KEFIR

Kefir is a fermented milk that tastes like yogurt. Contains a high concentration of B vitamins and calcium. The lactic bacteria that are present in kefir make it easy to digest; a perfect food for expectant mothers, colicky babies, invalids. It is good for the complexion, inflammation, conditions of the stomach, the intestinal tract and the liver.

For a drink, blend 1 cup kefir, 1 teaspoon vanilla and 1 cup chopped fruit (bananas or berries). Use kefir on granola, or hot whole grain cereals, or use it in pancakes or waffles.

KELP

Kelp is a seaweed and grows deep in the rocky bottoms of the ocean. Kelp contains 13 vitamins, 20 essential amino acids, and 60 trace elements. It is rich in iodine, B1, B2, niacin, pantothenic acid and vitamins A, B12, C and D. B12 content is important for vegetarians. The nutrients in kelp occur in a natural state of biological balance and, therefore, are very easy to assimilate. The high iodine content of kelp makes it valuable for the thyroid gland to function properly. Even a tiny amount of iodine lacking can cause nervous irritability and the inability to sleep. Kelp is a wonderful substitute for table salt.

SESAME SEED AND KELP SEASONING

6 tsp. ground sesame seeds
1 tsp. kelp

This is a wonderful seasoning to use on salads, fresh or lightly steamed vegetables or in grain dishes. Use as you would salt.

LECITHIN

Lecithin is considered the fuel which feeds energy to the nerves. It is stored in the myelin sheaths of the nerves and is used up constantly in nerve activity and health. Lecithin helps to build nerve and tissues, including brain tissues.

Lecithin contains inositol, choline and phosphorus which are essential to normal body functioning. Lecithin is quickly carried to the bloodstream, without undergoing digestive enzymatic action, where it is used for the brain and nerve system. Great for exhaustion and fatigue.

Lecithin reduces cholesterol in the body, helps to eliminate liver spots, dry skin, arthritis, psoriasis, stimulates sexual vigor and stimulates brain activity. It acts by emulsifying the fats in the body, arteries, and veins by supplying easily digested choline.

It reduces the cholesterol level in the blood and helps dissolve the plaques already laid down in the arteries. It helps in the assimilation of vitamins A and E.

LENTILS

Lentils are a valuable food and a good source of protein. Lentils are a complex carbohydrate and will give energy and nourishment. They digest easily and are beneficial for those with weak stomachs. Lentils contain B complex vitamins, A, C, calcium, iron, phosphorus, potassium, iron and magnesium.

They can be used in soups, casseroles and vegetables loaves. The sprouted lentils can be used in salads and uncooked loaves. Serve them with green vegetable salads to help balance the gas-causing elements.

LENTIL SALAD

1 C. lentil sprouts	1 small green pepper,
2 stalks chopped celery	chopped
2 green onions	2 C. leaf lettuce

Combine all ingredients and serve with dressing of your choice.

MACADAMIA NUTS

A very delicious nut. They are an excellent body-building food, high in calories. They are 93% fat and are very expensive. They are grown extensively in Hawaii and Australia, and are considered a delicacy. They are delicious in ice cream.

The shell is very hard and, unless you are willing to shell them yourself, it will be hard to get them fresh. Because of the high fat content, they will become rancid very quickly.

It is an excellent body-building food and is good for anemia and weakness in those recovering from sickness.

Macadamia nuts contain protein, fat and are high in calories and carbohydrates. They are high in calcium, phosphorus and iron.

MAPLE SYRUP

Pure maple syrup is an excellent substitute for white sugar. It is high in calcium, potassium, phosphorus, iron and trace minerals. It can be used to flavor puddings, cheese cakes, cereals and granola.

MAPLE DESSERT

1 pint heavy cream	Pinch of cardamom
3/4 C. pure maple syrup	1/4 C. chopped pecans
6 egg yolks	

Whip the cream until thick. In a double boiler heat the syrup until it is warm. Add well-beaten egg yolks slowly, stirring constantly. Add cardamom and stir the mixture until it thickens. Remove from heat and stir until it cools. When cooled fold in the cream. Pour in individual bowls or a pan to cut in squares. Chill in refrigerator or freezer. When ready to serve, sprinkle nuts on the top.

MILLET

Millet is an alkaline cereal and is easily assimilated by the body. It is a complete protein, and is rich in lecithin and calcium. It contains iron, phosphorus, B1, B2, B17 and niacin. It acts as an intestinal lubricant aiding in proper elimination. It is easily digested and an excellent food for babies and those with weak stomachs. High in dietary fiber.

MILLET CASSEROLE

Put 2 cups of cooked millet in a buttered baking dish, add 6 chopped green onions, 1/2 cup grated carrots, one small green pepper, 2 medium chopped tomatoes and 1 cup chopped mushrooms. Add vegetable seasoning or herbs for seasoning. Mix all together and top with 1 cup grated cheese. Bake in oven just until it is warm clear through.

MISO

Miso is a dark soybean paste that has been aged for three years. It is made from soybeans, barley, water, sea salt and koji rice (a fermented rice). It is a living food and is killed by temperatures over 104°F. It should be added to cooked foods just before serving the dishes.

Miso is an energy food and also helps in the digestion and assimilation of other foods. Miso is considered an alkalyzing food and tends to balance the acidic condition of the body when such foods as sweets, meats and white flour products create an acid condition of the body. Miso contains zybicolin, a substance which absorbs, attracts and eliminates radioactive products such as strontium from the system. It also helps where air pollution is prevalent. It is called the macrobiotic yogurt. It is similar to fermented milk, and is rich in easily assimilated protein.

Miso can be used in hot water as a soup: 1-1/2 tsp. miso in 2 cups of hot water. Add to soups for bouillon flavor. Add at the end of cooking. To preserve the nutritious properties do not boil.

MISO SAUCE

1 heaping T. miso
5 T. Tahini
1 C. pure water

1 tsp. fresh grated orange rind
1/4 tsp. fresh grated lemon rind

Mix all ingredients together except the grated rinds and miso. Cook over low heat for about 20 minutes. Add the orange, lemon rind and miso.

MOLASSES

Blackstrap molasses is a byproduct of the sugar refining industry. It is the residue, left over when the sugar cane is crushed and processed to obtain refined white sugar. This residue is a valuable source of minerals and vitamins. This is the way that white sugar loses all its nutrients of vitamins and minerals.

Molasses is rich in iron and B6. Research has found that B6 is needed for the proper assimilation of iron. Both iron and B6 occur naturally in molasses, which makes it a valuable food to supply iron the body can utilize. Molasses is a good source of other B vitamins, such as B1 and B2. Molasses contains copper, calcium, phosphorus and potassium. One tablespoon of molasses contains as much calcium as a glass of milk and as much iron as ten eggs. It contains phosphoric acid, and along with potassium strengthens the cells, especially in the brain and nerves.

Molasses is good for anemia, constipation, nervous system, menstrual problems and blood disorders. It can be used for colitis, one teaspoonful is dissolved in three pints of warm water and used as an enema. It can be used in compresses for infected tissue and as a mouthwash for pyorrhea. It can be applied directly to wounds to help in healing.

OATMEAL

Oatmeal is a very nutritious whole grain. The steelcut oatmeal has the highest nutritional value. It is an easily digestible cereal for children. The old fashioned oatmeal is richer in vitamins and minerals. It takes longer to cook but is more valuable. It would be better to alternate oatmeal with millet, brown rice and whole wheat. That way you will receive a well-rounded diet in the grains--with more nutritional benefits.

Oatmeal is rich in inositol as well as B1 (thiamine). It is rich in iron and phosphorus. It is 16.7% protein. It also contains calcium, sodium and potassium. It is a good food for the nerves, urinary system, reproductive organs and the heart muscles. For fever: boil one ounce of oats to a quart of pure water for 1/4 hour. It is a nourishing broth for infants.

MUESLI

2 T. oats	*1 T. ground almonds*
6 T. pure water	*1 T. ground sunflower seeds*
2 T. pure lemon juice	*2-3 T. almond milk*
	1 tsp. pure maple syrup

Soak oats overnight in pure water. Add lemon juice and almond milk until smooth. Add grated fresh apple. Sprinkle nuts and seeds, add more almond milk if needed.

This recipe can be used with any fresh fruit in season, such as strawberries, raspberries, blueberries, bananas, peaches and apricots. Yogurt can be used instead of milk, if you wish.

OLIVE OIL

Pure olive oil retains all its natural ferments and is very digestible. The cold-pressed oil is the best to use. It lubricates the mucous membranes of the intestines and does not prevent nutritive elements from being absorbed.

Olive oil stimulates the secretion of hepatic and pancreatic juices. It is an excellent food for the liver. It is beneficial to assimilate the proteins from vegetables. Imported Italian or Spanish oil is the highest quality with its sweet flavor.

Olive oil is high in calories, 124 in one tablespoon. It contains vitamin C, iodine, small amounts of vitamin E.

Use in salad dressings and mayonnaise. Olive oil oxidizes less rapidly than other oils; therefore it does not become rancid very easily and needs not be refrigerated.

PEANUTS

Peanuts are very nutritious. They are very rich in the essential amino acids and unsaturated fatty acids. Peanuts have been found to strengthen the capillaries. They help prevent an excessive loss of blood as well as help to reduce the body's vulnerability to infection and improve the efficiency of the cardiovascular system.

Peanuts help in chronic cases of constipation. Raw peanuts are the most nutritious. They can be purchased at a health food store. Make your own peanut butter. Spanish peanuts are softer and easier to grind smooth. It can be done in a blender or in a seed grinder.

The supermarket peanut butter is sweetened and heavily salted. If sodium in your diet is a problem, it would be better to make your own.

They are rich in vitamins E and B and trace minerals. They are high in potassium, calcium, magnesium and phosphorus. They have a fair amount of vitamin A.

Peanuts can be used in soups, sauces, casseroles and ground in salads.

PEAS, DRIED

Split peas are very nutritious and can be used in a variety of ways. There are both green and yellow peas. They are rich in protein, sodium, potassium, magnesium, phosphorus, iron, vitamins A and B and calcium.

Use in soups and vegetable loaves.

DRY SOUP MIX

1 C. green split peas
1 C. yellow split peas
1 C. barley

1 C. lentils
1 C. millet
1 C. brown rice

Mix all together and store in a large can or gallon jar. Use 1-1/3 cup with 2 quarts of water. For seasoning add vegetable seasoning, kelp, onions, carrots, celery and canned tomatoes and garlic.

PECANS

Pecans are rich in linolenic acid, an unsaturated fatty acid that is essential for growth, energy and health. It aids in the production of lecithin, fat-digesting enzymes, and the beneficial intestinal bacteria that produces B vitamins.

The linolenic acid also aids in maintaining proper weight by helping to prevent water retention. It helps satisfy hunger. Pecans are high in calories--1/3 cup equals about 178 calories. Pecans contain protein, calcium, phosphorus, iron, potassium, B vitamins and magnesium.

PINE NUTS

They are also called piñon or pignoli nuts. They are a tasty nut found as seeds in several different kinds of pine trees.

Pine nuts are an excellent food for building strength and energy to the body.

They are eaten raw or can be mixed in casseroles and stuffings. They are excellent in tomato dishes, sautéed in olive oil, garlic and onion. Good with stuffed zucchini and eggplant.

Raw pine nuts contain protein, iron, calcium, phosphorus, potassium and traces of niacin, B1, B2, and vitamin C. High in fat content and calories, moderate carbohydrates.

PISTACHIO NUTS

A delicious nut, especially in its natural state without salt and red dye. It contains a good amount of linolenic acid, one of the unsaturated fats which has been found to help regulate cholesterol. It aids growth of healthy skin and hair, as well as proper gland function. They are moderately rich in carbohydrates and fats. They contain a good supply of potassium, which aids the heart, nerves and muscles. They are high in iron, vitamin A and protein. Also contains magnesium, phosphorus and B complex vitamins.

All nuts should be chewed thoroughly for proper digestion. They can be ground fine and sprinkled on food or made into nut butter.

PUMPKIN SEEDS

Pumpkin seeds are very beneficial for prostate disorders and bladder problems. They help to destroy intestinal worms.

They are also rich in phosphorus and higher in iron than any other seed. Contains niacin and is high in vitamin E and polyunsaturated fatty acids.

PROPOLIS

Propolis is a gift from the bees. It is rich in biologically active vitamins (especially the B vitamins), minerals and (for anti-bacterial activity,) flavonoids. Flavonoids exhibit therapeutic properties. They have a beneficial action on the capillary system. Acts as a diuretic and increases bile production. The flavonoids also have antibiotic, antiparasitic, anti-coagulant and anti-bacterial properties.

The flavonoids in propolis are in a highly concentrated form--about 500 times that of oranges. Also contains concentrated antibiotic properties.

It is felt that the flavonoids prevent the rapid oxidation of vitamin C, helping to strengthen the body's immunity against infection and disease. Useful for treating ulcers, rheumatism, arthritis, flu, upper respiratory diseases, radiation damage and enteritis.

REJUVELAC

Rejuvelac is a very healthy enzyme drink. It acts as a protection against harmful organisms in the intestinal tract. It is rich in proteins, carbohydrates, B complex vitamins, vitamins E and K. The enzymes help the friendly bacteria to grow, such as lacto-bacillus bifidus. It helps the large intestine maintain its natural, healthy, vitamin-producing environment. This produces a clean colon which helps prevent debris from collecting on the colon walls.

Many diseases of old age are related to enzyme deficiency in the foods eaten, in the digestive tract, and in the cells. Rejuvelac is a pre-digested food. The proteins are broken down into amino acids and the carbohydrates into simple sugars. These nutrients are readily assimilated by the body, with little energy going for digestion.

REJUVELAC

1 C. wheat berries (organic, soft pastry wheat)
3 C. pure water
A quart jar with a wide mouth

Be sure to use untreated wheat berries. Wash the wheat and remove any old or bad ones. Use your hands to scrub, and let the bad ones float to the top so they can be discarded. Soak the wheat berries for 48 hours. After 48 hours, pour off the rejuvelac, which is ready to use. It will keep for several days without refrigeration. Good rejuvelac has a pleasant odor and tastes somewhat sour with a lemon taste. Keep in a dark and warm place while soaking. 73°F. is the ideal temperature for soaking. Pour two more cups of pure water into the jar of wheat berries. Let this ferment for 24 hours before pouring off. It can be repeated again for 24 more hours. The wheat berries can be soaked a total of three times.

RICE POLISH

A very nutritious food to use on cereals, in baking and topped on fruit for breakfast. Use it like you would wheat germ or bran. Rice polish is very high in B complex vitamins, calcium and vitamin A.

ROYAL JELLY

Royal jelly is considered to be a tissue rebuilder and is regarded as a food for the glands. It has a rejuvenating effect to help promote growth and glandular health. It has been used in Russia for hypertension. It contains acetylcholine, which dilates and strengthens the blood vessels. It also contains high amounts of pantothenic acid which has been found to play a vital role in reproduction. Royal jelly contains vitamin E which stimulates fertility and promotes healthy cells.

Royal jelly helps to normalize metabolism, has a diuretic effect, helps in preventing obesity, builds resistance to infections, regulates the functioning of the endocrine glands and is good for arteriosclerosis and coronary deficiency.

RYE

Rye is the hardiest of all cereal grasses. It is a muscle builder and considered a brain food. It is rich in manganese, phosphorus, potassium and iron. It contains the B complex vitamins, as well as calcium. It contains 13% protein. Sprouted rye makes a nutritious live food with enzymes and easily assimilated minerals and vitamins. Use rye sprouts raw in salads, in sprouted breads and in soups.

SPROUTED SALAD

1 C. alfalfa sprouts
1 C. mung bean sprouts
1/2 C. rye sprouts
1 bunch watercress,
  chopped
2 C. leaf lettuce

1/4 C. chopped green
  onions
4 T. minced parsley
2 large tomatoes, chopped
1 large avocado, sliced
  small
1/2 C. ripe olives

Chop all ingredients in a large salad bowl for serving. Toss lightly and add dressing of your choice. Vinaigrette dressing is very good.

SAUERKRAUT

Sauerkraut is a bone and blood builder with its lime and iron content as well as vitamins and essential minerals. Intestinal catarrh is helped with sauerkraut juice soup.

If cabbage is a problem to digest, homemade sauerkraut should be easier to assimilate. It is a great food for the winter, especially if it is hard to get fresh vegetables.

Fermented foods have known to help heal arthritis, scurvy, ulcers, colds, digestive disorders and even cancer. Fermented foods can build health as well as prevent disease. Its natural lactic acid and fermentive enzymes have a beneficial effect on metabolism as well as elements to heal disease. The lactic acid destroys harmful bacteria in the intestines and helps in digestion and assimilation of necessary nutrients.

HOMEMADE SAUERKRAUT

Cabbage, red and green   *Juniper berries*
Onions   *Carrots*
Green Peppers   *Kelp*
                               Dill

Save outer layer of cabbage. Grate vegetables. Layer cabbage in the bottom of an earthenware pot or krock about 10 inches deep. Sprinkle juniper berries, layer of carrots, onion, green peppers. Press each layer down so that the cabbage will be saturated in its own juice. Repeat the procedure. When the container is full, cover with outer layer of cabbage and heavy stone to weigh it down. Leave at room temperature for 1 to 3 weeks (longer if cool weather). Remove the foam or mildew from the top; it is ready to eat. Store in a glass jar in the refrigerator.

SESAME SEEDS

Sesame seeds are very nourishing and contain 50% more protein than meat and twice as much calcium as milk. They are rich in lecithin and fatty acids which help to dissolve cholesterol. They contain potassium, iron, phosphorus and vitamin E.

Sesame seeds are used to make tahini and humus and are used in cereals, salad dressings and spreads and to make milk for baby's formulas. Sesame seed milk is excellent for lubricating the bowels.

SESAME MILK

Use 1/2 cup sesame seeds in 1 cup pure water, blend for about three minutes. Strain and use instead of milk. Make a drink using bananas, dates and ice cubes.

SPIRULINA

Spirulina is a plankton which thrives in alkaline, fresh water ponds. It is always a deep, dark green. It has a unique, slightly marine aroma. The flavor is mild, and the taste can be compared to mushrooms or nuts.

Spirulina is rich in vitamins and minerals and protein. Two heaping tablespoons of spirulina powder provide about 13 grams of complete protein. It is about 60% to 70% protein compared to 45% for whole dried eggs. It contains B12 and a teaspoon of spirulina has two and a half times the B12 as contained in the same amount of liver powder. A vegetarian can supply his B12 requirements with 3 grams of spirulina per day. Rich in B1, B2 and B3, A, E and high in iron. It is also very high in chlorophyll.

It will enrich the high blood count by providing easily assimilated iron to the organs, improving anemic conditions. It will counteract toxins, cleansing and deodorizing bowel tissues, purifying the liver and helping in liver problems. It is useful in weight loss, for its high content of the amino acids phenylalanine and tyrosine help suppress hunger in some people by helping in biochemical changes in the brain. It will also increase energy, while decreasing the appetite.

SUNFLOWER SEEDS

Sunflower seeds are rich in unsaturated oil, containing approximately 25% protein. They are rich in natural sugar and easy to assimilate, rich in concentrated minerals. They are also rich in methionine which is often lacking in vegetable proteins. Sunflower seeds are a complete protein of the highest quality. They help in promoting normal growth of the tissues in the body and two tablespoons equal 15 grams of protein. The amino acids, which are the building blocks of proteins, are needed for growth and cell repair for enzymes, hormones, antibodies and blood cells. Amino acids are also used in actual structure of all cells. One half cup of sunflower seeds contain 350 milligrams of magnesium. This mineral is nourishing for the pituitary glands. Contain natural fluorine, B vitamins, vitamins D and E, iron, calcium, PABA and pantothenic acid. Good for weak eyes, strengthens fingernails, helps tooth decay and dry skin.

Sunflower seeds can be used in salads, cereals, soups, casseroles and with fruit and roasted nuts. Many people on slimming diets are deficient in oils, but sunflower seeds are a natural for oils that help to satisfy hunger. The fiber and pectin act as roughage and prevent constipation. They keep the colon pockets clean.

RAW SUNFLOWER AND ALMOND ROAST

1 C. raw sunflower seeds,
    ground
3/4 cup raw almonds,
    ground

1 tsp. soy sauce
2 tsp. cold pressed oil
Kelp or other seasoning to
    taste

Mix all together and form into loaf, store in refrigerator.

TAHINI

Tahini is a sesame seed butter. Two tablespoons of tahini is equivalent in protein to a 16 ounce steak. It is digested and assimilated into the bloodstream in about 1/2 hour. (It takes about 5 hours or more to digest, assimilate and metabolize meat.)

Tahini can be purchased at health food stores. When it is mixed with tamari (soy sauce) it is tasty. It is also used over fresh or lightly steamed vegetables, and grain dishes such as millet and brown rice.

Mix with lemon juice for a salad dressing. It is a concentrated food and a little goes a long way.

TAHINI SAUCE

1 C. sesame seeds
2 T. sunflower oil
1/2 C. pure water

1 tsp. mineral salt
1/4 C. fresh lemon juice

Mix seeds, oil and water in blender until seeds are finely ground. Add salt and lemon juice. If too thick add more water.

TAHINI SPREAD

1-1/2 T. sesame tahini
2 T. lemon juice

2 tsp. tamari (soy sauce)
*Dash of kelp and cayenne
    pepper*

Mix all together and use on sandwiches instead of butter or mayonnaise.

TAMARI

Natural soy sauce made from soybeans. It is fermented soy sauce and should be used sparingly since it does contain salt. Use in place of salt. It is excellent when used with rice, millet, soups and nut and grain dishes.

TEMPEH

Tempeh is a fermented soybean patty, with a nutty aroma and soft chewy texture. It is best when cooked. Protein is 18% to 20%, which is about twice that of hamburger.

Tempeh can be used as mock chicken in salads or as a tempeh burger on a whole wheat bun with homemade mayonnaise, alfalfa sprouts and tomatoes. It can be diced for mixed vegetable dishes, soups, sauces, salads and in sandwiches.

TEMPEH VEGETABLE STEW

1 lb. tempeh
*2 large tomatoes, or
    2 cups canned*
2 large potatoes, cubed
2 carrots, cubed
*1 red or green pepper,
    chopped*

1/2 C. natural soy sauce
2 cups water
6 T. oil, cold pressed
2 cloves garlic, pressed
1 large onion

Sauté onion and garlic in oil for about 3 minutes and add all of the ingredients and simmer for about 40 minutes. Seasoning should be added when done. Use kelp, vegetable seasoning or herb seasoning to taste. If you are not used to this seasoning add sea salt.

TOFU

Tofu is a soybean curd. It is a white cake of pressed curds made from coagulated soymilk. It looks like cheese. It is a complete plant protein, containing all the eight essential amino acids needed by the human body for growth and regeneration. Tofu is highly nutritious, relatively inexpensive, easily digestible, versatile to cook with and free from chemical toxins. It contains no cholesterol, a protein equal to chicken, low in calories (8 ounces contain 147 calories), more calcium than 8 ounces of milk and more iron than 4 eggs. Tofu contains vitamin E, B complex, iron, phosphorus, potassium, choline, a natural source of lecithin and linolenic acid. Japanese doctors actually recommend tofu for starch-restricted diets, diabetes, heart diseases and circulatory disorders.

Tofu has a bland flavor which allows it to blend into numerous recipes. A great substitute for daily products as well as meat. Use as cheese in everything from pizza to cheesecake. Add tofu to salads and vegetable dishes. Sauté with tomato sauce, onions, garlic to use with spaghetti. Also use in dips and dressings.

RASPBERRY DESSERT

1-1/2 C. tofu
1 10-oz. frozen raspberries,
*   drained*
1 tsp. pure vanilla
1/2 C. honey

2 T. fresh lemon juice
1 ripe banana
1/2 tsp. cardamom

Blend all ingredients together. Chill, then serve. Serves about 6 persons.

TRITICALE
(Trit-i-kay-lee)

Higher in protein than wheat, it contains about 16% digestible protein. It is a cross between rye and wheat and makes it superior in protein than wheat. It is high in lysine and methionine, two important amino acids. Use it in 50-50 portions with whole wheat when making bread.

It has a nutty, chewy flavor. It can be sprouted, used in casseroles.

VEGETABLES

Vegetables are very important in the everyday diet. Fresh vegetables are ideal and should be organically grown--if you can obtain them. They are more nutritious than canned, dried or frozen. Vegetables are rich in blood- and bone-building vitamins and minerals. The average American diet is lacking in fresh vegetables. They should be eaten raw and as often as possible.

ASPARAGUS

Asparagus helps break up oxalic acid crystals in the kidneys and in the muscular system. Aspargine is the active substance beneficial in kidney problems. It contains a good supply of protein and is very high in vitamins A and C, as well as potassium; rich in iodine, sulphur and silicon. The iodine content inhibits cell growth or cancer. It is good for rheumatism and neuritis. The vitamin A content is good for healthy skin and good eyesight and helps in digestion, energy and healthy bones, muscles and nerves.

Asparagus is best steamed lightly, and eaten with seasonings or used in salads or cream soups. Asparagus is an excellent bulk food and high in chlorophyll.

ASPARAGUS SALAD

2 C. asparagus, diagonally cut	2 tsp. apple cider vinegar
1 tsp. cold pressed oil	1 to 2 tsp. honey
1 tsp. sesame seeds	1 tsp. tamari (soy sauce)
	1/2 tsp. kelp

Steam asparagus lightly, sauté sesame seeds in oil. Mix all ingredients together and chill. Serve cold on a bed of leaf lettuce.

ARTICHOKE

Artichokes are a good source of vitamin A, B complex and potassium. They also contain vitamin C, iron and calcium. The artichoke is an effective diuretic to help remove toxins from the kidneys and is useful in liver ailments and dropsy. It is good to use in anemia, acidity, diarrhea, jaundice, catarrh, halitosis, glandular problems, obesity, neuritis and rheumatism. The high calcium and potassium aid muscles, nerves, bones and heart. Potassium aids against water retention.

One large artichoke is about 8 calories. They are best prepared steamed until they are tender. The leaves are usually picked off and eaten one at a time. They are good with lemon butter or just fresh lemon or vinaigrette dressing. Don't throw away the liquid--it can be used in apple or grape juice.

ARTICHOKE WITH ITALIAN SEASONING

4 artichokes
1/4 C. olive oil
14 C. onion, chopped
1 clove garlic, minced
1 tsp. kelp or mineral
     salt

1 tsp. oregano
1/2 tsp. rosemary, minced
1/2 tsp. basil
1/4 tsp. sage
2 T. parsley, chopped

Wash and cook artichokes until partially cooked, with cover on. Remove from water, drain and reserve the cooking water. Sauté all ingredients in a saucepan until lightly browned. Place the artichokes upright in a round pan. Pour about one inch of the cooking water in the pan. Spoon the sautéed onion mixture over the artichokes, scooping some into the centers of the artichokes. Cover and simmer for 30 minutes. Use the liquid to dip the artichokes in while eating.

BEETS

Beets are best eaten raw. They will assimilate much better when used in their natural state. Beets are recognized for their blood-building powers. The mineral content stimulates enzyme activity through the lymphatic system and to the circulation of the blood. Beets are good food for the kidneys and bladder. They help in preventing calcium deposits because of their high potassium and sodium. They help regulate menstruation, are good for anemia, low blood sugar, liver problems, dysentery, skin problems and the nerves.

Beets contain vitamin A, C and G, B complex and some protein. They also contain iron, calcium, potassium, phosphorus and sodium. Raw beet juice is excellent for the kidneys. It has been used to clear kidney gravel from the system. It is used one tablespoon at a time, taken alone and throughout the day.

Beets can be shredded or sliced and served over salads. Cooked beets should be eaten with the skins on to benefit from all the vitamins and minerals. Honey and lemon juice are a tasty addition to raw beets, added on top of green beans, cauliflower or other vegetables.

BEETS IN ORANGE SAUCE

4 C. cooked beets
1 tsp. arrowroot
1/3 C. beet juice
2/3 C. orange juice
1/3 C. lemon juice
1 T. orange peel, grated.

2 T. cider vinegar
1-1/3 T. honey
1/2 tsp. mineral salt or
sea salt
2 T. butter

Thicken the arrowroot in the beet juice and stir over heat until it is smooth. Combine the orange juice, lemon juice, vinegar, honey and salt. Cook until thickened. Add butter, orange peel and beets.

BAMBOO SHOOTS

Excellent in salads or stir-fried vegetables. Contain vitamin A, C and B complex, calcium for the nerves and iron to build the blood, also contain phosphorus, potassium and niacin. Good for constipation, high blood pressure, toxemia and worms.

They are good in Chinese dishes. Excellent with stir-fried vegetables, especially good with mushrooms.

CHOP SUEY

1/4 C. safflower oil
1 small onion, sliced
1 carrot, diagonally cut
1/2 C. green pepper, cut
in strips
2 C. Chinese cabbage,
sliced
1 C. mushrooms, sliced

2 C. mung bean sprouts
1 C. bamboo shoots
1 large tomato, peeled
1 C. pea pods
1/2 C. almonds, chopped
1 tsp. arrowroot
Tamari sauce to taste

Stir-fry onion in oil, turning constantly. Add carrots and stir-fry. Add each vegetable in turn until the pea pods. Add almonds, stir and cover and let steam for about 4 or 5 minutes over low heat. Pour off any liquid in a pan and add arrowroot and tamari sauce. Cook over low heat until it thickens. Add sauce to vegetables and stir. Cover and heat through, add water if needed. Heat just until the vegetables remain crisp. Serve over brown rice.

BROCCOLI

Several chemicals in broccoli have been found to inhibit cancer in animals. Broccoli is high in sulphur, and sulphur foods help rid the body of built-up toxins. Broccoli contains vitamins A, B, and C, calcium, iron, potassium, E and K. Broccoli is good for obesity, constipation, high blood pressure and the glands.

MARINATED BROCCOLI

4 C. broccoli, small pieces
2 C. mushrooms, sliced
1 C. red onion

Dressing:
1/3 C. honey   *1 tsp. celery seeds*
1 tsp. tamari   *1 C. cider vinegar*
1 tsp. paprika   *1 C. cold pressed oil*

Chill all together overnight. Serves 8.

BRUSSELS SPROUTS

Brussels sprouts are a member of the cabbage family, and is a protection against cancer. It is rich in sulphur which has a cleansing and antiseptic properties.

They should be cooked lightly steamed but firm in texture. They go well with mushrooms, chestnuts, cheese. It helps in the proper digestion of protein.

BRUSSELS SPROUTS AND CHEESE

4 C. Brussels sprouts   *1/2 C. parmesan cheese,*
3 cloves garlic, pressed   *grated*
1/4 C. olive oil   *Kelp to taste*
                               Paprika, dash

Wash and trim sprouts. Sauté garlic in olive oil for a few minutes and add Brussels sprouts and stir them around in the oil to coat. Sprinkle with kelp and paprika; add a few tablespoons of water and the grated cheese. Place in a casserole dish with a cover and bake in oven ten minutes. Serve with more cheese on top. Serves 4 to 6.

CABBAGE

Cabbage is another healing vegetable which is rich in sulphur and also contains calcium and iodine. It stimulates the appetite, supplies nitrogen. The chlorophyll in cabbage is a cleanser and enriches the blood. The raw juice has germicidal properties. The juice is well known to heal stomach ulcers with its vitamin U content. It has been found that patients heal three times as fast with raw cabbage juice.

The juice can be mixed with honey for coughing and hoarseness. The glutamine content has been used to treat alcoholism. It is good for anemia, fatigue, infections, intestinal parasites, stones and arthritis.

It is good lightly steamed, sliced thinly and used with olive oil and lemon to enhance flavor.

CABBAGE COLESLAW

3 C. green cabbage, sliced	*1 T. honey*
1/2 C. green peppers, sliced	*1/4 tsp. white pepper*
	Dash of paprika
1/2 C. almonds, chopped	

Dressing:

1/2 C. mayonnaise	*1 T. honey*
1/2 C. yogurt, plain	*1/4 tsp. white pepper*
2 T. lemon juice	*1/4 tsp. paprika*

Stir ingredients together and pour over salad and toss.

CARROTS

Carrots are rich in alpha-gamma carotene, which is transformed into vitamin A when the carrot is eaten. It contains a chemical called daucarine which is a strong vasodilator of the coronary blood vessels. Carrots promote normal elimination, while preventing diarrhea. They are considered a cleansing food and have an effective means of changing the intestinal flora from a putrefactive to a non-putrefactive type. They give the body energy. Five ounces of fresh carrot juice contain over 30,000 IU units of vitamin A. Carrots should be eaten raw as often as possible, especially the juice, in raw soups, grated and seasoned with lemon and olive oil.

Fresh carrot juice is wonderful for babies, as it has more calcium than milk or baby formulas, as well as vitamin A. It is a good substitute for baby's milk after weaning. Carrot soup is excellent for diarrhea. Diarrhea could be serious for it weakens the body, loses nutrients and food is not absorbed when it goes through the body too fast. Vitamins A, D, E and I are easily lost.

CARROT SOUP

2 C. grated carrots
Enough water to cook until soft
1/2 C. almond nut cream
1/2 tsp. kelp (important for providing sodium)

Blend until smooth.

CAULIFLOWER

Cauliflower is a member of the cabbage family and has been recommended as an anti-cancer food. It is a good blood purifier and food for the nerves and heart. Cauliflower is rich in potassium and sulphur. Contains vitamins A, C and B complex, calcium, phosphorus and some iodine.

CAULIFLOWER AND TOMATOES

1 medium head cauliflower *1/4 C. onions*
Juice of 1/2 lemon *1 tsp. kelp*
2 small tomatoes, chopped *1 tsp. basil*
1 T. tomato paste *1/2 tsp. oregano*
2 T. olive oil

Sauté onion in oil. Stir in washed cauliflower that has been tossed with lemon juice. Combine all other ingredients, add to cauliflower and stir. Let the mixture simmer for about ten minutes.

CELERY

Celery is an alkaline food and is rich in calcium and is an excellent food for the nerves. It is good for kidney problems, arthritis, rheumatism, constipation, asthma, high blood pressure. It helps rid the body of catarrh. Good for phyorrhea, dropsy. Celery is good for insomnia with its calcium content. Helps chemical imbalance.

Celery and carrot juice are good for the nervous system. Use celery in salads, stews and soups. Celery and leaves are high in sodium, chlorine and chlorophyll. Celery stalks are high in potassium.

CELERY CREAM BALL

1 C. cream cheese (8 oz)   *2 T. pimento*
1 T. almond milk   *1/4 C. cheddar cheese,*
1 C. celery, chopped   *grated*

Soften cream cheese with almond milk; add celery, pimento and cheddar cheese. Mold into one big ball or small balls and roll in ground pecans. Serve with crackers or place around a vegetable salad.

CORN

Fresh corn is very tasty uncooked, especially in salads. It is also good roasted leaving the corn in the jackets. Corn contains vitamin A, calcium, phosphorus, iron, potassium, magnesium and silicon. It is considered a great brain, bone and muscle building food.

CORN SALAD

2 ears fresh corn   *2 T. parsley*
1 C. tomatoes, chopped   *White pepper, paprika and*
                                   kelp to taste

Cut corn off cob. Add tomatoes, parsley and seasonings. Serve on a bed of leaf lettuce.

CUCUMBERS

The peelings of cucumbers are rich in silicon, and the cucumbers are high in calcium, potassium, sulphur, enzymes. Carrot, celery and cucumber juice promote hair growth. Good for high and low blood pressure. They aid digestion, and are useful to eat with protein, for they contain the enzyme erepsin to digest protein. They are good for boils, rashes and pimples and the juice is helpful for pyorrhea.

Cucumbers are rich in vitamin C and B1, which help in circulation, irritability and depression. They also contain B2 which helps in low blood sugar and eye problems. They are high in potassium. Cucumber juice is beneficial as an astringent for the skin. Cucumber and celery juice is a cooling drink for summer. Cucumbers are rich in sodium, which is a cooling mineral.

CUCUMBER NUT SALAD

1 bunch fresh watercress
1/4 C. almonds, ground
1 medium chopped cucumber

Top with a sour cream dressing.

JERUSALEM ARTICHOKE

Jerusalem artichokes are not a true artichoke so they are being called sunchokes because of their misleading name. They have the taste of water chestnuts with a mild flavor. You can use them as you use water chestnuts. They are a natural source of insulin and are called the diabetic's potato. They contain vitamin A, C and B complex and the minerals potassium, phosphorus, calcium, sodium and iron.

They can be grated raw and used in soups, vegetables and salads.

JERUSALEM ARTICHOKE SALAD

4 Jerusalem artichokes,   *1/2 C. celery, chopped thin*
     grated   *1/3 C. parsley, minced*
2 carrots, grated   *2 radishes, grated*

Combine and use with homemade mayonnaise.

LETTUCE

Lettuce should be used in the diet daily--the dark leafy kind. It has cleansing properties and is calming to the nerves. It contains trace amounts of lactucin, a chemical that has sedative qualities. It stimulates circulation, and the fiber is excellent for aiding elimination.

TOSSED FRESH SALAD

1 C. red leaf lettuce   *1/2 C. sliced mushrooms*
1 C. romaine lettuce   *1/4 C. sliced radishes*
1/2 C. radish sprouts   *1/4 C. grated raw beets*
1/2 C. sliced red cabbage   *1/4 C. cauliflower, chopped*

Toss all ingredients together and serve with your favorite dressing.

MUSHROOMS

Mushrooms are very popular for their unique flavor and taste appeal. The mushroom is rich in some of the B complex vitamins. Contains some protein, rich in potassium, sodium, sulphur, phosphorus and some vitamin D.

Use in casseroles, salads, sautéed in butter and garlic.

SOUR CREAM MUSHROOM SAUCE

1/4 C. minced onions
2 C. mushrooms, sliced
2 T. ghee or butter
1 T. whole wheat flour

1/2 C. sesame cream
1 C. mock sour cream
Sprig of parsley, minced
1/2 tsp. paprika
1/4 tsp. kelp

Sauté onions in ghee or butter, blend flour and add sesame cream, mushrooms, parsley, paprika and kelp. Fold in sour cream before serving. Good over brown rice or millet.

OKRA

Okra is very mucilaginous and good for urinary, alimentary and the lungs. Provides bulk for the digestive tract and helps keep the bowels clean and prevents constipation. It contains mucin which has been beneficial in aiding digestion. The mucin tends to neutralize hydrochloric acid. The dried powder can be used with hot water and used as a poultice to apply on bruises or sores.

It is delicious used in gumbo soups, stews, soups, and creole dishes. It is high in silicon and selenium, strengthens capillaries and helps to cleanse clogged veins.

It contains vitamins A and C and some B complex vitamins, calcium, potassium and iron.

OKRA CASSEROLE

2 C. okra, sliced
1 medium onion, chopped
1 clove garlic, minced
1 C. tomato supreme, or
blended fresh
tomatoes
1 tsp. oregano

1 C. mushrooms, sliced
1 small green pepper
1/2 C. brown rice
Grated mild cheese

Mix all ingredients together except cheese. Pour into a casserole dish. Sprinkle cheese on top. Bake for 1 hour at 350°F.

OLIVES

Olives are rich in potassium, and heart muscles need potassium. Olives can be used in Spanish dishes, casseroles and in salads.

OLIVE AND CREAM CHEESE SPREAD

4 oz. cream cheese	*1/4 C. ripe olives, chopped*
1/4 C. yogurt	*1 green onion, minced*
1 tsp. lemon juice	*2 T. green pepper, minced*
1/2 tsp. curry powder	

Soften the cream cheese and add yogurt, lemon juice and curry powder. Blend in olives, green onion and green peppers. Serve with whole wheat crackers or a bread of your choice.

ONIONS

Onions are rich in potassium and have antiseptic qualities, and lower triglyceride levels. They are a cancer fighter vegetable when used often. The active principles are not destroyed by heat. They are a good source of silicon to help in nerves and mental fatigue.

GREEN SALAD

1 C. spinach	*1 C. celery, sliced*
1 C. red lettuce	*1/4 C. green onions,*
1 C. romaine lettuce	*chopped*
1 C. watercress	*3 T. parsley, chopped fine*

Serve with your favorite dressing or use one from this book.

PARSLEY

Parsley is a very valuable vegetable and will fight garlic and onion breath. It is rich in vitamins A, C and B complex. It is rich in natural iron and chlorophyll and a good source of calcium, potassium, magnesium and some sodium. It is good for asthma, anemia, bleeding gums, menstrual problems, liver, high blood pressure and urinary problems.

Parsley should be ground so that nutrients can be well absorbed to break down the cellulose around the nutrients so that the vitamins and minerals and enzymes can be absorbed into the cells of the body.

PARSLEY CUCUMBER SALAD

12 C. parsley	1/2 C. sweet onions, sliced
1 C. cucumbers, sliced	2 large fresh tomatoes, chopped

Dressing:

1/2 C. feta cheese	1/4 tsp. oregano, dried
1/4 C. sunflower seed oil	1/2 C. sesame seeds, ground
2 T. lemon juice	1 tsp. paprika
1 clove garlic, minced	Dash white pepper

POTATOES

Potatoes should be cooked with the skins on to prevent a loss of essential active nutrients. They are high in potassium, phosphorus, sulphur, chlorine, and are an excellent source of B complex vitamins. They contain protein and some vitamin C.

Potatoes should be grated and added to soups uncooked. They are good for eczema and other skin problems, externally and internally. The raw potato juice has been used successfully on warts. Good for colds and bronchial and digestive problems. They are good for removing excessive toxins in the system.

HOT POTATO SALAD

4 C. cooked potatoes, diced with peelings on

Sauté potatoes in:

1/4 C. unsalted butter

When sautéed add:

2 T. tamari or soy sauce	1/2 C. ground toasted sunflower seeds
1/2 C. parsley, chopped	
1/2 C. watercress	Dash cayenne pepper
2 C. chopped celery	Sesame and kelp salt to taste

SPINACH

Spinach is very rich in magnesium and chlorophyll, a good vegetable for the nerves. Good for the glands, anemia, high blood pressure, constipation, obesity and heart. It contains iron and copper. Excellent source of calcium and vitamin E to supply oxygen to the cells.

SPINACH AND MUSHROOM SALAD

1 bunch spinach	*1/2 tsp. garlic, minced*
1/2 C. raw mushrooms, sliced	*1/2 C. whole wheat croutons*
3 T. parmesan cheese, grated	

Wash spinach thoroughly, dry and tear into small pieces. Add all ingredients and toss with a french dressing.

SQUASH

Summer squash is high in vitamins A, C, B1, B2 and B3, potassium, magnesium and iron. It is easy to digest. Zucchini can be used raw in salads to benefit from its nutrients. It can be used in casseroles or in stuffings. Winter squash contains vitamins A and C and is high in potassium. Both kinds contain calcium and iron.

STUFFED ACORN SQUASH

2 acorn squash, cut in half and seeded	*1 sweet apple, cored and chopped*
1/4 C. pure maple syrup	*Sunflower seeds*
1/4 C. pecans, ground	*2 T. butter*
	Cinnamon

Combine syrup, pecans and apple. Fill squash with mixture, sprinkle with sunflower seeds and dot with butter. Place in a baking dish, cover and bake for about 1 hour at 350°F.

TURNIPS

Turnips are rich in vitamins A and C, and a good source of natural calcium to build bones and teeth. Contain phosphorus, iron and sulphur. Good for anemia, blood purification, high blood pressure, liver problems, bladder problems and constipation.

TURNIP SOUP

3 C. sesame milk or skim
   milk
1/4 C. onions, chopped
2 C. turnips, cooked
   and mashed

1 C. potatoes, cooked and
   mashed
1/4 C. parsley, minced
Kelp
Paprika

Cook together milk, onion, turnips and potatoes. Add kelp and paprika to taste. When done sprinkle parsley on top when serving.

WATERCRESS

Watercress is an excellent source of vitamins A and E. It is also rich in potassium. It is an excellent food for losing weight. It helps rid the body of retained water. Rich in calcium and sulphur. It is a vegetable to use often in the prevention of diseases.

It is a tasty treat to add to salads.

WATERCRESS NUT SALAD

1 bunch watercress
2 C. romaine lettuce
1 T. sweet red onions
2 T. black olives

2 stalks celery, diced
1 C. chopped walnuts
2 tsp. fresh parsley

Toss all ingredients together and serve with mild vinaigrette dressing.

VINEGAR, APPLE CIDER

Contains malic acid which is similar to the hydrochloric acid manufactured by the stomach for digestive purposes. It is an effective digestive aid. It helps maintain the balance between the acids and alkalis of the body chemistry. It is high in potassium for a healthy nervous system. Contains phosphorus, calcium, some iron, chlorine, sodium, magnesium, sulphur, fluoride and silicon.

SALAD DRESSING

1/4 C. cider vinegar	*1 clove garlic, cut in pieces*
3/4 C. safflower oil	*1/2 tsp. paprika*

Put in a jar with a lid on and shake all together. Always shake before using.

VINAIGRETTE DRESSING

6 T. oil
2 T. cider vinegar
1/4 tsp. kelp
1 T. chopped onion
Also add parsley, chives and garlic to taste

WALNUTS

Walnuts are a muscle-building food. Buy the walnuts that have not been bleached with lye to brighten them. They are beneficial to the teeth and gums. Good for constipation problems.

They are high in complete protein, unsaturated fat, starches, some calcium, potassium and magnesium. Contains phosphorus and sulphur. Walnuts contain a small amount of vitamins A and B complex and are a good source of vitamin E.

Walnuts are an excellent nut to use in cookies, candy, granola, fruit salads and nut loaves.

WHEAT

Wheat is a staple food for half the world population. It is considered the staff of life in our daily bread. It is rich in protein, B complex, B1, B2 and B6, niacin, inositol, biotin, folic acid, choline, calcium, iron and other essential minerals.

The hard wheat is very good for storage. The fresh ground wheat is very high in vitamin E.

WHEATGRASS

Wheatgrass is the young green shoots of the wheat plant, which can be easily grown on a window sill in one week. Wheatgrass juice dilates the blood vessels, creates super-oxygenation of the brain and is a specific for treating cancer. Wheatgrass contains the elements that reverse the growth of cancer. (See <u>How I Conquered Cancer Naturally</u> by Eydie Mae.)

Wheatgrass is rich in chlorophyll and most essential nutrients. It is a detoxifier, alkalizer and healer. Chlorophyll is an astringent and germicidal and strengthens cells. Health clinics have chosen wheatgrass as a nutritional supplement because of a high chlorophyll, vitamin and live enzyme content.

Wheatgrass juice has been found to help as a gargle, sinus wash and ear drops. The grain of the wheat contains all the elements of which the body is composed, including rebuilding and revitalizing materials. Grains and sprouts are perfect foods because they contain the eliminating and assimilating elements, including valuable minerals.

Wheatgrass juice must be used as it is juiced. Juicing the wheatgrass releases the vital live elements.

WHEATGRASS COCKTAIL

8 oz. wheatgrass juice *1 small green pepper*
1 qt. fresh carrot juice *Several sprigs parsley*
1 fresh tomato *Kelp to taste*

Blend all ingredients together. Keep in refrigerator and use within a day or two.

WHEY

Whey is the mild residue, a creamy white liquid, which is leftover from cheese making. It has the highest content of natural sodium of any other food. Sodium has the ability to dissolve calcium deposits around the joints. Arthritis is benefitted from whey since it dissolves the calcium deposits and enables the bloodstream to carry them out of the body.

Whey helps to feed the acidophilus and bifidus bacteria in the intestines and prevent the development of harmful putrefactive bacteria which lead to auto-toxemia. Whey, which contains lactose, is the best natural food for these bacterias. Whey can also aid in the assimilation of nutrients from the food eaten. Helps to prevent constipation, internal sluggishness, gas and bowel putrefaction when used regularly.

Whey contains rich amounts of B complex vitamins, especially B1 and B2 which are very important for preserving a youthful appearance and preventing premature aging. The dried variety is good mixed with fruit or vegetable juices. Start with one tablespoon of powdered whey and work up to three times a day. Use in health drinks and in casseroles.

WILD RICE

Wild rice is very nutritious and delicious, but it is also very expensive. It is excellent mixed with brown rice or millet in casseroles. Add to soups and stuffings. It is rich in protein, B complex vitamins, iron and phosphorus.

YOGURT

Yogurt is a cultured milk product that is custard-like in texture with a sour taste. It is made with milk where lactic cultures have been added. With controlled temperature, the milk sugar is converted into beneficial lactic acid. The lactic acid acts as a cleanser as well as an antiseptic for the gastro-intestinal tract. It is easily digestible. It is excellent for lactase-deficient people. The bacteria used to make yogurt produces lactase. It breaks down milk sugar into lactic acid, and bacteria which cause putrefaction. Gas cannot live in lactic acid. The yogurt bacteria manufactures the B complex vitamins in the intestine via the intestinal flora.

Yogurt contains some antibiotic properties. All types of pathogenic bacteria and harmful germs are killed within five hours. When yogurt is eaten over a long period of time no other bacteria but the friendly kind appear in the stools. Plain yogurt is high in protein, lots of calcium, vitamin A and B complex. Eight ounces supplies 20% of the daily protein allowance.

HOMEMADE YOGURT

1 quart of milk
1 can evaporated milk
2 C. water

1 C. non-instant powdered milk
6 T. plain yogurt culture

Combine milk, canned milk, water and powdered milk. Warm the 2 cups water slightly, add powdered milk and blend well in blender. Add yogurt and blend all together. Put in pint jars, cover and put in warm oven (on/off) in water and leave about 8 hours or overnight. Refrigerate before serving.

RECIPES FOR HEALTH

NUTRITIOUS BREAKFAST

SUPER BREAKFAST CEREAL

1/2 C. oatmeal
1 C. plain yogurt
2 T. orange juice
1 T. honey
1/2 C. raisins

1/4 C. almonds, chopped
1 T. sesame seeds
1/2 C. chopped peaches
1/2 C. chopped apples
1/2 C. sliced bananas

Fold all ingredients together. You can substitute sunflower seeds for sesame seeds, pecans for almonds.

BUCKWHEAT CREPES

1/2 C. buckwheat flour
1/2 C. whole wheat
    pastry flour
1/4 C. wheat germ

1 C. milk
1/2 C. water
1/2 tsp. mineral salt
3 eggs 3 T. cold-pressed oil

Combine flours, eggs, milk, water, salt and oil. Mix in blender. Batter should be thick, but if it is too thick the crepe will curl up at the edges when cooking. Just add a little more milk.

Heat the skillet and spread butter and oil mixture, butter alone will burn. Pour 1/3 Cup of crepe batter onto pan and swirl to cover entire surface or tilt the pan to cover bottom. Cook crepe about one minute and flip over to cook other side. The second side need not be brown for it to be done.

Topping Suggestions:

Blueberry sauce with sour cream or whipping cream. Strawberries with whipping cream or sour cream.

BUCKWHEAT PANCAKES

3 C. buckwheat flour
1 C. whole wheat flour
4 tsp. baking powder,
    aluminum free
1 tsp. mineral salt

3 C. buttermilk
2 C. yogurt
4 eggs
1/4 C. cold-pressed oil
6 T. honey

Sift dry ingredients together. Blend liquid into dry ingredients. Cook on hot greased griddle. Serves 6.
Serve with pure maple syrup or blueberry sauce.

BUCKWHEAT PANCAKES

1 C. buckwheat flour
1-1/4 C. whole wheat flour
1/2 C. wheat germ
1 T. baking powder,
    aluminum free
3 egg yolks

6 T. butter
1 T. honey
3 C. buttermilk

Fold in:
3 egg whites, beaten stiffly

Stir all ingredients together and fold in the egg whites last. Fry the pancakes on a hot, slightly greased griddle. Serve with butter and pure maple syrup.

EASY GRAIN CEREAL

1/2 C. bran
1/2 C. wheat germ
1/2 C ground sesame seeds
2 T. lecithin granules

1/2 C. ground sunflower
    seeds
1 C. ground almonds
1/4 C. ground chia seeds

Grind all ingredients in blender and use on breakfast fruit such as bananas, peaches, or in applesauce. This can be added to peanut butter for sandwiches.
This can be added to muffins or pancakes, pizzas or homemade breads.

RAW GRANOLA #1

*6 C. raw oatmeal (baby
    oat)*
*1 C. ground sunflower
    seeds*
1 C. ground sesame seeds
1/4 C. ground chia seeds
1 C. flaxseeds, ground

1 C. shredded coconut
1 C. ground almonds
1-1/2 tsp. grated orange rind
1/2 tsp. cardamom
1 C. date sugar
1/2 C. warm honey

Mix all together and drip warm honey and stir. Keep in a tight jar in a cool place. Can be stored in freezer.

The granola acts as an intestinal broom and cleanser. The best method is cooking in the over at 200°F. for about an hour, stirring often.

RAW GRANOLA #2

1 C. sprouted triticale
*1 C. ground sunflower
    seeds, coarse*
*1 C. ground sesame seeds,
    coarse*
*1 T. chia seed (soaked over-
    night in apple juice)*

1 C. coarse ground almonds
10 T. apple juice
1 C. light figs, chopped
1 C. dates

Mix all together and moisten with apple juice.

RAW OAT CEREAL

Raw cereals are rich in silicon and valuable for health bowel activity.

1/2 C. baby oats
1 T. ground almonds
1 T. ground sesame seeds

1 tsp. date sugar
*1 T. raisins soaked in
    water*

Add bananas, fresh peaches, fresh berries, ground sunflower seeds, sesame seeds, coconut, cashews.

Add rice polishings, flaxseed meal, wheat germ, bran.

RAW OATS WITH FRUIT MUESLI

2 T. baby oats
6 T. spring water
2 T. lemon juice
1/4 grated fresh apple

1 T. ground almonds
1 T. ground sunflower seeds
2-3 T. almond milk
1 tsp. maple syrup

Soak oats overnight in spring water. Add lemon juice and almond milk until smooth. Add grated unpeeled apple. Sprinkle nuts and seeds; add more almond milk if needed.

This recipe can be used with any fresh fruit in season, such as strawberries, raspberries, blueberries, apples, bananas, peaches, apricots. Yogurt can also be added for variety.

RAW WHEAT WITH FRUIT

2 T. wheat flakes
6 T. water
2 T. lemon juice
2 T. ground sesame seeds

1 T. honey or maple syrup
1 small banana
1 tbs. ground almonds
Almond milk to moisten

Soak wheat flakes overnight. Mix juice, ground nut and honey.

Dried fruit may be used. Soak overnight, grind and add to cereal.

GRANOLA

5 C. rolled oats
3 C rolled wheat
2 C. wheat germ
1 C. rice polishing
1 C. almonds
1 C. pecans
1 C. walnuts

2 C. sunflower seeds
1 C. bran
2 C. coconut, unsweetened
1 C. flaxseeds, ground
1 C. sesame seeds
1/2 C. chia seeds, ground

Mix dry ingredients together.

1-1/4 C. honey
1/4 C. maple syrup
1/2 C. date sugar

1 T. vanilla, pure
1 C. raw oil mixed with...
1 C. hot water

Mix thoroughly all other ingredients. Spread out in a shallow baking pan. Bake at 325°F. for about 30 minutes or until dry and golden brown, stirring often to prevent burning.

GRAPE NUTS   (Used as a cereal or pie crust)

3 C. whole wheat flour
1 C. sour milk
1/2 C. honey
1/2 C. date sugar
1 C. ground walnuts

1 tsp. pure sea salt or
* mineral balanced salt*
1-1/2 tsp. baking powder
1 T. pure vanilla
1/2 C. sesame seeds

Blend all ingredients in a mixer. Place in a 12 x 18 inch pan and cook for 15 minutes at 350°F. Cut in squares and turn over and place back into the oven at 200°F. for about 30 minutes longer.

When done take out and break into small pieces and cook again.

WHEAT BERRIES

1 C. whole wheat
3 C. spring water

1/2 tsp. sesame kelp salt
* or sea salt*

Rinse grain. Add slowly to boiling water and add salt. Stir grain with a fork and place lid on pan and reduce heat and simmer for one hour.

It makes a good breakfast food by adding milk or nut milk and a little pure maple syrup.

It can be used in casseroles and ground and used in breads or added to other grain for main dishes or added to cookies for a crunchy taste.

FRUITS AND SEEDS

1/4 C. ground sunflower
* seeds*
14 C. ground sesame seeds

1/2 C. white figs or dates
* or half of each*
1/2 C. spring water

Soak seeds and dry fruit overnight in spring water. Blend all ingredients together in a blender. Put over fresh apples, bananas or peaches.

Makes a nourishing quick energy breakfast.

WHEAT CEREAL

1/2 C. cooked wheat berries
1/4 C. raisins (unsulphured)
1 tsp. pure maple syrup

Mix together and top with a teaspoon of ground almonds and nut milk.

BULGHUR

4 C. spring water
2 C. whole wheat berries

Cook the whole wheat berries for one hour. Drain off any liquid that has not been absorbed by the wheat. Spread the wheat on a cookie sheet. Place in the oven at 225°F. Toast the wheat until it is dry, about one hour. Stir so the drying will be even.

Let the wheat cool, then crack it in the blender or in a grinder.

HEALTHY DRINKS

APPLE CHAMOMILE DRINK

A drink to soothe and calm the nerves

4 C. raw apple juice
4 C. chamomile tea
1/4 tsp. cinnamon

1/4 tsp. cardamom
1/4 tsp. ginger
Malt sugar to taste

Can be served hot or cold. Enjoy.

ORANGE SPICE TEA

4 C. spearmint tea
4 C. fresh or frozen
    orange juice
1/2 fresh lemon

1/4 tsp. cinnamon
Dash cardamom and cloves
Malt sugar to taste

Can be served hot or cold.

ENERGY DRINK

2 C. sesame seed milk or
    unsweetened fruit
    juice
2 bananas, frozen
2 T. sunflower seeds
2 T. sesame seeds

2 T. lecithin
10 almonds
2 T. wheat germ
1 tsp. chia seeds
1 tsp. pure vanilla

Blend until smooth. A high energy drink. This makes 2 good servings. Drink slowly and chew.

ENERGY DRINK

Blend together:

8 oz. papaya juice *1 T. wheat germ*
1 fresh peach *1 T. chia seeds*
2 T. protein supplement *2 oz. plain yogurt*
1 T. rice polishings *1 T. sunflower seeds*

The papaya juice contains protein digestive enzymes. The protein supplement provides protein and natural B complex. The yogurt makes the drink more digestible and helps prevent gas formation. The sunflower seeds offer nutrition and energy along with unsaturated fatty acids. The chia seeds also produce energy and are very high in vegetable protein.

GINGER ALE

1 C. fresh ginger root *1 quart pure water*
chopped and *6 T. honey*
unpeeled *Juice of 4 lemons*
Rind of 4 lemons, grated *1 quart cold soda water*
(organically grown) *Powdered vitamin C*

Add a quart of boiling water over chopped lemon rind and ginger and steep for five minutes. Strain and stir in honey or fructose (if you prefer) to taste. Chill, add lemon juice, soda water, vitamin C powder and ice. Wonderful drink for children with upset stomach and colds or flu.

HOLIDAY DRINK

2 quarts apple juice *Dash of allspice*
2-3 whole cloves *4 T. fresh lemon juice*
1 stick cinnamon *6 T. fresh orange juice*
1/2 tsp. cardamom

Heat the apple juice and spices. When ready to serve, add juices.

EGG NOG

3 egg yolks
1 tsp. vanilla
1 T. honey
3 C. freshly squeezed
    orange juice

4 ice cubes
1 T. whey powder
1 T. lecithin

Mix all together in a blender. Very nourishing.

PROTEIN TOMATO JUICE DRINK

8 oz. tomato juice or
    vegetable cocktail
1 heaping T. protein
    powder
1/2 tsp. kelp

1 tsp. olive oil
Dash cayenne
1 T. lecithin (granulated)
1 tsp. brewers yeast

Blend all together well. Serve chilled.

SEASONINGS WITHOUT SALT

Seasonings should be used to enhance the flavor, not to overwhelm the dish. They should complement the natural flavors of food.

We should learn to enjoy and relish the flavors of salads and other uncooked foods. Try vegetable salads without seasoning such as salt and pepper. They are refreshing and the taste is delicate. Too many seasonings can cause digestive and kidney problems. They can also stimulate digestion and cause overeating.

Try the following seasonings for food:

Dried lemon peel, garlic, paprika
Dried onion, garlic, celery seed
Kelp, watercress, dried vegetables, dried onions
Chili pepper, garlic, dried onion, cumin
Papaya seeds (dried and ground are a tasty
pepper substitute

HERB SEASONING BLENDS

SPECIAL HERB BLEND

1 oz. each basil, coriander, rosemary, cumin, sage and
thyme
1/2 oz. each celery seed, parsley, onion and marjoram
1/4 oz. each cayenne, garlic, kelp, watercress, mustard
and paprika

Grind the herbs in a flour mill, blender or with a mortar. When powdered, sift and shake to remove any large pieces.

You can add different herbs and taste until you get the taste you prefer.

SEASONINGS WITHOUT SALT

SESAME SEED AND BROTH SEASONING

6 T. sesame seeds, ground fine
2 T. vegetable seasoning broth

Mix together and use to season casseroles, soups and sprinkle on fresh salads.

SESAME SEED AND KELP SEASONING

6 tsp. sesame seeds, ground fine
1 tsp. kelp

This is a wonderful seasoning to use on salads, fresh or lightly steamed vegetables, or in grain dishes. Use as you would salt.

HERB SEASONING (use instead of salt)

1 T. garlic powder
2 tsp. onion powder
1 tsp. basil
1 tsp. marjoram
1 tsp. thyme
1 tsp. parsley

1 tsp. mace
1 tsp. savory
1/2 tsp. cayenne pepper
1/2 tsp. kelp
1/2 tsp. dulse

SEASONING BROTH

1 C. tamari
2/3 C. lemon juice
1/2 C. wine vinegar
3 T. dulse, powdered
1 clove garlic, minced

1 C. lecithin
1 T. okra powder
1 T. molasses
1 T. papain
1 T. parsley, dried

Use this seasoning in soups, casseroles and in cooking beans.

DELICIOUS DRESSINGS, TOPPINGS, MAYONNAISE, SEED AND NUT MILKS, SALSA AND ETC.

AVOCADO DRESSING

3 ripe avocados, mashed
1/2 C. lemon juice
2 cloves garlic, minced
1/2 C. chopped onion

1 tomato, chopped
1/2 tsp. kelp
1/2 tsp. paprika
Dash of cayenne

GREEN DRESSING

1 C. parsley, chopped
3/4 C. raw oil
1/4 C. lemon juice
1 small clove garlic

1 tsp. sesame kelp salt
1 tsp. paprika
2 T. sesame seeds

Mix until smooth in blender and serve on vegetable salads.

GREEN DRESSING

2 T. plain yogurt
3 T. mayonnaise
2 T. minced onion

1 tsp. lemon juice
1 T. spirulina
Kelp to taste

Blend all ingredients together. Use on fresh vegetables and salads.

SEED SALAD DRESSING

1 C. sesame seeds, ground
1/2 C. cold pressed oil
1/4 C. lemon juice
1-1/2 tsp. ground basil

1/8 tsp. tarragon
1/2 tsp. thyme
1/8 tsp. celery seed
2 T. soy sauce
Dash kelp

Mix in blender or shake in a pint jar. Use over salads, over soaked vegetables, casseroles or over whole grain.

ITALIAN DRESSING

1 C. pure olive oil
1/3 C. lemon juice
1/3 C. water
3 cloves garlic, minced

1 tsp. sweet basil
1 tsp. oregano
1 tsp. kelp
Dash thyme

Mix all ingredients together in a jar and shake well. Let set for awhile so all will blend together.

VINAIGRETTE DRESSING

1 C. sunflower seed oil
1/2 C. apple cider vinegar
1/2 C. water
1 clove garlic, pressed

1/2 tsp. sesame kelp salt
Dash white pepper
1 T. honey
1/2 tsp. dry mustard

Blend all ingredients. Add fresh green onions and fresh parsley. Blend together in a blender.

FRESH TOMATO DRESSING

4 ripe tomatoes
1/3 C. fresh lemon juice
1/3 C. olive oil
1 clove garlic minced

1/4 tsp. kelp
1 tsp. honey
1 tsp. paprika

Mix all ingredients together in a blender. Use on fresh salads, vegetable loaves, bean dishes and salads.

HERB DRESSING

12 T. safflower oil, cold
    pressed
4 T. fresh lemon juice
2 cloves garlic, pressed
1/2 tsp. dried parsley

1/2 tsp. summer savory
1/2 tsp. paprika
Dash of kelp or vegetable
    seasoning

Mix all ingredients together in a pint jar and shake well. Let stand in jar for awhile before using.

TAHINI DRESSING

1/4 C. tahini
1/4 C. lemon juice
1 crushed clove garlic

2 T. bran water
2 T. chopped parsley
2 small chopped green
    onions

Mix all ingredients in blender. Blend thoroughly. Serve over hot or cold vegetables.

GUACAMOLE

2 medium avocados,
    mashed
1 large peeled tomato
    chopped
1 T. red minced onion

1 T. fresh parsley
1 T. fresh lemon juice
Kelp to taste

Mix all ingredients together in a glass bowl and serve immediately. Use on salads, tacos, tostadoes or serve as a dip with chips.

AVOCADO SAUCE

2 ripe avocados
1 small can green chilis
2 hard-boiled eggs
    (optional)

2 T. red wine vinegar
2 T. fresh parsley
2 T. olive oil

Mash the avocados, chop the green chilis, eggs and parsley. Mix all together. Use on tacos and tostadoes.

VINAIGRETTE HERB DRESSING

6 T. sunflower oil
4 tsp. olive oil
6 T. fresh lemon juice
2 T. pure water

2 tsp. Dijon mustard
3 tsp. fresh chopped parsley
2 tsp. fresh chives
1/2 tsp. malt sugar

Put all ingredients in a pint jar and shake well.

MOCK SOUR CREAM

1 C. low-fat cottage cheese
1 T. lemon juice
2 T. nut milk (cashew or almond)
1 tsp. sesame kelp salt

Blend all ingredients thoroughly in a blender. Use on potatoes, casseroles and anything on which you would put sour cream.

BLUEBERRY SAUCE

Use on pancakes, waffles, ice cream and yogurt.

2 C. fresh or frozen
     unsweetened
     blueberries
2 T. pure maple syrup or
     honey
1 tsp. fresh lemon juice

1/2 C. pure water
1 T. arrowroot starch
1/4 tsp. cardamom

In a saucepan combine water, arrowroot and cardamom and cook over low heat until the mixture thickens. Add rest of the ingredients. Ready to serve.

FRESH TOMATO SAUCE

2 C. ripe fresh tomatoes
2 cloves garlic
1 T. red wine vinegar

1/2 tsp. rosemary
1/2 tsp. oregano
Kelp to taste

Stir all ingredients together in a blender. Use over stir fried vegetables, cooked rice or millet or other grains.

TOMATO SUPREME

This recipe is to be used in soups, stews, vegetable dishes, grain dishes, bean dishes and casseroles.

8 qts. tomatoes
8 garlic buttons
3 C. chopped onions
1 small can green chiles

2 C. green peppers
2 jalapeño pepper
1 long yellow pepper

Remove skins from tomatoes, blend all ingredients together and cook for about two hours. Prepare in quart jars and process in pressure cooker according to canning directions. Can enough to last all year.

SALSA   (Medium Hot)

4 peeled tomatoes
2 onions
1 Jalapeño pepper
3 T. cold pressed oil

4 tsp. lemon juice
Kelp and mineral salt
    to taste
1/4 tsp. each oregano and
    rosemary

Chop tomatoes, onions and pepper. Mix in salad oil, lemon juice and seasonings. Chill until ready to use.

FRESH SALSA

2 C. chopped ripe
    tomatoes
1 small can green chiles
1/2 C. chopped green
    onions

2 cloves garlic, pressed
Dash of cayenne
1 T. olive oil
Chili powder to taste

Blend 1 cup of the fresh tomatoes and garlic in blender. Add the rest of the ingredients and chill.

MAYONNAISE

1 C. safflower oil
2 egg yolks
2 T. fresh lemon juice
1 T. lecithin

1-1/2 T. apple cider vinegar
1 tsp. sesame kelp salt,
    more if needed
1/4 tsp. mustard powder

Mix egg yolks in blender and mix until thick. Add vinegar and blend about 30 seconds. Pour the oil, while the blender is running very slowly, in a thin stream. Add lemon juice, sesame kelp salt, lecithin and mustard powder. Blend until smooth.

CASHEW MAYONNAISE

1/2 C. raw cashews
1 C. pure water
1 tsp. kelp or mineral
    salt
1 T. lecithin

1/2 tsp. paprika
1/4 tsp. powdered mustard
1 C. safflower oil
4 T. fresh lemon juice

Blend the first 6 ingredients. Add lemon slowly. Pour the oil, while blender is running, in a thin stream.

MOCK MAYONNAISE

1 C. low-fat cottage cheese
2 T. cold pressed oil
1 T. water

1 T. cider vinegar
1 tsp. dry mustard
1/2 tsp. paprika

Mix all ingredients together in a blender. Blend until the mixture is smooth.

NUT MILKS

ALMOND MILK

1 C. almonds, ground
1 qt. pure water
2 T. pure maple syrup

Blend thoroughly in a blender until it is smooth. Strain through a strainer or cheese cloth.

SESAME MILK

1 C. sesame seeds
1 qt. pure water
2 T. pure maple syrup

Blend ingredients in a blender until smooth and strain off the milk.

COCONUT MILK

1-1/2 C. grated fresh coconut
1 qt. pure water
2 T. sunflower oil

Blend all together and strain off milk.

NUT AND SEED MILK

1/2 C. blanched almonds　　*1 qt. pure water*
1/2 C. sesame seeds　　*2 T. pure maple syrup*

Blend together in blender and strain the milk.

CASHEW MILK GRAVY

6 T. raw ground cashews　　*1 T. arrowroot*
1-1/2 C. pure water　　*2 tsp. soy sauce*

Grind nuts in water with blender and strain off the milk. Mix arrowroot with a little nut milk, put milk in saucepan and gradually add arrowroot mixture and stir until it thickens.

Use on nut loaves, vegetable and grain loaves. If you want a brown gravy add teaspoons of a vegetable broth seasoning.

MILK GRAVY

2 C. cashew milk
2 T. arrowroot
1 T. vegetable broth seasoning

Blend and cook over medium heat, stirring continually until thickened. Use for creamed peas, corn, broccoli or cauliflower. Use over brown cooked rice or millet.

POTATO TOPPING

1 C. creamed low-fat cottage cheese	Kelp to taste
1/3 C. buttermilk	Chopped chives
1 T. lemon juice	Chopped parsley

Mix all ingredients together. Add chives and parsley last.

SOUPS

BANANA AND PAPAYA SOUP

2 ripe bananas
1 ripe papaya
1 pint thick nut milk

1 T. pure maple syrup or
    honey

Mash the bananas and papaya. Add sweetener and nut milk, blend thoroughly, and warm only in a double boiler. Do not cook. Add a dash of cardamom.

BEAN SOUP

1 C. navy beans
4 C. pure water
1 C. grated carrots
1 small onion, grated

1/2 C. parsley, chopped
1 T. nut cream
1 tsp. lemon juice

Soak beans overnight in three cups of water. Cook beans in 4 cups water until tender. Blend the cooked beans and vegetables in a blender, add parsley, nut cream and lemon and let boil for a few minutes. Ready to serve.

BORSCHT (Beet Soup)

1-1/2 C. yogurt
1 T. fresh lemon juice
1/2 tsp. mineral salt or
    kelp

1 T. onion, minced
1 C. beets, cooked and diced

Combine all ingredients together. Mix in a blender for a few seconds at low speed. Serve chilled with chopped parsley sprinkled on top or with a teaspoon of yogurt.

CARROT SOUP

1/2 lb. carrots
1 C. cashew milk
Water

1 T. butter
Vegetable seasoning

Wash and cut carrots and steam until soft. Remove from heat and let cool. Pureé carrots in blender using water the carrots were cooked in. Put pureéd carrots in a pan and add cashew milk and not water to desired thinness. Do not boil after adding milk. Add seasoning and add butter just before serving.

CHILI CORN SOUP

3 T. oil
1 onion, chopped
1 green pepper, chopped
1 clove garlic, minced
3 stalks celery, chopped
1 qt. Tomato Supreme or
plain tomatoes

1 T. chili powder
1 tsp. oregano
1 tsp. basil
2 C. fresh or frozen corn
2 C. cooked pinto beans or
red beans
2 C. vegetable broth

Sauté oil with onion, pepper, garlic and celery. Cook until transparent. Add tomatoes, broth, seasonings and cook for 30 minutes. Add all other ingredients and cook for about 20 minutes. If you need to add more seasoning, add kelp or mineral salt.

CORN CHOWDER

2 C. fresh corn
1/4 C. chopped celery
1 medium chopped onion
1/4 C. water

4 C. milk
4 T. butter
1 tsp. sea salt
2 T. baco bits
Paprika

Sauté corn, celery and onion for 4 minutes. Add water and cover. Cook for 5 minutes. Scald milk and add butter, seasonings, baco bits and a dash of paprika. Makes about 4 to 6 servings.

CREAM OF TOMATO SOUP

4 large ripe tomatoes　　　*2 T. fresh chopped parsley*
1 C. nut cream　　　*1 T. ground fresh chives or*
　　　　　　　　　　　　　　green onions

　　　Blend peeled tomatoes in a blender and add the nut cream and other ingredients. Heat in a double boiler and add water if it is too thick.

DRIED PEA SOUP

1 C. dried split peas　　　*2 small carrots, grated*
4 C. pure water, cold　　　*2 T. chopped parsley*
1 medium onion, minced　　*1/2 C. nut cream*
1 C. celery, chopped　　　*1 tsp. vegetable salt or*
　　　　　　　　　　　　　　kelp

　　　Cook the peas in water after soaking overnight. Cook with vegetables for about two hours. When done add nut cream and seasoning.

GAZPACHO　(Chilled Soup)

2 C. pureéd fresh tomatoes　*1/4 C. olive oil*
1 large cucumber　　　　　*1/4 C. apple cider vinegar*
4 green onions　　　　　　*1 clove garlic, minced*
1 red pepper　　　　　　　*Kelp*
1 green pepper　　　　　　*Vegetable seasoning*
1/2 C. ripe olives

　　　Mix in blender, tomatoes, chopped cucumber, onions, red pepper, olive oil, vinegar, minced garlic, kelp and vegetable seasoning. Chill. Serve topped with minced green pepper and chopped ripe olives.

LENTIL SOUP

2 C. lentils
5 C. bran water
1 qt. tomatoes
2 stalks celery, chopped
1 large green pepper

2 large carrots, chopped
2 cloves garlic, minced
1/2 tsp. basil
1/4 C. tamari
Kelp or vegetable seasoning
   to taste

Combine all ingredients except kelp in a slow cooker. Cover and cool on low heat for about 6 hours. Season to taste.

MINESTRONE

1 qt. Tomato Supreme or
   lg. can stewed
   tomatoes
1 qt. water
3 T. vegetable seasoning
1 large onion, chopped
2 C. carrots, sliced
1/2 C. celery
2 potatoes, diced with
   skins on
2 C. pinto beans, cooked

1 corn on cob, cut off
1/3 C. millet, uncooked
1 C. peas, fresh or frozen
1/2 C. whole wheat
   spaghetti, broken
   into pieces
2 T. parsley, minced fresh
2 bay leaves
1 tsp. mineral salt or kelp
2 T. cold pressed oil
   (optional)

Combine Tomato Supreme, water, vegetable seasoning, onion, carrots, celery, onions, millet, parsley, bay leaves and mineral salt. Cook until millet is tender. Add rest of the ingredients and cook for about 15 minutes more. Add oil before serving.

OKRA AND BARLEY SOUP

1/2 pound okra
1 small onion
1 T. arrowroot

1/2 C. barley, cooked
3 C. nut milk

Steam the choped okra and onion until tender. Mix arrowroot with nut milk and cook slowly in double boiler along with okra, onion and cooked barley.

PARSLEY SOUP

2 C. vegetable broth
1 C. fresh parsley
1 C. yogurt

1/2 tsp. sesame kelp salt
Dash of cayenne

Mix all ingredients together in blender until smooth. Chill and serve with thin slices of lemon.

POTATO SOUP

4 large potatoes
3 C. water
2 T. raw cashew butter
1 small onion

4 stalks celery, chopped
1/2 C. fresh chopped parsley
1 tsp. vegetable salt

Steam potatoes with skins on in the water. Remove skin from potatoes and mash through dicer. Dissolve nut butter in 1 cup of warm pure water. Put all other ingredients together and cook in double boiler for about 20 minutes.

SOUP MIX

1 C. dry green split peas
1 C. pearled barley
1 C. millet

1 C. lentils
1-1/2 C. brown rice
4 C. dry minced onions

Combine all ingredients in a large container. Stir for even distribution. Store in a cool place. Use within 6 months.

SOUP STOCK

6 C. bran water
1-1/2 C. Soup Mix
1 tsp. kelp or mineral
    salt
3 carrots, sliced
2 stalks celery

1 qt. tomatoes
1 C. cabbage
1 C. broccoli
1/2 C. parsley
1/2 C. sesame seeds, ground

Cook Soup Mix in bran water until done. Add all other ingredients and cook until done.

RAW SOUP #1

Raw soups contain live enzymes that are essential to help prevent cancer and other diseases.

3 C. vegetable broth
1 C. tomato juice
1 T. ground chia seeds
   (optional)

1 T. olive oil
1/2 tsp. kelp
2 T. vegetable broth powder

Heat all ingredients and simmer for 10 minutes. Remove from heat and all the following raw vegetables:

1/2 C. grated carrots
1/2 C. grated celery
1/2 C. fresh sweet corm
1/2 C. fresh peas

1 small chopped onion
2 fresh tomatoes cut in
   small pieces
2 sprigs parsley, chopped

RAW SOUP #2

4 C. bran water or pure
   water
1 C. small cubes potatoes
   skin on

1 medium onion
2 T. vegetable broth powder
1 clove garlic

Simmer all ingredients together until potatoes are done. Remove from stove and add the following ingredients.

1 C. grated carrots
1/2 C. chopped celery
1/2 C. finely chopped green
   beans

1/2 C. chopped spinach
1/2 C. chopped parsley

Serve immediately for a live enzyme soup.

VEGETABLE BROTH #1

Homemade vegetable broth is a basis for soups and stews.

1 gallon pure water
2 large onions
2 leeks
1 C. fresh parsley

6 medium potatoes, scrubbed
with skins on
4 medium carrots
1 bay leaf

2 parsnips
2 turnips
4 ribs celery
1 medium green pepper

1/2 tsp. thyme
1/2 tsp. basil
1/2 tsp. rosemary
1 T. vegetable seasoning

Combine all ingredients in a large stainless steel pan with the gallon of water. Bring to boil, lower heat and simmer for about 1-1/2 hours. Strain and use for soups and stews.

VEGETABLE BROTH #2

6 medium potatoes
4 medium onions
2 ripe tomatoes, or 1 qt.
    Tomato Supreme
2 stalks celery

3 carrots
1 clove garlic
Kelp, vegetable broth
    seasoning to taste
3 qts. pure water

Put all the ingredients in the water and bring to a boil and simmer covered for about one hour. Add herbs of your choice after 45 minutes. Fresh parsley, basil or thyme.

VEGETABLE SOUP

2 T. cold pressed oil
1 medium onion

1 clove garlic
2 T. vegetable broth
    seasoning

Sauté oil, onion and garlic until transparent in color. Add 1 quart of pure water and the following ingredients and simmer for about thirty minutes.

1 C. chopped potatoes
    (skins on)
1/2 C. chopped carrots
1 C. chopped summer
    squash

1/2 C. fresh chopped
    mushrooms
1 stalk celery, chopped fine

After all is done add 2 sprigs of parsley and serve with whole wheat crackers.

YOGURT GAZPACHO

1-1/2 C. yogurt
4-1/2 T. olive oil
2 cloves garlic
1 green pepper
4 tomatoes, peeled and chopped

1 medium cucumber, peeled and chopped
1/2 tsp. basil
1/2 tsp. cumin
2 T. cider vinegar

Mix in a blender all the ingredients and chill well before serving.

VEGETABLE DISHES

ASPARAGUS AND SOUR CREAM

2 lbs. asparagus
1 C. sour cream
2 T. lemon juice

3 T. butter
Mineral salt to taste
1/2 C. whole wheat bread
     crumbs

Steam asparagus until tender, drain. Place in a shallow baking dish. Combine sour cream, mineral salt, lemon juice, warm and pour over asparagus. Brown the crumbs in butter and sprinkle on top. Bake at 350°F. for 5 minutes.

BEANS AND TOMATOES

2 lbs. fresh string beans
2 C. tomatoes
1 small green papper,
     diced
2 onions

3 tsp. honey
3 T. butter
2 tsp. vegetable broth
     powder
1/2 kelp

Sauté onions and green peppers in butter; add tomatoes, seasoning, honey. Simmer for 10 minutes. Add steamed green beans and heat through.

BROCCOLI

2 C. broccoli pieces
1 clove garlic

3 T. olive oil
1/2 lemon

Steam broccoli for about 5 minutes. Drain and sauté in olive oil and chopped garlic. Before serving, squeeze lemon juice on broccoli. You can also serve broccoli topped with mock sour cream.

BRUSSELS SPROUTS CASSEROLE

1 C. Brussels sprouts,
    steamed
1 C. red cabbage, chopped
2 red onions, chopped
2 C. carrots, sliced and
    steamed

1 C. potatoes, skins on,
    diced and steamed
2 T. mineral bouillon
1 T. mineral salt
1 tsp. kelp
2 T. olive oil
1 C. tomato juice

    Combine steamed Brussels sprouts, carrots and potatoes. Add all other ingredients and cover with tomato juice. Cook in oven for 30 minutes at 350°F.

CHOP SUEY VEGETABLES

1 C. green and red peppers
    sliced diagonally
1 C. celery, sliced
    diagonally
1/2 C. onions, sliced
1 small can water
    chestnuts, sliced
1 C. bamboo shoots
1 C. bean sprouts

1 C. bean sprouts
1 C. mushrooms, sliced
1/8 tsp. ginger
2 cloves garlic, minced
4 T. butter
4 tsp. tamari (soy sauce)
1 T. sesame seeds

    Cook vegetables lightly and serve over cooked brown rice or millet. Vegetables should be crunchy.

SWEET POTATO CASSEROLE

2 C. mashed, cooked,
    sweet potatoes
1 C. ripe mashed banana
1/3 C. yogurt or sour
    cream

1 egg
1/2 tsp. mineral salt
2 T. pure maple syrup

    Blend all ingredients together. Beat until smooth. Bake in a buttered casserole dish at 350°F for 20 minutes. Serves 4 to 6.

VEGETABLE CASSEROLE

*1 qt. Tomato Supreme or
    stewed tomatoes
1 C. carrots, sliced thin
    diagonally
1 C. green beans, sliced
    thin
2 small crookneck squash,
    cubed
1 medium onion, sliced*

*1/2 C. green peppers
1 tsp. mineral salt or
        vegetable seasonings
1/2 tsp. allspice
Juice of 1 lemon
2 T. olive oil*

Mix all ingredients together. Pour into a casserole dish. Bake for one hour at 350°F.

VEGETABLE STIR FRY

*1 C. carrots, sliced
1 C. red onions
1 C. broccoli, sliced
1 C. cauliflower
2 cloves garlic, minced*

*1/2 C. blanched almonds,
        chopped
1/4 C. sunflower seeds
2 T. soy sauce (natural)
1/2 tsp. basil
1/4 tsp. cumin*

Heat two tablespoons ghee or butter or cold-pressed oil in wok or frying pan. Add carrots, onions, garlic and herbs, stir thoroughly and cover and let cook for five minutes. Stir occasionally and you may add a few tablespoons of water if vegetables get too dry. Add broccoli and blanched almonds, stir; cover and cook for about 3 minutes. Add cauliflower, sunflower seeds and soy sauce and stir thoroughly. Cover and cook for about two minutes.

Serve over millet, brown rice or other grain and use vegetables in season such as zucchini, green peppers, Brussels sprouts and cabbage. Add fresh corn, mushrooms or bean sprouts.

FRUIT SALADS

AMBROSIA

Mix together:

1 C. orange segments
1 C. pineapple tidbits, unsweetened

Pour 1/2 C. fresh orange juice and 1 T. honey over fruit. Sprinkle 1/4 C. ground almonds on top.

APPLE SAUCE

4 juicy apples
1 C. nut butter

1 T. honey
1 tsp. fresh lemon juice

FRUIT DELIGHT

1 C. dates
1 C. white or dark
  figs

3/4 C. almonds, ground
1/4 C. sunflower seeds,
  ground

Mix all ingredients together and run through food chopper. Press the mixture into a buttered pan. Let mixture set overnight and cut into squares.

FRUIT NUT SALAD

2 C. red delicious apples,
  chopped
1 C. fresh pineapple,
  diced
3/4 C. fresh orange sections,
  chopped

1/2 C. pitted dates, chopped
1/2 C. walnuts, chopped
1/4 C. sesame seeds

Dressing:

1/2 C. yogurt
1/4 C. cream cheese

3 T. orange juice concentrate
1 T. pure maple syrup

Combine all fruits and nuts. Mix the dressing and put over salad.

GLAZED FRESH FRUIT

*1 C. fruit and berry
    juice, unsweetened
    (frozen section)
1 T. arrowroot or corn-
    starch
1/4 tsp. ginger
1/2 tsp. cardamom*

*2 C. fresh strawberries
1 C. apples, chopped
1 C. seedless grapes, halved
1 C. fresh peaches, sliced*

Stir arrowroom and seasonings in juice over stove and bring to a boil; cook for one minute. Toss fruit together and fold in juice mixture and stir to coat well. Chill. Serves 6.

MIXED FRUIT COMPOTE

*2 apples
1 C. dried fruit (apricots,
    white figs, prunes)
1/3 C. currants
1/2 stick cinnamon*

*Thin lemon slice
1/4 C. almonds, ground
1/2 lemon, juiced
2-1/2 C. water*

Slice apples in chunks and put in saucepan with all other ingredients except currants. Bring to a boil, then simmer on low heat, covered, for about 30 minutes. Remove the cinnamon stick and lemon slice. Stir in currants and serve for breakfast. Makes about 4 servings.

PEACH SALAD

*2 large peaches
1 C. raspberries, fresh*

*1/2 C. pecans, chopped
Mock sour cream*

Pare and halve peaches, remove stones and fill with mixture of raspberries and pecans and moisten with mock sour cream.

PINEAPPLE WALDORF SALAD

*1 C. celery hearts
1 C. apples
1 C. fresh pineapple
1/4 C. chopped walnuts*

*Raisins (optional)
Home-made mayonnaise
Leaf lettuce*

Combine celery hearts, apples, pineapple, nuts and raisins. Add mayonnaise. This salad is also delicious without mayonnaise. Place on leaf lettuce.

STRAWBERRY JELL SALAD

*2 C. fruit and berry
     juice (frozen)*
3 T. agar-agar flakes
3 T. honey

2 C. strawberries, sliced
2 bananas, sliced
1 T. fresh lemon juice

Dissolve the agar-agar in the juice by bringing to a boil and simmer on low for about 5 minutes. Cool, add the strawberries, bananas, honey and lemon juice. Chill in a mold. Serves 6.

SUMMER SALAD

*4 peaches, scrubbed but
     not peeled*
1 C. whole strawberries
1 C. whole raspberries
1/2 C. finely chopped celery

1/4 C. pecans, chopped
1 T. honey
*1/2 C. heavy cream
     (optional)*

Mix fruit and nuts. Drizzle honey. Whip cream and fold into fruit.

WINTER FRUIT SALAD #1

2 Red Delicious apples
4 ripe bananas
1/2 fresh pineapple

2 pears
1/2 C. pecans

Dice apples, slice bananas, dice pineapple and pears. Add chopped nuts.

Dressing:

1/4 C. undiluted frozen orange juice
1 T. almond butter
4 oz. cream cheese

together and fold into fruit mixture. Serves 4.

WINTER FRUIT SALAD #2

2 C. fresh pineapple
1 C. bananas
1 C. strawberries

1/2 C. fresh coconut
1/4 C. chopped almonds
1/4 tsp. cardamom

Blend 1/2 cup of yogurt mixed with pineapple juice to sweeten and add to the salad.

YOGURT AND FRUIT

2 C. yogurt
2 C. frozen or fresh
      blueberries or
      strawberries
2 ripe bananas, sliced

1 apple, grated
Pure maple syrup
1/2 C. almonds, ground

Fold fruit into yogurt, sweeten with maple syrup to taste. Garnish with ground almonds.

VEGETABLE SALADS

ALFALFA AND ARTICHOKE SALAD

2 C. alfalfa sprouts
1 C. Jersualem artichokes,
    sliced
1 C. tomatoes, sliced
    lengthwise

1 small avocado, diced
1 small green pepper, diced
1 C. carrots, grated
1 C. celery, chopped

ARTICHOKE SALAD

1 pkg. frozen artichoke
    hearts
1 cucumber
4 small tomatoes
1 C. raw mushrooms
1/2 C. black olives,
    sliced

3 small green onions,
    sliced
1/4 C. sunflower seeds
1/4 C. sesame seeds
1/2 C. cheese

Combine all together. Good with Italian dressing or one or your choice.

BEET SALAD

2 C. red cabbage, shredded
1 C. beets, grated, raw
1 C. carrots, grated

1 C. parsnips, grated
1 C. watercress
2 T. parsley, minced

Arrange the shredded cabbage on a platter. Stir French dressing separately with carrots, parsnips and beets, and place them separately on the cabbage bed. Sprinkle parsley and watercress on the top.

CABBAGE SALAD

1-1/2 C. shredded red
    cabbage
1/4 C. red onion, sliced
    thin
1 small tomato, chopped

1/4 C. chopped parsley
1/4 C. oil and vinegar
    dressing

Toss and marinate in refrigerator for three hours.

CABBAGE SLAW

1 small purple cabbage, grated
1 small purple onion, sliced thin
1/2 C. radish sprouts

Toss all together and serve with your favorite dressing.

CARROT SALAD

2 C. carrots, grated   *1/4 C. ripe olives, chopped*
1/2 C. pine nuts, ground   *2 green onions, chopped*

Mix all together and moisten with homemade mayonnaise. Serve on a bed of red leaf lettuce.

CARROT RAISIN SALAD

2 C. grated carrots   *4 T. ground sunflower seeds*
1/2 C. raisins   *2 C. romaine lettuce,*
                              chopped

Place whole leaves of lettuce around flat salad bowl. Mix all ingredients together including 2 cups chopped romaine lettuce.

Dressing:

1 C. plain yogurt mixed with a squirt of lemon and 2 T. raw honey.

CAULIFLOWER SALAD

2 C. cauliflower, chopped   *1/2 C. radishes*
1/2 C. almonds, ground   *Kelp to taste*

Mix all ingredients together and moisten with homemade mayonnaise or mock mayonnaise.

CELERY SALAD

2 C. celery, chopped   *2 T. pimentos*
1 C. carrots, grated   *2 green onions*

Mix all together and fold in mock sour cream dressing. Serve on a bed of leaf lettuce.

CABBAGE AND NUT SALAD

1 small head cabbage
1 C. pecans, ground
1 C. celery, chopped

Chill cabbage in ice water, drain and mix all together and moisten with homemade mayonnaise.

GARBANZO BEAN SALAD

1 C. cooked garbanzo
*   beans*
1/2 C. chopped celery
1/2 C. chopped green
*   peppers*
1 C. sharp cheese

2 T. canned pimento
1 T. chopped onions, red
1/2 tsp. dry mustard
Mayonnaise to moisten

Mix all ingredients together. Stir in just enough homemade mayonnaise to moisten.

FRESH SALAD

3 C. leaf lettuce
1 C. endive
3 large tomatoes, ripe
1 bunch watercress

2 ripe avocados
1 C. (medium can) ripe
*   olives cut in rings*

Dressing:

1/2 C. homemade
*   mayonnaise*
1/2 C. plain yogurt
2 T. chopped fresh olives

2 T. chopped fresh parsley
1 tsp. dried basil
1/4 C. grated cheddar cheese

FRESH AVOCADO SALAD

2 C. fresh corn, off cob
1 large avocado, diced
2 small tomatoes, diced
1/4 C. green pepper,
    diced

1 T. olive oil
1 tsp. cider vinegar
Kelp and broth seasoning
    to taste

Blend all ingredients together and serve on a bed of leaf lettuce. Top with homemade mayonnaise or salsa.

FRESH CORN SALAD

2 fresh ears sweet corn,
    cut off the cob
1 C. fresh diced tomatoes
1 C. grated zucchini
2 chopped green onions

1/4 C. chopped green
    peppers
1/4 tsp. thyme
1/4 tsp. marjoram
1/4 tsp. paprika
Dash of kelp

GARBANZO SALAD

4 C. romaine and leaf
    lettuce
1 C. garbanzo beans,
    cooked

1/4 C. parsley
1 large tomato
1/4 C. green onions

Toss and serve with vinaigrette dressing.

GARDEN SALAD

3 C. leaf lettuce
1/2 C. fresh peas, shelled
1/2 C. carrots, grated
1/2 C. zucchini, grated

1 C. mung bean sprouts
1 cucumber, sliced
1/2 avocado
1/2 C. mixed sunflower
    seeds and ground
    almonds

Mix all ingredients together. Serve with herb dressing or dressing of your choice. You can top with sliced mushrooms.

GREEK SALAD

1 C. spinach
2 C. leaf lettuce
1 C. feta cheese, diced
1 C. black olives, sliced

1 small cucumber, sliced
2 tomatoes, sliced length-
    wise
1/2 green pepper

Toss all together and add 2 T. olive oil, 2 T. wine vinegar and sesame salt to taste.

GREEN BEAN SALAD

2 C. steamed, fresh
    green beans
1 small onion, sliced
    thin

1 cucumber, sliced thin
1 C. mock sour cream
2 T. lemon juice

Combine all ingredients together. Chill before serving.

JERUSALEM ARTICHOKE SALAD

2 C. grated Jerusalem
    artichokes
3 stalks celery, diced

1/4 C. parsley
3 carrots, grated
1 green onion, sliced

Lemon Oil Dressing:

1/2 C. olive oil
2 T. fresh lemon juice
1 T. honey

1 tsp. lemon rind, grated
1/4 tsp. kelp
1/2 tsp. paprika

Blend all ingredients together.

LAYERED VEGETABLE SALAD

This is a complete salad meal. It contains easily digestible quality protein along with vitamins, minerals and live enzymes.

*4 C. romaine and
  leaf lettuce
1/2 C. ground sunflower
  seeds
1 C. buckwheat sprouts
1 small cucumber, diced*

*1 large tomato
1 small green pepper
1 avocado
1 C. alfalfa sprouts*

Use salad oil with fresh lemon juice for the dressing.

Break up the lettuce and use half of it on the bottom of a salad bowl. Layer half of the other ingredients, add the rest of the lettuce and then another layer of the same ingredients.

LEAF LETTUCE SALAD

*1 C. green leaf lettuce
1/2 C. fenugreek sprouts
1/2 C. red clover sprouts*

*1/2 C. red cabbage, grated
1/4 C. turnips, grated*

LENTIL SALAD

*2 C. lentils, cooked and
  drained
3 T. apple cider vinegar
2 T. olive oil*

*1 T. parsley, minced
1 onion, chopped
1 celery stalk, chopped
1 tsp. kelp*

Marinate lentils overnight in oil, vinegar and kelp. Combine other ingredients with lentil mixture and chill. Serve with chopped salad green and sprouts

LIMA BEAN SALAD

*2 C. cooked lima beans
4 hard boiled eggs,
  mashed
1 C. chopped celery
1/2 tsp. chili powder*

*1/4 C. chopped green pepper
4 tsp. chopped onions
1/2 C. homemade
  mayonnaise*

Add all ingredients together and mix well. Chill before serving.

OLIVE AND PEPPER SALAD

1 C. chopped green bell
    peppers
1/2 C. chopped sweet red
    peppers
1/4 C. chopped black
    olives

1/4 C. chopped green onions
1 C. chopped celery
1/2 C. radishes

PINTO BEAN SALAD

2 C. pinto beans, cooked
4 T. hot chili sauce
1/4 C. bell peppers,
    chopped
1/2 C. Bermuda onion,
    chopped
1/2 C. black olives,
    chopped

1/4 C. homemade
    mayonnaise
1/4 C. apple cider vinegar
1/4 C. chopped celery
1 T. pimiento, chopped
1/2 tsp. kelp

Mix all together, chill until ready to serve.

POCKET BREAD FILLING

1 C. raw corn or steamed
    lightly
1/2 C. chopped tomatoes
1/2 C. chopped green
    peppers
1/4 C. red onion, chopped

2 T. chopped parsley
2 T. chopped watercress
1/2 C. cheese (from health
    store)
1/2 C. chopped ripe olives

Mix all ingredients together. Blend 1/4 C. fresh lemon juice
or cider vinegar, 1/8 tsp. dry mustard and 2 T. cold-pressed oil. Mix
with filling. Serve in pocket bread. Makes filling for 4 pocket breads.

POTATO SALAD

6 medium potatoes,
    boiled
1 C. grated carrots

1 C. cooked green beans
1 small red onion, chopped
1 C. chopped celery

Dice potatoes with skins on, cut raw carrots in small pieces. Cut cooked green beans lengthwise.

Dressing:

1 clove garlic, crushed
1-1/2 T. vegetable oil
1 T. lemon juice
1 T. thyme
1 C. chopped fresh
    mushrooms

1 T. chopped chives
1/2 C. plain yogurt
1/4 C. buttermilk
2 T. mayonnaise
1 T. prepared mustard
Kelp to taste

Sauté garlic in oil. Add mushrooms. Add lemon juice and thyme.

Combine all other ingredients. Cool sautéed mixture. Mix all together and serve over potato salad

POTATO AVOCADO SALAD

2 C. cooked diced potatoes
    with skins on
1 C. diced avocado
4 grated hard cooked
    egg yolks
1/2 C. chopped celery

1 C. peas, very lightly
    steamed
1/2 tsp. sesame kelp salt
Dash cayenne pepper

Moisten salad with mayonnaise and a dash or two or white vinegar. Garnish with sprouts, cherry tomatoes and radishes.

SEED AND VEGETABLE SALAD

3 C. leaf lettuce
1 C. watercress
1 C. alfalfa sprouts
1/2 C. grated carrots
1/2 C. grated raw beets
1/2 C. red cabbage
1/2 C. chopped celery

2 medium tomatoes, chopped
1 corn on cob, cut off
1/4 C. fresh peas or frozen
1/2 C. sunflower seeds
1/4 C. sesame seeds
1/4 C. pine nuts
Handful parsley

SPRING SALAD

1 C. watercress
1 C. dandelion greens
1/2 C. wheat sprouts
1 small red onion

1/4 C. Jerusalem artichokes,
  grated
Bunch parsley leaves

Wash greens and pat dry. Tear into small pieces. Grate artichokes into salad. Chop onion and serve with oil and lemon dressing.

SPROUT SALAD

1 C. alfalfa sprouts
1/2 C. lentil sprouts
1/2 C. watercress, minced

1 C. yogurt
1 T. tamari sauce
1 tsp. kelp

Toss all together and serve chilled.

SPROUT AND SEED SALAD

1 avocado
1 cucumber
2 C. mung sprouts
1 C. alfalfa sprouts
1/2 C. radish sprouts
2 C. leaf lettuce

1 summer squash
8 T. sunflower seeds
2 T. sesame seeds
2 ripe tomatoes
Kelp to taste
Olive oil

Toss all together and add kelp, olive oil and a little lemon juice to taste. Makes 4 servings.

RAW BEET SALAD

4 large beets
1 C. alfalfa sprouts
2 C. romaine lettuce

1/4 C. radish sprouts
1/2 C. mung bean sprouts

Grate the beets fine and toss with greens and add herb dressing.

STUFFED PEPPERS

2 large green peppers
    cut in half
1/2 C. celery, chopped
1 C. watercress, chopped
1 tomato, chopped

3 green onions, chopped
1 C. peas, fresh or frozen
2 hard cooked egg yolks
Homemade mayonnaise to
    moisten

Prepare green peppers and chill in cold water for a few hours. Mix all other ingredients together and fill the green pepper halves just before ready to eat.

SUMMER SALAD

1 C. fresh peas
4 carrots, thinly sliced
3 celery stalks, thinly
    sliced
6 radishes, sliced
1 green pepper, thinly
    sliced
6 green onions with stems
Kelp to taste

2 ears corn, cut off cob
4 C. cooked new potatoes,
    diced
1 C. lightly steamed green
    beans
Boston lettuce leaves
2 hard boiled eggs (optional)
3 large tomatoes, cut in
    thin slices

Add all ingredients together except the eggs and tomatoes. Chill in refrigerator. Toss all ingredients with herb vinaigrette dressing. Add kelp to taste.

Arrange mixture into salad bowl lined with washed lettuce leaves. Garnish top with chopped eggs or ground sunflower seeds. Garnish with sliced tomatoes.

SUPREME COLE SLAW

1 C. red cabbage, grated
1 C. green cabbage, grated
1 C. Jerusalem artichokes,
    grated
1 C. carrots, grated

1/2 C. celery, chopped
1/2 C. almonds, ground
2 T. fresh lemon juice
3 T. olive oil

Add all vegetables together and toss. Add olive oil and lemon juice. Toss and serve.

TOMATOES AND SPROUTS

1 C. alfalfa sprouts
1 C. fenugreek sprouts
1 small grated beet

2 small diced tomatoes
1/2 C. green peppers

VEGETABLE CORN CHIP SALAD

3 C. torn lettuce, leaf
2 medium diced ripe
    tomatoes
1/4 C. green onions
1 7-oz. can mild green
    chiles, diced
1-1/4 C. cooked pinto beans
1 C. grated cheese, mild

1 C. ripe avocado (optional)
1 C. fresh corn, cut off cob
1/2 C. diced ripe olives
2 C. corn chips, unsalted
    and crushed

Dressing:

1/4 C. yogurt
1/4 C. sour cream

4 T. French dressing
1 T. chili powder

WATERCRESS SALAD

1 bunch watercress
1/4 C. carrots, grated
1/4 C. almonds, ground

6 radishes, sliced
1/4 C. sesame seeds, ground

Blend all ingredients together after washing watercress thoroughly and serve with natural Italian dressing.

WINTER VEGETABLE SALAD

2 C. romaine lettuce
2 C. leaf lettuce
1 C. red cabbage
1 C. cauliflower
1 C. broccoli
1 C. grated carrots

1 red pepper
1 green pepper
1 grated beet
1/4 C. green onion with tops
1/2 C. ground sunflower seeds

Italian Dressing:

3/4 C. cold pressed oil
1/4 C. fresh lemon juice
1/2 tsp. kelp

1/2 tsp. paprika
1 clove garlic, sliced

Add all ingredients in a jar. Shake well and let sit for awhile so garlic penetrates into oil. You can discard garlic before serving, or it can be eaten.

MAIN MEATLESS DISHES

ALMOND LOAF

1 C. finely ground
  almonds
4 medium potatoes
1 medium onion
1 grated carrot
4 T. butter

2 egg yolks
1 C. powdered milk
1 C. mushrooms
Vegetable seasoning

Sauté onion and sliced mushrooms in butter. Wash and grate potatoes, skin on; mix all ingredients together and pour into a greased 9 x 5 loaf pan. Bake at 350°F for 1 hour.

BAKED RICE AND MILLET

1-1/2 C. cooked brown
  rice
1/2 C. cooked millet
2 eggs, beaten
2 C. milk

2 T. butter
1 T. tamari soy sauce
1 C. chopped almonds
1/4 C. chopped sunflower
  seeds

Mix all ingredients. Pour into 1-1/2 quart casserole dish. Bake 30 minutes at 350°F.

BARLEY NUT CASSEROLE

1 C. barley
1/2 C. chopped almonds
1/2 C. fresh mushrooms
2 T. chopped parsley
2 C. vegetable broth

1/2 C. green onions
2 T. butter
1 T. miso (soybean paste)
1 T. apricot kernels, ground

Sauté mushrooms and onions gently. Place in casserole with all other ingredients. Bake in oven, covered, for 45 minutes at 350°F. (or until barley is tender). Serve with a fresh vegetable salad.

BEAN BURGERS

2 C. pinto beans, cooked
1 C. brown rice, cooked
2 eggs
2 cloves garlic, pressed
1/4 C. wheat germ
1/4 C. sunflower seeds,
    ground

1/4 C. almonds, ground
2 T. wheat bran
Season wheat bran with
    vegetable salt, kelp
    or miso

Mix all ingredients together. Roll patties in wheat bran. Fry in a small amount of oil. May use as burger patties or serve with nut milk gravy.

BEAN BURGERS #2

2 C. pinto beans, cooked
1 C. cooked barley, ground
1/2 C. whole wheat bread
    crumbs

2 T. chopped onions
1/2 C. mild cheese, grated
2 T. vegetable seasoning

Mash beans and add remaining ingredients. Make into patties and place on a buttered cookie sheet and bake at 400°F for 10 minutes. Turn patties over and bake another 10 minutes. Makes about 8 patties.

BEAN LOAF

1 C. pinto or lima beans,
    cooked
1/2 C. garbanzo beans
    cooked
3 T. butter
1 C. onions, chopped
1 C. carrots, grated
1/4 C. mushrooms,
    chopped

1/2 C. mung bean sprouts
2 eggs, beaten
1 tsp. savory
1/2 tsp. rosemary
1/4 C. tahini
1/2 C. cashews, ground
1 tsp. vegetable seasoning

Sauté mushrooms and onions in butter. Mix all ingredients together and pour into a buttered loaf pan. Cook for 1 hour at 35(̄ Serve with fresh tomato sauce and brown rice. Serves 4 to 6.

BEAN AND MILLET SUPPER

1 C. pinto beans, cooked
1 C. millet, cooked
1/4 C. almonds, ground
3 T. butter
1 C. onions, chopped
1 C. mushrooms, chopped
1/2 C. green peppers

1/2 C. celery, chopped
1 tsp. vegetable broth
    seasoning
3 tsp. lemon juice
1/8 tsp. rosemary
1/8 tsp. sage

Sauté with butter the onions, peppers, mushrooms and celery. Add seasonings and lemon juice with 1/2 cup of water. Cook on low heat for about 10 minutes. Add beans, millet and almonds. Serves 4 generously.

BEAN SUPREME

2 C. cooked pinto beans
1/2 C. chopped onions
1/2 C. green peppers
2 cloves garlic, pressed
2 T. olive oil

8 oz. tomato puree
1/4 C. parsley
1/2 tsp. marjoram leaves,
    crushed
1/2 tsp. paprika

Sauté onions, green peppers and garlic in olive oil. Stir all ingredients together and simmer covered for about 30 minutes.

BEANS, CROCK POT STYLE

1/2 lb. white navy beans
1 C. pure water
1/2 C. molasses
1/4 C. tamari (soy sauce)

2 tsp. dry mustard
1/2 C. honey
1 large onion, minced
1/2 tsp. kelp

Combine all ingredients and cook on low heat in a crock pot until done about 10 hours.

BEAN LOAF

2 C. cooked pinto beans,
    blended
1/2 C. cooked millet,
    blended
1/4 C. tomato sauce

1/2 C. chopped onions
1 tsp. mineral salt
1 tsp. kelp

Combine ingredients together and pour in an oiled loaf pan.
Baste with oil occasionally. Bake at 350°F. for about 45 minutes.

BROCCOLI QUICHE

2 C. broccoli
1 C. fresh sliced
    mushrooms
1/2 C. onions, chopped
1 clove garlic, pressed
2 T. butter
6 eggs, beaten

1 C. half & half
2-1/2 C. Swiss cheese,
    grated
1/2 tsp. mineral salt
1/8 tsp. nutmeg
1 tsp. basil
1/4 C. minced parsley
Dash of vegetable seasoning

Sauté broccoli, onions, mushroom in butter. Cook until
onions are transparent. Mix eggs, cream, cheese, salt, nutmeg, basil,
parsley and vegetable seasoning. Mix all ingredients in a buttered two
quart casserole. Bake for 30 minutes at 350°F.

BUCKWHEAT GROATS

2 C. buckwheat groats
2 eggs, lightly beaten

1 tsp. vegetable salt
4 C. pure water, boiled

Cook groats and eggs in a heavy skillet over a high heat for a
few minutes. Stir constantly to keep eggs from sticking. Add boiling
water and reduce heat and simmer, covered, for about 30 minutes. Add
vegetable salt before serving.

BULGHUR PILAF

1 C. bulghur
1/2 C. butter
1/2 onion, chopped
1 clove garlic

2 C. vegetable broth
1/4 lb. sliced mushrooms

Melt butter and sauté onions and garlic and mushrooms. Add bulghur, hot vegetable broth and kelp or mineral salt to taste. Bring to a boil, lower heat and cook for 30 minutes.

BULGHUR PILAF

1 C. bulghur
3 T. butter or ghee
2 T. chopped green onions

2 C. vegetable broth
1/2 tsp. kelp or mineral
    salt

Sauté bulghur and onions in butter and cook until golden brown. Add vegetable broth and seasonings. Bring to boil and reduce heat to simmer and cook for 15 minutes. Serve with a vegetable salad.

CHEESE ENCHILADAS

12 corn tortillas
2 C. mild cheese, grated
1/2 C. onions
1 small can diced green
    chiles
1 tall can enchilada sauce

1 small can tomato sauce
1 pint sour cream or mock
    sour cream
Black olives (optional),
    sprinkle on top

Heat enchilada sauce and tomato sauce and add 1 small can of water. Mix the cheese, onions and chiles. Dip tortilla in the hot sauce mix to soften. Place about 2 T. of the cheese mixture on tortilla, top with a heaping tablespoon of sour cream; roll the tortilla and place seam side down and put in a baking dish. When all tortillas are rolled up pour the rest of the enchilada sauce on the top and sprinkle top with cheese and olives. Bake in 350°F. oven for about 30 minutes.

CHILI BEANS

1 C. dried pinto beans
2 C. water
1 T. cold pressed oil
1 large onion, chopped
1 clove garlic, minced
1 green bell pepper,
    minced

1 qt. canned tomatoes or
    Tomato Supreme
1 T. chili powder
1 tsp. paprika
1 T. blackstrap molasses
1/2 tsp. cumin

Presoak beans over night. Throw away the soaking water. Add boiling water to cover and cook for at least 30 minutes. Discard the cooking water. This gets rid of the tri-saccharides that are the culprit that causes gas.

Add fresh water (about 2 cups or more) and resume cooking until done. Add remaining ingredients and continue to cook for about 1 hour.

COTTAGE CHEESE BALLS

1 C. cottage cheese
4 oz. cream cheese
1/2 C. cheddar cheese,
    grated

1 T. pimentos
1/2 C. ripe olives, chopped

Cream cottage cheese and cream cheese; then mix all ingredients together. Form into small balls and roll in chopped parsley or watercress and serve on bed of lettuce with carrots and celery sticks.

DAL

3 C. pure water
1 C. dried lentils
1 tsp. mineral salt (or
    sesame kelp salt)
1 tsp. turmeric
1 onion, chopped

2 cloves garlic, minced
1 tsp. cumin
1/4 tsp. cardamom, ground
2 T. ghee or melted butter
Juice of 1 lemon

Rinse and clean lentils. Bring water to boil and add lentils. Lower heat and simmer, covered, for 45 minutes.

Heat ghee in a small frying pan and sauté the onion and garlic until a golden color. Add turmeric, cardamom, cumin, salt (or kelp) and cook for 1 minute. Add onion mixture to lentils when done; continue to simmer for about 15 minutes. The lemon juice is to be added just before serving. Serve over brown rice or millet.

ENCHILADA CASSEROLE

1 pkg. corn tortillas
2 C. enchilada sauce
1 pt. mock sour cream
1 can chopped green chiles

1 can sliced black olives
4 small green onions
2 C. grated cheese

Soften tortillas in cold pressed oil or steam to soften. Pour about 1/2 C. enchilada sauce into a glass dish. Place a layer of tortillas over the sauce. In a bowl, mix the mock sour cream, grated cheese, olives, onions and chiles. Spoon this mixture over tortillas in dish. Top with 1/2 C. enchilada sauce. Add second layer of tortillas. Pour the remaining enchilada sauce over the casserole. Cover and bake at 350°F. for about 20 minutes. Serve in squares.

Enchilada Sauce:

1 small can tomato paste
1/2 C. vegetable broth
1 can green chili salsa

2 tsp. chili powder
1 tsp. paprika
1/4 tsp. cumin

Mix all ingredients together and simmer for 15 minutes.

FRESH VEGETABLE CASSEROLE

2 C. cooked millet
1 C. grated cheddar cheese
1 medium fresh tomato,
    cut in chunks
1/2 medium green pepper

4 small green onions
1/4 C. chopped parsley
1/4 C. chopped almonds
1/2 C. sour cream for top

Fold all the ingredients into the cooked millet except the sour cream. Spread sour cream on top of mixture. Put in oven at 350°F. long enough for the cheese to melt. This dish makes a complete meal, and each cup of millet gives you almost your daily requirement of protein.

This recipe is packed full of protein, vitamins and minerals. It is very filling. Millet does not put fat on like wheat does. Millet should be used often while you are losing and maintaining your weight.

GARBANZO BEAN FILLING

1 C. cooked garbanzo beans	*2 T. fresh lemon juice*
1 clove garlic, minced	*1 T. sesame tahini*
Dash kelp and cayenne	*Chopped parsley*

Mix cooked beans with all other ingredients. Add tomatoes, radishes, watercress, olives, onions and cheese. Add lemon juice. Serve in pocket bread.

GARBANZO STEW

1 qt. Tomato Supreme or	*1 C. potatoes, skins on*
tomatoes	*1/4 C. millet*
1 qt. pure water	*1 tsp. mineral salt*
1 C. garbanzo beans	*1 T. vegetable powder*
1 C. carrots	

Soak garbanzo beans overnight in 2 cups water. Cook beans in 1 quart Tomato Supreme or tomatoes (canned), and one quart of water. Cook until tender. Add millet and cook thirty minutes. Add chopped carrots, diced potatoes, salt and vegetable powder.

KASHA

1 C. buckwheat	*2 C. water*
1/4 C. butter or ghee	*3 T. honey*
1 large onion, chopped	*3 T. vinegar*
3 medium cloves garlic,	*3 T. tamari*
minced	*1 tsp. vegetable seasoning*
1/4 lb. mushrooms, sliced	

Sauté onion and mushrooms. Add buckwheat, water, honey, vinegar and tamari. Boil, then lower heat and cook for 30 minutes.

LENTIL AND NUT LOAF

2 C. cooked lentils	*1 tsp. garlic, minced*
1 C. cooked millet	*1 egg*
2 medium onions, chopped	*1/2 C. almond milk*
1 C. fresh tomatoes,	*1 tsp. kelp or mineral salt*
blended	
1/2 C. almonds, ground	

Sauté onion in olive oil. Blend lentils, add onions and tomatoes. Mix all other ingredients and pour into oiled loaf pan. Sprinkle parmesan cheese on top. Bake at 350°F. for 30 minutes.

LIMA BEAN ROAST

2 C. lima beans, cooked	1 C. ripe tomatoes
1 C. walnuts, ground	2 T. olive oil
3 green onions	1 tsp. kelp or mineral salt

Blend all together in blender and place in buttered loaf pan. Bake at 350°F. for 45 minutes. Baste with lemon juice and unsalted butter.

MILLET NUT LOAF

2 C. cooked millet	1 medium onion
1 C. walnuts, almonds, pecans ground fine	1 egg
	1/4 C. red pepper
2 tsp. vegetable seasoning broth	4 medium ripe tomatoes

Blend together and bake in oven at 350°F for one hour. Serve with homemade tomato sauce.

MOZZARELLA AND ALMOND PATTIES

1 C. millet, cooked and blended	1/4 C. green peppers, chopped
3 C. mozzarella cheese	2 T. onions, chopped
1/4 C. rice bran	1 T. celery, chopped
1/4 C. butter, melted	1 tsp. vegetable seasoning broth
2 T. parsley, minced	1 tsp. Italian seasoning
4 eggs, beaten	4 T. almond milk, or raw milk

Mix all ingredients together and form into patties. Bake in oven at 350°F for 30 minutes. Serve with fresh tomato sauce.

NUT BURGERS

Sauté the following:

3 T. butter
1 onion, chopped
1/4 C. fresh parsley,
    minced
1/4 C. red pepper, chopped
1 T. sesame salt

1 clove garlic, minced
1 tsp. sweet basil
1/2 tsp. rosemary
1/8 tsp. sage
1/8 tsp. thyme

Grind the following nuts and seeds finely and add to sautéed vegetables:

1/2 C. almonds
1/4 C. sunflower seeds

1/4 C. pecans
1/4 C. sesame seeds

Add:

1/4 C. sesame milk
2 eggs, beaten

1 C. cheddar cheese, grated
1/2 C. jack cheese, grated

Combine all ingredients thoroughly and shape into patties. Bake in the oven at 350°F. for about 20 minutes. Serve on whole wheat hamburger buns.

PECAN CELERY PATTIES

1 C. pecans
6 stalks celery
3 T. ripe olives
3 green onions

1/4 C. watercress
1/4 C. parsley
1 avocado
Dash of sage or kelp (more
    if needed)

Grind celery, onions, parsley and watercress. Drain the juice. Grind the pecans fine and mash the avocado, chop the olives; combine all together and shape into patties. Serve on red leaf lettuce and top with paprika and 1 whole olive.

PECAN CHEESE BALLS

4 oz. cream cheese,
    softened
2 T. softened butter
1 C. grated natural cheese
    (health store)

1 T. chopped olives
1 T. pimientos
1 C. finely chopped pecans

Mix cream cheese and butter together. Stir in cheese, olives and pimientos. Chill in refrigerator for 2 to 3 hours. Shape into 1" balls or into one large ball and serve with whole wheat crackers. Roll in chopped pecans. Keep in refrigerator until ready to serve.

PINTO BEAN STEW

2 C. pinto beans, cooked
4 C. vegetable broth
1 C. carrots, sliced
1/2 C. broccoli, sliced
1/2 C. zucchini
1/2 C. celery, sliced
3 large tomatoes, peeled
    and chopped

1/4 C. clarified butter or
    olive oil
1/4 C. millet
1/4 C. brown rice
1 T. vegetable seasoning
1 T. kelp

Sauté onions and garlic in butter or oil in a large stew pan. Add all ingredients and water if needed. Bring to a boil, reduce heat and simmer about 45 minutes until rice and millet are cooked.

POTATO SUPREME

Bake 1 potato for each person.

In a saucepan sauté 2 cups mushrooms in 4 tablespoons butter with one clove minced garlic. Simmer lightly; do not let mushrooms get soggy.

Open up potatoes; put in butter, grated cheese, sour cream, chopped black olives and chopped chives. Top with sautéed mushrooms. Use your imagination for baked potatoes (chili, stroganoff, etc).

RAW NUT LOAF

1 C. almonds, ground
1/4 C. oats
1 T. parsley, chopped

1 T. celery, chopped
1 tsp. paprika

Moisten with cashew cream. Press into a mold and chill for several hours. Serve with a fresh vegetable salad or fruit salad.

REFRIED BEANS

3 C. cooked pinto beans
1 C. chopped onions

3 T. cold pressed oil
Kelp to taste

Sauté onions in oil until soft. Stir in beans and mash. Cook slowly for about 5 minutes, stirring. Serve alone or use to make burritos with mock sour cream and grated cheese wrapped in flour tortillas.

RICE AND NUT CASSEROLE

2-1/2 C. vegetable stock
1 C. brown rice
1/4 C. ground sesame
    seeds
1/2 C. fresh corn

1 C. chopped tomatoes
2 T. sweet basil
1/2 C. chopped almonds
4 chopped green onions

Sauté onions in 1 tablespoon olive oil; add stock and bring to boil. Stir rice slowly. Reduce heat and simmer for about 45 minutes. Add corn, sesame seeds, tomatoes, basil and almonds. Simmer for about 15 minutes more.

SEED LOAF

1-1/2 C. sunflower seeds
1/2 C. sesame seeds
1 C. carrots, grated

1 small red pepper, chopped
1/4 C. parsley, minced
3 medium ripe tomatoes,
    chopped

Soak the seeds overnight in rejuvelac. Grind seeds. Mix all ingredients together and season with olive oil, 1 clove pressed garlic, dash of rosemary, basil and ground caraway seeds (more if needed). Form into a loaf. Use raw tomato sauce for topping.

SOYBEAN AND BULGHUR CASSEROLE

1/2 C. dried soybeans
1 C. bulghur wheat
1 C. boiling water
2 T. olive oil
1 onion, chopped
1 quart tomatoes or
    Tomato Supreme

1 green pepper, chopped
Kelp or mineral salt to taste
1/2 tsp. cayenne pepper
2 T. parsley, minced
2 C. feta cheese, crumbled
1 tsp. cumin

Soak soybeans in water to cover overnight. Drain and put beans in blender and add 1 cup fresh water and blend until smooth. Pour 1 cup boiling water over bulghur and set aside.

Preheat oven to 350°F. Heat oil in skillet and sauté onion and green pepper until tender. Add soybeans, then bulghur, kelp, cayenne and parsley.

Oil a three quart casserole and spread half the mixture in the bottom, sprinkle half the cheese. Combine the tomatoes and cumin and spread half over the cheese. Repeat the soybeans mixture, cheese then tomatoes. Cover and bake 1 hour. Uncover and cook 10 minutes longer. Serves 8.

SPANISH MILLET LOAF

2 C. cooked millet	2 beaten eggs
1 C. whole wheat bread crumbs	2 T. vegetable seasoning
	1 C. ground almonds
1 small can green chiles	2 T. olive oil
1 C. canned tomatoes	1 tsp. chili powder

Combine all ingredients together. Pour into a buttered loaf pan. Cook for 45 minutes at 350°F. While cooking baste with butter two or three times. It may be served with uncooked salsa.

STUFFED PEPPERS

6 green peppers, large	1 C. almonds, ground fine
2 T. butter or ghee	1 C. cheese, grated
4 small onions	4 eggs, beaten
1 C. cooked brown rice	Vegetable seasoning to taste
1 C. cooked millet	

Remove the pulp and seeds of the peppers. Sauté onions in butter. Mix all the other ingredients with the onions and butter. Stuff each pepper until full. Arrange the peppers open end up in a baking dish. Pour water into the dish to barely cover the bottom. Bake for 30 minutes at 350°F. Leftover stuffing can be used for a casserole.

STUFFED PUMPKIN

2-4 lb. pumpkin or acorn squash	1 C. green apples
2 C. brown rice (cooked)	1 C. ground walnuts
1 C. wild rice (cooked)	1 tsp. poultry seasoning
2 C. whole wheat bread crumbs	1-1/2 tsp. vegetable broth
1 large onion, chopped	1/2 C. butter or cold pressed oil
1 C. chopped celery with tops	Soy sauce to taste
	Mineral salt or vegetable seasoning

Combine all dry ingredients. Sauté onions and celery in butter or oil and mix well. Add soy sauce and salt (or vegetable seasoning). Add all together. The stuffing should be moist. If you like a drier stuffing use less liquid.

Cut the top off the pumpkin. Remove the seeds and any stringy pulp. Pack the stuffing loosely in the pumpkin. Put the lid on the pumpkin and bake on an oiled baking sheet for about 1-1/2 hours at 325°F.

When you serve the stuffed pumpkin, scoop out the pumpkin along with the stuffing.

TABOOLEY

2 C. sprouted wheat berries	2 C. leaf lettuce
2 cucumbers	3 large tomatoes
1 bunch parsley	6 small green onions

Mix all ingredients together. Serve on a romaine lettuce leaf.

THANKSGIVING NUT LOAF

2 C. cooked millet	1 egg
1 C. pecans, ground fine	1/2 C. red pepper
1 T. vegetable seasoning broth	4 large ripe tomatoes
1 medium onion, grated	2 T. ground or soaked chia seeds

Blend all ingredients together. Pour into bread loaf pan and bake for 1 hour at 350°F. It can be served with homemade ketchup or tomato sauce, or with a mushroom sauce.

The millet is an alkaline cereal with large amounts of iron, magnesium, potassium and protein.

TOSTADOES

12 corn tortillas
Cold pressed oil
Refried beans (warmed)
1 onion, chopped
3 medium fresh tomatoes,
    chopped

1-1/2 C. grated cheddar
    cheese
1-1/2 C. shredded leaf
    lettuce
1/4 C. chopped green chiles
1/2 C. black olives

Brush the tortillas with oil and place on a cookie sheet. Cook until crisp in a 400°F. oven for about 5 minutes. Turn once. Remove from oven. Cover each tortilla almost to the edge with warmed refried beans. Top beans with onions, tomato, cheese, green chiles, olives and lettuce. Top with sour cream and guacamole

TOFU AND VEGETABLES

12 oz. pkg. tofu
4 T. butter
1 C. carrots, sliced thin
2 green peppers, sliced
    thin
1 C. water chestnuts,
    sliced
1/2 C. onions, sliced thin
1 C. mung bean sprouts

1/4 tsp. kelp
3 T. tamari
1 T. honey
1 T. apple cider vinegar
1-1/2 T. arrowroot or
    cornstarch

Stir fry carrots, peppers, onions, water chestnuts and tofu for about 3 minutes in the butter. Add seasonings and sprouts just to heat through. Dissolve arrowroot in 1/4 cup of water and cook until thick. Serves 4.

BREADS

SESAME BREAD STICKS (Unleavened)

2 C. sifted whole wheat
    flour
1 T. date sugar or honey
1/2 tsp. sea salt (or omit)

3 T. cold pressed oil
1/2 tsp. cinnamon
3/4 C. cold water

    Add all ingredients together and stir well. Knead. Round up into little balls. Roll into pencil-like strips 8" long and 1/2" around. Place on a greased cookie sheet. Bake for 30 minutes at 350°F.

GRAHAM CRACKERS

2 C. whole wheat graham
    flour
1 C. whole wheat pastry
    flour
1/2 C. ground sesame seeds
2 T. arrowroot

1/2 C. cold pressed oil
1/2 tsp. kelp
1/2 C. water
1/2 C. molasses

    Work the oil into all the dry ingredients. Blend together the water and molasses. Knead the dough and roll out thin; cut into squares and prick with a fork. Bake at 300°F. for 25 minutes.

MILLET CRACKERS

1 T. dried yeast (bakers)
1/2 C. lukewarm water
1/2 C. hot water
1/2 C. dried apricots

1/2 C. dries light figs
1 C. cold pressed oil
3 C. millet flour
1 C. whole wheat pastry
    flour

    Pour the yeast in the lukewarm water. Pour the hot water in a blender and add apricots and figs; blend until fine. Combine yeast and fruit together. Stir in oil and the flours. Dough should be stiff; add more flour if needed. Roll out thin on floured board. Cut into squares. Place on oiled cookie sheet. Let stand for 15 minutes before baking at 300°F. for about 30 minutes.

ALMOND-SUNFLOWER SEED MUFFINS

*1 C. ground sunflower
    seeds
1 C. ground almonds
1/4 C. ground sesame seeds*

*1/2 C. wheat germ
1/2 C. rice polishings
1/2 C. unsweetened coconut*

Combine dry ingredients. Add the following ingredients but fold in egg whites last.

*3 egg yolks
2 T. honey
2-1/2 T. cold pressed oil*

*1 C. orange juice
3 beaten egg whites*

Fill greased muffin tins 3/4 full and bake at 350°F. for about 25 minutes.

BLUEBERRY MUFFINS

*1-3/4 C. whole wheat
    pastry flour
1/4 C. wheat germ
4 tsp. baking powder
    (aluminum free)
1/2 tsp. pure vanilla
1 tsp. sea salt*

*1 egg
6 T. cold pressed oil
1/4 C. honey
1 T. lecithin
1 C. sesame milk
1 C. blueberries (fresh
    or frozen)*

Blend all dry ingredients together. Beat egg, oil, honey and lecithin together and stir into dry ingredients. Add milk and fold in blueberries. Put in muffin tins. Bake for about 25 minutes at 375°F.

BANANA BREAD

*1 C. whole wheat flour
1/2 C. dried white figs
1/2 C. sunflower seeds,
    ground
1/4 C. sesame seeds,
    ground*

*1/2 C. honey
2 ripe bananas, mashed
1/2 tsp. cardamom*

Blend all ingredients together. Mix well; roll out in a thin layer on a cookie sheet. Cut into slices, dry for several hours.

CHAPATIS

1-1/2 C. whole wheat pastry flour
1/2 C. water--more if needed
1 T. cold pressed oil

Mix the flour, water and oil. Knead the dough until it is smooth and elastic. Pinch off the dough into balls. Should make about eight. Flatten the dough in the palm of your hand and roll it out on a floured surface into a circle about seven inches in diameter.

Use an iron or stainless heavy griddle. Cook each side until brown. Needs to be a hot pan and will dry out if it is not hot enough. Keep pan clean from burned flour before cooking another.

BRAN MUFFINS

1 C. bran
1-1/2 C. whole wheat
pastry flour
1-1/4 tsp. baking powder
(aluminum free)
1 egg, beaten

3/4 C. milk
1/4 C. honey
2 T. cold pressed oil
1 tsp. orange rind

Mix all ingredients together. Spoon batter into greased muffin tins. Bake for 20 minutes at 400°F or until muffins begin to pull away from pans. Makes 12 muffins.

For a special treat add a cup of grated fresh apples.

CHEESE CORN BREAD

2 eggs
1/4 C. cold pressed oil
2 T. minced onion
2 T. minced green pepper
2 tsp. baking powder

3/4 C. thick yogurt or
sour cream
1/4 C. ground sesame seeds
1 C. yellow corn meal
2 C. cheddar cheese, grated

Combine eggs and oil and blend well. Add all other ingredients and mix well. Grease an 8 x 8 pan and pour in batter and bake at 350°F. for about 40 minutes.

CORNBREAD

1 C. corn meal
1/2 C. whole wheat flour
1/2 tsp. baking powder
(aluminum free)
1/4 C. wheat germ
2 T. cold pressed oil

1/4 tsp. sea salt
1 egg
1/4 C. honey
1/2 C. yogurt

Mix oil, egg, honey and yogurt. Add salt and baking powder. Stir in flour and corn meal slowly. Butter an 8 x 10-inch glass baking dish. Bake at 400°F. for about 30 minutes until golden brown.

CORN TORTILLAS

2 C. yellow corn meal
ground fine
1/2 C. whole wheat pastry
flour

1 tsp. sea salt or substitute
1/4 C. warm water--more if
needed

Mix corn meal, flour and salt together; add water in small amounts. Stir until dough is stiff. Roll dough into a medium-sized ball. Pat the mass of dough into a thin round cake. Bake tortillas on a buttered griddle. Turn so both sides are done.

NUT AND SEED BREAD

3/4 C. ground almonds
1/4 C. ground sunflower seeds
1/2 C. wheat flour

Mix all together. Moisten with pure water. Spread thinly on a cookie sheet. Dry at room temperature for a few hours.

PECAN BREAD

2 C. whole wheat
pastry flour
1/2 C. wheat germ
2-1/2 tsp. baking powder
1/2 tsp. allspice

1 C. date sugar or
3/4 C. honey
2 eggs, beaten
1 C. buttermilk or yogurt
2 T. cold pressed oil
1 C. chopped pecans

Sift flour, wheat germ, baking powder and allspice. Add the date sugar (or honey) and eggs, buttermilk and oil. Stir well. Fold in pecans. Pour into a loaf pan. Makes on 9-inch loaf pan. Bake at 325°F. for about 40 minutes. Cool in pan for about 10 minutes.

POCKET BREAD

2 T. yeast
2-1/2 C. bran water or
plain water
2 tsp. honey

2 tsp. sea salt or natural
seasoning
2 T. cold pressed oil
6 C. (about) whole wheat
flour

Add all ingredients except 3 cups whole wheat flour and mix well, at least 100 strokes. Let sit for 20 minutes. Add the remaining 3 cups flour. Knead for about 10 minutes. Divide the dough into 20 pieces, rolling with rolling pin into 4-inch round balls about 1/4-inch thick. Place on ungreased cookie sheet, cover and let rise in warm place for about 2 hours.

Cook on bottom rack in oven for 5 minutes at 500°F. Then move bread to a higher rack and bake until puffed up (about 4 minutes). When sliced, the bread will have a pocket in which to put a sandwich filling.

RYE BREAD

4 T. dry yeast
1/2 C. molasses
6 C. warm bran water or
plain water
1 C. wheat germ
2 T. sea salt or salt
substitute

5 C. rye flour
10 C. whole wheat flour
4 T. lecithin
8 T. cold pressed oil

Dissolve 4 T. dry yeast into a mixture of 1/2 cup molasses and 6 cups warm bran water. Add T. sea salt and 5 cups rye flour and 3 cups whole wheat flour and blend well. Beat at least 100 times--very important! Let stand for about 20 minutes.

Mix in 8 T. cold pressed oil and gradually blend in the remaining 7 (about) cups of whole wheat flour. Knead, cover and let rise for about 1/2 hour. Should double in bulk. Do not let it rise too high.

Form into 4 large loaves, place in greased loaf pans and let rise for about 1/2 hour. Bake in 350°F. oven for about 1 hour.

SPROUTED WHEAT BREAD

2 T. dry yeast
2-1/2 C. bran water
1/4 C. honey
3 T. cold pressed oil

1 T. sea salt or sesame
kelp salt
5-6 C. whole wheat flour
2 C. wheat sprouts, ground

Soften yeast in warm liquid. Add honey, oil and salt; mix well. Gradually add 4 cups flour to water/yeast mixture. Beat for at least 100 times and let stand for 20 minutes.

Add 2 cups sprouted wheat and the rest of the whole wheat flour. Knead dough until smooth and elastic. Put in oiled pan, turning dough over to coat with oil. Let rise until it is double in bulk. Punch down and divide in loaves. Let rise in oil loaf pans until volume has doubled. Bake in oven at 350°F. for about 45 minutes to 1 hour.

WHOLE WHEAT BREAD (No-Fail Whole Wheat Bread)

Dissolve 4 T. dry yeast into a mix of 1/2 C. honey or molasses and 6 C. warm water. Add 2 T. sea salt and 8 C. whole wheat flour and blend well. Beat at least 100 times. Let stand for about 20 minutes.

Mix in 10 T. cold pressed oil and about 1 C. bran and 1 C. wheat germ, and 6 C. more flour. Knead; cover and let rise for about 1/2 hour. It should double in bulk. Do not let it rise too high.

Form into 4 loaves. Place in greased loaf pans and let rise for about 1/2 hour. Bake in a 350°F. oven for 45 minutes to 1 hour.

DESSERTS

SANDWICH COOKIES

1/2 C. butter softened
1/3 C. honey, warmed
1 egg, separated

1 tsp. pure vanilla
1-1/4 C. whole wheat pastry
    flour

Cream butter, honey, egg yolk and vanilla. Add egg white and beat well. Gradually stir in flour until blended. Wrap dough in wax paper and chill at least 1 hour.

When chilled, roll out on lightly floured surface. Cut into round cookies on lightly greased cookie sheet. Bake 8 to 10 minutes at 350°F.

Use cream cheese filling between two cookies.

<u>Cream Cheese Filling:</u>

8 oz. cream cheese,
    softened
1 T. raw honey

1 tsp. pure vanilla
1/2 C. almonds, ground

Mix all together in blender. Refrigerate and use on celery sticks or on sandwiches and crackers.

MAPLE NUT COOKIES

2 egg yolks
1/3 C. pure maple syrup
1/3 C. butter
1/2 tsp. soda
1 T. sour cream
2 T. wheat germ

1/8 tsp. sea salt
1/2 tsp. pure vanilla
1 C. whole wheat pastry
    flour
3/4 C. chopped walnuts

Beat egg yolks, then add butter, maple syrup, soda mixed with sour cream, salt, vanilla and wheat germ. Mix well. Stir in flour, mix thoroughly, then add chopped walnuts and chill. Preheat oven to 325°F. Drop dough by the teaspoonful on a greased cookie sheet. Top with half walnut. Bake in preheated over for about 13 minutes.

ORANGE COOKIES

Beat together:

1/2 C. butter or sunflower oil	*2 eggs*
1/2 C. raw honey	*2 T. undiluted orange juice*
	1 tsp. grated orange peel

Stir in:

1 C. whole wheat pastry flour	*1 tsp. baking powder (health store)*
1/4 C. rice bran	*1 tsp. sea salt*
1/2 tsp. cardamom	

Add:

1 C. baby flake oats
1/2 C. almonds, ground fine

Drop by teaspoonful on oiled cookie sheet. Bake 10-12 minutes at 350°F.

CARROT-PINEAPPLE CAKE

2 eggs	*1 C. pecans, chopped*
1/2 C. honey	*1-1/4 C. whole wheat pastry flour*
3/4 C. oil	
1/4 C. buttermilk	*1 tsp. mineral salt or sea salt*
1-1/2 C. carrots, grated	
1 C. crushed pineapple, drained	*1-1/2 tsp. baking powder*

Beat eggs and add warm honey, oil and buttermilk. Stir in carrots, pineapple and nuts. Sift flour, salt and baking powder. Fold into carrot mixture. Pour into a greased 8 x 8-inch pan in a preheated oven at 300°F. for 1 hour.

Use cream cheese frosting for topping.

Cream Cheese Topping:

1/4 C. cream cheese
1/4 C. creamed cottage
    cheese

2 T. raw honey or 3 T. pure
    maple syrup
1/2 tsp. pure vanilla

Blend all together and use to frost carrot cake or use on cookie sandwiches.

PIE CRUST

2 C. grapenuts crumbs
8 T. melted butter

Mix together. Press in 2 tins and let cool in refrigerator. Fill with any fruit filling of your choice.

FLAKY PASTRY

Makes one double crust pie.

3/4 C. butter or
    margarine
2 C. whole wheat pastry
    flour

1-1/4 tsp. sea salt
1/2 C. ground walnuts
1/4 C. cold water

Mix butter, salt and walnuts into flour until mixture is crumbly. Add water slowly and mix with a fork. Do not handle dough too much or it will make it tough. Add flour if needed.

Divide dough in half. Grease the pie pan and coat it with a light dusting of flour. It keeps the pie from sticking to the pan and makes it easier to cut.

For the apple pie put 1/2 on the bottom, prick with a fork. Put apple mixture in pie crust. Put remaining crust on top and prick with a fork. Top with milk and smooth evenly over the top.

APRICOT PIE

1 C. yogurt
8 oz. cream cheese
1 T. honey
Juice of 1/2 lemon

Dash of sea salt
1/4 C. pecans
1/2 C. apricots--fresh,
    frozen or dried

Blend all together and then fold in nuts. Pour into a pastry shell and refrigerate until well chilled.

HONEY APPLE PIE

6 tart apples, unpeeled
    sliced thin
1/3 C. butter, melted
2 T. fresh lemon juice
2 T. whole wheat flour
1/2 C. honey, soft

1/2 tsp. cinnamon
1/4 tsp. nutmeg
1/4 tsp. cloves
1/2 tsp. cardamom
1/2 tsp. sea salt

Mix honey, flour, spices and salt together. Place half of the apples in a pie crust. Pour half the mixture and add remaining apples and the rest of the honey toppinng. Top with lemon juice and butter. Place top crust on and flute edges. Bake for 1 hour at 375°F.

HONEY PUMPKIN PIE

Blend together:

1 C. canned milk
3 eggs
2 C. cooked pumpkin
1/2 C. unsulphured
    molasses
1/2 C. date sugar

1 tsp. cinnamon
1/2 tsp. salt
1/2 tsp. ginger
3/4 tsp. nutmeg
1/8 tsp. cloves

Pour filling into an unbaked pie shell and bake about 50 minutes at 350°F. Whipping cream topping makes a special treat.

PUMPKIN WALNUT PIE

1-1/2 C. cooked pumpkin
3 T. molasses
1 C. canned milk
2 beaten eggs
1/2 C. honey
1/4 tsp. nutmeg

3/4 tsp. sea salt
1 tsp. cinnamon
1/4 tsp. ginger
1/2 C. light cream
1 C. ground walnuts

Combine pumpkin, honey, molasses, salt and spices and mix all together. Add eggs, milk and cream. Mix thoroughly and add nuts. Pour into unbaked pastry shell. Bake at 425°F. for about 45 minutes. When ready to serve top with whipping cream.

WALNUT AND RAISIN PIE

1 C. raisins	*1/2 C. honey*
1 C. walnuts	*2 eggs*
1 C. sour cream or	
canned milk	

Stir eggs and add all other ingredients. Use an unbaked whole wheat pastry shell and cover the top with pastry. Bake at 350°F. for about 45 minutes.

WALNUT BRAN LOAF

1-1/2 C. milk	*1/2 tsp. baking soda*
1/3 C. molasses	*1/2 tsp. salt*
1 C. whole bran	*2 T. honey*
1 C. unbleached flour	*1 egg, slightly beaten*
1 C. whole-wheat flour	*1/4 C. oil*
3 tsps. baking powder	*1/2 C. walnuts, chopped*
	coarse

Mix milk, molasses and bran; let stand until bran is soft. In large bowl mix flours, baking powder, soda, salt and honey; set aside. Stir egg and oil into bran mixture, then add to flour mixture, stirring just to moisten. Stir in walnuts. Pour into greased 9x5x3-inch loaf pan. Bake in preheated 350°F. oven 50 to 55 minutes or until pick inserted in center comes out clean. Cool in pan 10 minutes. Invert on rack. Wrap cool loaf airtight. Will keep in cool, dry place up to 1 week. Freezes well up to 2 months.

AVOCADO MOUSSE

2 packets unflavored	*4 oz. cream cheese, softened*
gelatin softened in	*1 C. drained pineapple*
1/2 C. orange juice	*1/2 C. hot pineapple juice*
1 large ripe avocado	*1/4 C. honey*
1 T. fresh lemon juice	
1/2 C. plain yogurt	

On low heat soften gelatin in the orange juice. In a blender put avocado, lemon juice, yogurt and softened cream cheese. Blend until smooth. Fold in pineapple. Add honey, hot pineapple juice and gelatin-orange juice mixture. Add this to the avocado mixture and fold together. Pour into a mold and chill.

BAKLAVA

1 Box Filo pastry
    (1 lb. box)
1 C. melted butter

4 C. finely chopped walnuts
2 C. honey
2 tsp. ground cinnamon

Sauce for top after it is baked:

1 C. honey
1 tsp. ground cloves
1 tsp. finely grated orange
    peel

1 tsp. ground cardamom
2 tsp. lemon juice

Brush 4 pastry sheets with melted butter as you layer them into the pan. Combine walnuts, honey and cinnamon. Spread about 1/8 of the mixture over the filo sheets in the pan. Cover with 4 more sheets brushed with the melted butter, then spread another 1/8 of the walnut mixture. Repeat until you have used all the filo sheets and the walnut mixture. Brush 4 or 5 more sheets with butter and place on top.

With a very sharp knife, cut pastry to form diamond-shaped pieces. Top with remaining butter and bake in preheated oven for about 50 minutes at 350°F. or until top is crisp and golden brown.

While baklava is baking, combine remaining ingredients, heat to boiling, then lower heat and simmer mixture for 8 to 10 minutes. Remove the baklava from oven and top immediately with hot syrup. Cool.

DATE NUT DESSERT

8 oz. pitted dated,
    soaked overnight
1/2 C. orange juice
1 tsp. lemon juice

1/2 tsp. grated lemon rind
1/2 C. chopped walnuts
4 oz. cream cheese
2 stiffly beaten egg whites

Combine all ingredients together and bake at 300°F. for about 15 minutes.

GRANOLA CRUST APPLES

1/4 C. chopped dates
1/4 C. raw honey
1/2 C. chopped walnuts
2 T. grated lemon peel
1 C. ground granola (see
    homemade recipe)

1 tsp. cinnamon
6 cooking apples
1/2 C. raw melted butter
    (unsalted)

Slice peeled apples and put in a baking dish. Combine dates, honey, walnuts, and lemon peel. Sprinkle over the apples. Combine granola, cinnamon and sprinkles over the top and dot the butter over the granola mixture. Cook at 400°F. for about 30 minutes. Can be served with or without whipping cream.

MAPLE TOFU CHEESECAKE

1 C. graham cracker crumbs, 1/4 C. honey and 1/3 C. melted butter. Mix together and press into 9-inch pie pan.

1/3 C. orange juice	1/2 C. pure maple syrup
1 envelope unflavored gelatin	2 T. lime juice
2 C. mashed tofu	8 oz. cream cheese
1/2 tsp. vanilla (pure)	1 large banana

Pour orange juice into top of double boiler. Sprinkle the gelatin over the liquid. In blender mix together tofu, banana, maple syrup, vanilla and lime juice and cream cheese and add heated gelatin mixture. Blend the filling until smooth. Pour into crust. Refrigerate at least 3 hours. May be topped with strawberries or blueberries.

RASPBERRY YOGURT DESSERT

2 C. raspberry, fresh or frozen	5 oz. cream cheese
1 C. yogurt	1-1/2 T. honey

Mix all ingredients in a blender. Serve in dessert dishes. Serves 6.

ORANGE ICE CREAM

3 C. orange juice	1/4 C. honey
2 C. cashew cream	3 T. apple juice

Mix ingredients together. Freeze; when nearly frozen blend and freeze again until firm.

CANDY

WALNUT POPCORN

1 C. honey	*4 C. popcorn (popped)*
1 tsp. vanilla	*1 C. walnuts, chopped*
3 T. butter	*1/4 C. sesame seeds*

Bring honey to boil in a saucepan and simmer, while stirring, until it reaches the crack stage (about 10-15 minutes). When done remove from heat and stir in butter and vanilla. Mix popcorn, walnuts and sesame seeds in a large bowl. Pour honey over mixture and toss to coat all popcorn. Pour the mixture onto a buttered cookie sheet and let it harden.

HONEY CARAMEL TURTLES

1-1/2 C. honey
1/2 C. butter
2 C. light cream

Combine honey, butter and 1 cup of cream in a saucepan. Bring to a boil, stirring frequently, and cook until mixture begins to darken and thicken. Add remaining cup of cream and continue to cook until mixture forms a fairly firm ball when dropped into cold water or reaches 244°F. Place about five half walnuts on wax paper, pour caramel slowly over nuts. When cool add melted carob chips that have been melted in a double broiler over the caramel walnuts.

LEMON-HONEY NOUGAT

3 egg whites (room
    temperature)
3/4 C. honey

1-1/2 T. grated lemon peel
1 tsp. vanilla

Beat egg whites until stiff. Cook honey over medium heat until it reaches 250°-265°F. (the hard ball stage). Test often, honey cooks quickly. Pour honey very slowly into egg whites, beating constantly. Stir in lemon peel and vanilla. Beat until candy is very thick. Drop by spoonsful on a buttered cookie sheet. Cool.

MAPLE NUT FUDGE

2 C. pure maple syrup
3/4 C. canned milk
1 tsp. pure vanilla

2 T. butter
1 C. pecans or walnuts,
    chopped fine

Combine maple syrup and canned milk into a stainless steel saucepan. Cook to the soft ball stage (234°-240°F.). Do not stir while cooking; remove from heat and cool to 110°F. Beat with a hand mixer on low speed until candy thickens and loses its gloss. When candy is cool stir in nuts, butter and vanilla. Spoon on buttered pan.

NATURAL CANDY

1/2 C. raw butter
1 C. raw honey
1-1/2 C. quick-cooking
    oatmeal
1 C. flaked coconut
1 C. coarsely chopped
    walnuts

1/2 C. toasted wheat germ
1/3 C. sesame seeds
1/2 C. pecans
1 tsp. cinnamon

Melt raw butter and honey. Add remaining ingredients. Heat until bubbly for five minutes, stirring occasionally. Allow mixture to cool so it can be handled. Form into one-inch balls. Keep in the refrigerator.

ORANGE FIG BALLS

1 C. baby oats
1 C. light figs
1/4 C. ground sesame seeds
1/2 C. ground walnuts

1 tsp. orange rind
4 T. concentrated orange
    juice
4 T. water

Blend together. Roll in a ball and roll in unsweetened coconut.

PROTEIN FRUIT BARS

1 C. white raisins
1/2 C. honey
1/2 C. powdered milk
1/2 C. wheat germ
2 T. sesame oil, or other

1/3 C. whole wheat pastry
    flour
1/2 C. bran
1/2 C. each: chopped
    walnuts, pecans and
    sunflower seeds

Use white grape juice to moisten

Pour ingredients into an oiled 8-inch square pan. Bake about 35 minutes at 300°F. Cool before cutting. Keep in refrigerator.

SESAME PEANUT BUTTER BALLS

3/4 C. peanut butter
1/2 C. honey
1 tsp. vanilla
3/4 C. powdered milk

1 C. oatmeal
1/4 C. sesame seeds
2 T. boiling water

Combine all ingredients and roll into balls. Roll finely chopped walnuts or pecans. You can toast seeds in 200°F. oven for 20 minutes or until light brown.

ENERGY STICKS

1 C. honey
1 C. peanut butter

1-1/2 C. powdered milk
    (add more if too soft)

Mix and shape into finger size pieces. Roll in wheat germ, sesame seeds or raw coconut. Freeze.

BIBLIOGRAPHY

BAKER, Elizabeth and Dr. Elton, The Uncook Book. Drelwood Publications.

BESTWAYS MAGAZINES, 1980 to 1985 issues.

BOND, Dr. Harry C., Natural Food Cookbook. Melvin Powers Wilshire Book Co.

CAMPBELL, Diane, Step-By-Step to Natural Food. CC Publishers.

CARROL, Anstice and Vona, Embree De Persiis, The Health Food Dictionary with Recipes. Weathervance Books, New York.

COTTRELL, Edith Young, The Oats, Peas, Beans and Barley Cookbook. Woodbridge Press.

DUQUETTE, Susan, Sunburst Farm Family Cookbook. Woodbridge Press.

FATHMAN, George and Doris, Live Foods, Nature's Perfect System of Human Nutrition. Ehret Literature Publishing Co.

HEWITT, Jean, The New York Times Natural Foods Cookbook. Avon Books.

HURD, Frank J., D.C. and Rosalie, B.S., A Good Cook......Ten Talents.

JENSEN, Bernard, Ph.D., Food Healing for Man and the Chemistry of Man. Bernard Jensen, Publisher.

KADANS, Joseph M., Ph.D., Encyclopedia of Fruits, Vegetables, Nuts and Seeds for Healthful Living. Parker Publishing Co., Inc.

HUNSBERGER, Eydie Mae and Loeffler, Chris, Eydie Mae's Natural Recipes for the Live Foods Gourmet. Production House Publishers.

LET'S LIVE MAGAZINES. 1980 to 1985.

MALSTROM, Stan, N.D., M.T., and Marie Myer, Own Your Own Body. Woodland Books.

MINDELL, Earl, Earl Mindell's Vitamin Bible. Rawson, Wade Publishers, Inc.

PESHEK, Robert J., D.D.S., Students' Manual for Balancing Body Chemistry with Nutrition. Published by Color Coded Systems, Riverside, CA.

ROBERTSON, Laurel, Carol Flinders and Bronwen Godfrey, Laurel's Kitchen.

SALAMAN, Maureen, M.Sc., Nutrition: The Cancer Answer. Stratford Publishing.

TARR, Yvonne Young, The New York Times Natural Foods Dieting Book. Ballantine Books, New York.

TENNEY, Louise, Today's Herbal Health. Woodland Books.

TODAY'S HERBS, Newsletter. Woodland Books.

WENTZLER, Rich, The Vitamin Book. Gramercy Publishing Co., New York.

WIGMORE, Dr. Ann, Recipes for Longer Life. Rising Sun Publications, Boston, MASS.

ZURBEL, Runa and Victor, The Vegetarian Family, with Recipes for a Healthier Life.

INDEX